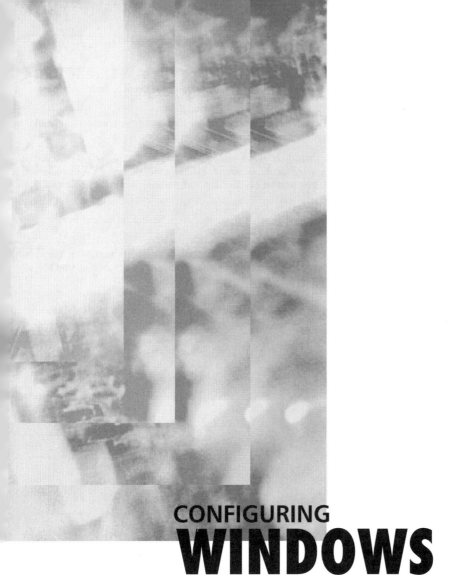

CONFIGURING
WINDOWS 2000
SERVER SECURITY

SYNGRESS®

KEY	SERIAL NUMBER
001	IL89F7NE9M
002	7AMLM26411
003	EKAM3IRH3H
004	YH67BA56NB
005	MMYY77FBV2
006	87NUD481B5
007	7B6VLUNV31
008	H5FNALUR43
009	12MNG673FD
010	IY7698BV4M

PUBLISHED BY
Syngress Media, Inc.
800 Hingham Street
Rockland, MA 02370

Configuring Windows 2000 Server Security

Printed in the United States of America

1 2 3 4 5 6 7 8 9 0

ISBN: 1-928994-02-4

Copy Editor: Adaya Henis
Technical Editor: Stace Cunningham
Indexer: Robert Saigh
Product Line Manager: Julie P. Smalley

Proofreader: James Melkonian
Graphic Artists: Emily Eagar,
Vesna Williams, and Reuben Kantor
Co-Publisher: Richard Kristof, Global Knowledge

Acknowledgments

We would like to acknowledge the following people for their kindness and support in making this book possible.

Richard Kristof, Duncan Anderson, Jennifer Gould, Robert Woodruff, Kevin Murray, Dale Leatherwood, Shelley Everett, Laurie Hedrick, Rhonda Harmon, Lisa Lavallee, and Robert Sanregret of Global Knowledge, for their generous access to the IT industry's best courses, instructors and training facilities.

Ralph Troupe and the team at Rt. 1 Solutions for their invaluable insight into the challenges of designing, deploying and supporting world-class enterprise networks.

Karen Cross, Kim Wylie, Harry Kirchner, John Hays, Bill Richter, Michael Ruggiero, Kevin Votel, Brittin Clark, Sarah Schaffer, Luke Kreinberg, Ellen Lafferty and Sarah MacLachlan of Publishers Group West for sharing their incredible marketing experience and expertise.

Peter Hoenigsberg, Mary Ging, Caroline Hird, Simon Beale, Julia Oldknow, Kelly Burrows, Jonathan Bunkell, Catherine Anderson, Peet Kruger, Pia Rasmussen, Denelise L'Ecluse, Rosanna Ramacciotti, Marek Lewinson, Marc Appels, Paul Chrystal, Femi Otesanya, and Tracey Alcock of Harcourt International for making certain that our vision remains world-wide in scope.

From Global Knowledge

At Global Knowledge we strive to support the multiplicity of learning styles required by our students to achieve success as technical professionals. As the world's largest IT training company, Global Knowledge is uniquely positioned to offer these books. The expertise gained each year from providing instructor-led training to hundreds of thousands of students worldwide has been captured in book form to enhance your learning experience. We hope that the quality of these books demonstrates our commitment to your lifelong learning success. Whether you choose to learn through the written word, computer based training, Web delivery, or instructor-led training, Global Knowledge is committed to providing you with the very best in each of these categories. For those of you who know Global Knowledge, or those of you who have just found us for the first time, our goal is to be your lifelong competency partner.

Thank your for the opportunity to serve you. We look forward to serving your needs again in the future.

Warmest regards,

Duncan Anderson

President and Chief Executive Officer, Global Knowledge

Contributors

Stace Cunningham (CCNA, MCSE, CLSE, COS/2E, CLSI, COS/2I, CLSA, MCPS, A+) is a Systems Engineer with SDC Consulting located in Biloxi, MS. He was an instrumental force in the design, engineering, and implementation of an enterprise network consisting of 12,000 nodes. He held the positions of Network Security Officer and Computer Systems Security Officer while serving in the United States Air Force. He also was an active contributor to The SANS Institute booklet "Windows NT Security Step by Step". Stace has been working with Windows 2000 since Microsoft released the first beta and is pleased to see the new security features present in the operating system.

Stace has participated as a Technical Contributor for the IIS 3.0 exam, SMS 1.2 exam, Proxy Server 1.0 exam, Exchange Server 5.0 and 5.5 exams, Proxy Server 2.0 exam, IIS 4.0 exam, IEAK exam, and the revised Windows 95 exam. In addition, he has coauthored 16 books published by Microsoft Press, Osborne/McGraw-Hill, and Syngress Media as well as performing as a technical reviewer for several books published by Microsoft Press, Osborne/McGraw-Hill, and Syngress Media.

His wife Martha and daughter Marissa are very supportive of the time he spends on the network of computers located in his house. Without their love and support he would not be able to accomplish the goals he has set for himself.

Debra Littlejohn Shinder (MCSE, MCP+I, MCT) is an instructor in the AATP program at Eastfield College, Dallas County Community College District, where she has taught since 1992. She is Webmaster for the cities of Seagoville and Sunnyvale, TX, as well as the family website at www.shinder.net. She and her husband, Dr. Thomas W. Shinder, provide consulting and technical support services to Dallas area organizations. She is also the proud mom of a daughter, Kristen, who is currently serving in the U.S. Navy in Italy, and a son, Kris, who is a high school chess champion. Deb has been a writer for most her life, and has published numerous articles in both technical and non-technical fields. She can be contacted at deb@shinder.net.

Thomas W. Shinder, M.D. (MCSE, MCP+I, MCT) is a technology trainer and consultant in the Dallas-Ft. Worth metroplex. Dr. Shinder has consulted with major firms including Xerox, Lucent Technologies and FINA Oil, assisting in the development and implementation of IP based communications strategies.

Dr. Shinder attended Medical School at the University of Illinois in Chicago, and trained in Neurology at the Oregon Health Sciences Center in Portland, Oregon. His fascination with interneuronal communication ultimately melded with his interest in internetworking and led him to take down his shingle and focus on Systems Engineering. Tom works passionately with his beloved wife, Deb Shinder, to design elegant and cost efficient solutions for small and medium sized businesses based on Windows NT/2000 platforms.

Brian M. Collins (MCNE, CNI, MCSE, MCT, CTT) is a technical trainer for Network Appliance Inc (NASDAQ: NTAP), a premier provider of Network Attached Storage, as well as a consultant and trainer through his own company Collins Network Engineering. Brian is an 18-year veteran of technology industries and has worked as a network engineer, trainer, software developer and consultant for government, Fortune 500 companies, and small business. His hobbies include hiking, golf, and operating systems. Brian lives in the redwood forest of Boulder Creek, California, 30 miles from California's Silicon Valley.

D. Lynn White (MCPS, MCSE, MCT, MCP+I) is president of Independent Network Consultants, Inc. Lynn has more than 14 years in programming and networking experience. She has been a system manager in the mainframe environment as well as a software developer for a process control company. She is a technical author, editor, trainer, and consultant in the field of networking and computer-related technologies. Lynn has been delivering mainframe, Microsoft-official curriculum and other networking courses in and outside the United States for more than 12 years.

Garrick Olsen (A+, Network+, MCP+I, MCSE+I, CNE) currently works for MicroAge in Anchorage, Alaska as a Network Technician. Questions and comments can be submitted to golsen@gci.net.

Contents

Preface

Security has always been important to computer networks, but the network landscape has changed immensely over the last several years, with the public swarming in droves to the Internet, organizations hooking their private networks to the Internet, and the burgeoning effect of electronic commerce. Organizations must make every effort possible to protect their data (such as new product information), their business partners' data (such as confidential agreements), and their customers' data (such as credit card information).

There are now many "script kiddies" on the Internet, since the public has unprecedented access to the Internet, unlike the old days, when only researchers and scientists utilized ARPANET. The "script kiddies" can easily find the information they seek, since it is freely available on underground Web sites. No longer do they need an in-depth knowledge of programming languages and Unix. They can simply download executable programs to help them work their way into an organization's network, or at least a portion of it.

What can network managers and network administrators do about this threat to their organizations' networks? Convince their management to cut all ties to the Internet? I doubt that is going to happen; networks are strategic to organizations' achieving their goals, as well as allowing them to maintain a competitive edge in some circumstances. Should they switch from the operating system they are using to a different operating system? Not really; all operating systems have security vulnerabilities, regardless of what the operating system zealots say. The only secure computer is the one that is not powered on, and that is locked in a room with no windows! Managers and administrators must make sure to take every precaution they can to ensure the security of their networks.

Securing an organization's network has been made easier with the enhanced security present in Windows 2000 Server. Don't get me wrong; Windows 2000 Server greatly enhances the security available for a Windows-based network, but Microsoft cannot allow it to become stagnant. For example, the key size used for the Encrypting File System (EFS) must increase as technology advances. This is necessary to protect the integrity of the information being protected by EFS. Also, just because an organization rolls Windows 2000 Server out enterprisewide, this does not mean that it is now secure. Network managers and network administrators must actively implement the security measures within Windows 2000 Server correctly for their particular organizations. Implementation must be carefully considered, and this is why a network security plan is extremely important. I cannot stress enough the importance of the network security plan. I can imagine that Windows 2000 Server will probably receive some bad press from organizations that do not take the time to properly develop a network security plan, instead implementing it willy-nilly and then having it blow up in their faces.

Organization

The book starts with a chapter on the security migration path for Windows 2000 Server and moves on to Chapter 2, which examines the default access control settings. Chapters 3 through 9 deal with specific portions of the new security features present in the operating system. Chapter 10 provides a Security Fast Track to Windows 2000.

- Chapter 1. Provides a brief overview of Windows 2000 Server security. Examines the problems and limitations of Windows 2000 Server security as well as considerations for upgrading and migrating. Discusses the network security plan.

- Chapter 2. Discusses the Access Control Settings for both the file system and registry that are configured during Windows 2000 Server setup. The chapter also discusses the default user rights and group memberships for the different built-in groups.

- Chapter 3. Provides an overview and history of the Kerberos protocol and also details the use of Kerberos within Windows 2000 Server.

- Chapter 4. Covers Windows 2000 Distributed Security Services, including Active Directory and security, multiple security protocols, enterprise and Internet Single Sign-on, Internet security, and interbusiness access for distributed partners.

- Chapter 5. Provides a look into the Security Configuration tool set available for use in Windows 2000. Aspects covered include configuring security, analyzing security, group policy integration, and using the available tools.

- Chapter 6. Discusses the Encrypting File System, starting with using EFS, moves on to user operations, and concludes with a look into the architecture that makes up EFS.

- Chapter 7. The discussion of IPSec includes an overview of several methods used to break into networks, the architecture of IPSec, and concludes with information on deploying Windows IPSec in the organization. This chapter includes a walkthrough exercise.

- Chapter 8. Provides a look into the use of smart cards in Windows 2000 including the interoperability, smart card base components, and enhanced solutions.

- Chapter 9. A discussion of the concepts of Public Key Infrastructure (PKI) is followed by a look at the components in Windows 2000 PKI, including certificate authorities, enabling domain clients, and public key security policy. The chapter concludes with an applications overview and instructions for preparing for Windows 2000 PKI.

- Chapter 10. Provides a fast-track look at Windows 2000 security and why you need to know about it. The chapter includes a historical perspective of Windows NT security as well as information on important features or design changes implemented in Windows 2000.

Audience

This book is intended primarily for network managers and network administrators who are responsible for implementing security in Windows 2000 environments. However, the book is also useful for people that are interested in knowing more about the new security features available in Windows 2000 Server. The book is designed to be read starting with Chapter 1 and ending with Chapter 10. Readers who want a quick understanding of the information contained in the book can read Chapter 10 first.

Chapter 1

The Windows 2000 Server Security Migration Path

Solutions in this chapter:

- **Brief Overview of Windows 2000 Server Security**

- **Windows 2000 Server Security White Paper**

Brief Overview of Windows 2000 Server Security

Why should you worry about security in your network environment? There are several reasons. First, you need to be sure that only authorized users have access to your network. Without this level of security, anyone can use your network resources and possibly steal sensitive business data. Second, even if your network utilizes login security, a mechanism must be in place to protect data from users who do not need access to it. For example, personnel in the marketing department do not need access to data used by the payroll department. These two mechanisms help to protect network resources from damage and unauthorized access. As networks become more evolved and organizations are more dependent on them, additional protections must be put in place to maintain network integrity.

Security for Microsoft's network operating system has been greatly enhanced with the arrival of Windows 2000 Server. It is obvious from the improvements that have been made in this version that the software giant does take security seriously. Some of the new features include:

- Multiple methods of authenticating internal and external users
- Protection of data stored on disk drives using encryption
- Protection of data transmitted across the network using encryption
- Per-property access control for objects
- Smart card support for securing user credentials securely
- Transitive trust relationships between domains
- Public Key Infrastructure (PKI)

Windows 2000 Server Security White Paper

Windows 2000 Server security goes well beyond the security available in earlier versions of the network operating system. In today's ever-changing global environment, the more security that can be provided by a network operating system, the better off the organizations that use it will be, since organizations depend heavily on their information systems.

Why the Change?

The change in security in Windows 2000 Server is necessary as more organizations use the operating system for mission-critical applications. The more widely an operating system is used in industry, the more likely it is to become a target. The weaknesses in Windows NT came under constant attack as it became more prevalent in industry. One group, L0pht Heavy Industries, showed how weak Windows NT's password encryption for the LAN Manager hash was. Because the LAN Manager hash was always sent, by default, when a user logged in, it was easy to crack the password. It was good that L0pht Heavy Industries revealed this weakness in the network operating system. Microsoft made provisions for fixing the problem in a Service Pack release, but in Windows 2000 Server it has replaced the default authentication with Kerberos v5 for all Windows 2000 domain-controller-based network.

Differences in Windows 2000 Server Security

One of the enhancements to the security in Windows 2000 Server is that Windows 2000 Server supports two authentication protocols, Kerberos v5 and NTLM (NT LAN Manager). Kerberos v5 is the default authentication method for Windows 2000 domains, and NTLM is provided for backward compatibility with Windows NT 4.0 and earlier operating systems, as well as all Windows 2000 network computers. (See Chapter 3, "Kerberos Server Authentication.")

Another security enhancement is the addition of the Encrypting File System (EFS). EFS allows users to encrypt and decrypt files on their system on the fly. This provides an even higher degree of protection for files than was previously available using NTFS (NT File System) only. (See Chapter 6, "Encrypting File System for Windows 2000.")

The inclusion of IPSec (IP Security) in Windows 2000 Server enhances security by protecting the integrity and confidentiality of data as it travels over the network. It's easy to see why IPSec is important; today's networks consist of not only intranets, but also branch offices, remote access for travelers, and of course, the Internet. (See Chapter 7, "IP Security for Microsoft Windows 2000 Server.")

Each object in the Active Directory can have the permissions controlled at a very high granularity level. This per-property level of permissions is available at all levels of the Active Directory. (See Chapter 4, "Secure Networking Using Windows 2000 Distributed Security Services.")

Smart cards are supported in Windows 2000 Server to provide an additional layer of protection for client authentication as well as to provide secure e-mail. The additional layer of protection comes from an adversary's needing not only the smart card but also the Personal Identification Number (PIN) of the user to activate the card. (See Chapter 8, "Smart Cards.")

Transitive trust relationships are a feature of Kerberos v5 that is established and maintained automatically. Transitive trusts rely on Kerberos v5, so they are applicable only to Windows 2000 Server–only domains. (See Chapter 4.)

Windows 2000 Server depends heavily on Public Key Infrastructure (PKI). PKI consists of several components: public keys, private keys, certificates, and certificate authorities (CAs). (See Chapter 9, "Microsoft Windows 2000 Public Key Infrastructure.")

For IT Professionals

Where is the User Manager for Domains?

There are several changes to the tools used to administer the network in Active Directory. Users and groups are administered in a new way. Everyone who is familiar with User Manager for Domains available in Windows NT 4.0 and earlier versions will now have to get used to the Active Directory Users and Computers snap-in for the Microsoft Management Console (MMC) when they manage users in a pure Windows 2000 domain. The MMC houses several new tools used for managing the Windows 2000 Server environment, such as the QoS Admission Control and Distributed File System. The MMC also includes old tools, such as the Performance Monitor and Event Viewer. Table 1.1 shows the differences between some of the tools used in Windows NT 4.0 and those used in Windows 2000 Server.

Table 1.1 Tools Used in Windows NT 4.0 and Windows 2000 Server

Windows NT 4.0	Windows 2000 Server
User Manager for Domains	Active Directory Users and Computers is used for modification of user accounts. The Security Configuration Editor is used to set security policy.
System Policy Editor	The Administrative Templates extension to group policy is used for registry-based policy configuration.
Add User Accounts (Administrative Wizard)	Active Directory Users and Computers is used to add users.
Group Management (Administrative Wizard)	Active Directory Users and Computers is used to add groups. Group policy enforces policies.
Server Manager	Replaced by Active Directory Users and Computers.

Problems with and Limitations

Windows Server 2000 maintains compatibility with downlevel clients (Windows NT 4.0, Windows 95, and Windows 98), so it uses the NTLM and LM authentication protocol for logins. This means that the stronger Kerberos v5 authentication is not used for those systems. NTLM and LM is still used, so the passwords for those users can be compromised. NTLMv2, released in Service Pack 4 for Windows NT 4, is not supported in Windows 2000. Figure 1.1 shows a packet capture of a Windows 98 client logging on a Windows 2000 Server domain. The Windows 98 machine is sending out a broadcast LM1.0/2.0 LOGON Request.

Figure 1.2 shows a Windows 2000 Server responding to the request sent by the Windows 98 client. The Windows 2000 Server responds with a LM2.0 Response to the logon request.

Figure 1.1 A Windows 98 client sends a LM1.0/2.0 LOGON request.

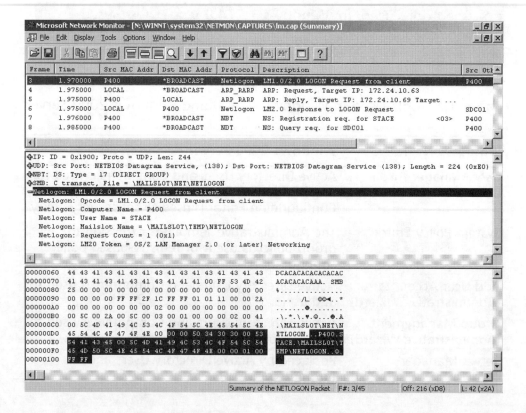

Figure 1.2 Windows 2000 Server responds with a LM2.0 Response to the Windows 98 logon request.

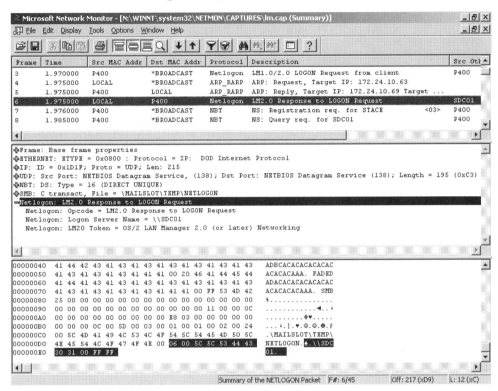

NTLM is used to authenticate Windows NT 4.0, but LM is used to authenticate Windows 95 and Windows 98 systems. NTLM is used to authenticate network logons in these cases:

- Users in a Windows NT 4.0 domain authenticating to a Windows 2000 domain

- A Windows NT 4.0 Workstation system authenticating to a Windows 2000 domain controller

- A Windows 2000 Professional system authenticating to a Windows NT 4.0 primary or backup domain controller

- A Windows NT 4.0 Workstation system authenticating to a Windows NT 4.0 primary or backup domain controller

The difficulty with using NTLM or LM as an authentication protocol cannot be overcome easily. The only way to get around using NTLM or LM at the moment is to replace the systems using earlier versions of Windows with Windows 2000 systems. This probably is not economically feasible for most organizations.

Windows NT 3.51 presents another problem. Even though it is possible to upgrade Windows NT 3.51 to Windows 2000 Server, Microsoft does not recommend running Windows NT Server 3.51 in a Windows 2000 Server domain, because Windows NT 3.51 has problems with authentication of groups and users in domains other than the logon domain.

What Is the Same?

Windows 2000 Server has grown by several million lines of code over the earlier versions of Windows NT, so it may be hard to believe that anything is the same as in the earlier versions. NTLM is the same as it was in earlier versions because it has to support down-level clients.

Global groups and local groups are still present in Windows 2000 Server with an additional group added.

Built-in groups such as Backup Operator, Account Operator, Server Operator, Print Operator, and Administrator still exist. NTFS permissions are still present in the new NTFS5.

Otherwise, for security purposes, this is a new operating system with many new security features and functions for system administrators to learn about.

Upgrading/Migrating Considerations

Upgrading/migrating from Windows NT 4.0 to Windows 2000 Server is a totally different issue than it was when you upgraded from Windows NT 3.51 to Windows NT 4.0. Windows 2000 Server includes several new security features that were not present in any earlier version of Windows NT, so it is important to carefully consider, before implementation, exactly how you will take advantage of the new security features in the operating system.

Network Security Plan

One security item to consider before upgrading/migrating to Windows 2000 Server is the development of the Network Security Plan. Without it, you may not have as secure a network as possible, given the new tools available in Windows 2000 Server. Depending on the size of your network, you may actually need more than a single Network Security Plan. Organizations that span the globe may need a different plan for each of their major locations to fit different needs. Smaller organizations may find that they need only a single plan. No matter what size your organization is, a Network Security Plan is extremely important. Microsoft recommends that, at a minimum, these steps be included in your plan:

- Security group strategies
- Security group policies
- Network logon and authentication strategies
- Strategies for information security

Security group strategies are used to plan the use of the three group types: universal, global, and local. Universal is a new group that was not present in Windows NT 4.0, so make sure you include it in your plan. You need to decide how you will use the existing built-in groups and what new groups you will need to create when you formulate your Network Security Plan.

After you have defined the group strategies necessary for your organization, move on to the security group policies, including: Active Directory Objects, File System, Registry, System Services, Network Account, Local Computer, Event Log, and Restricted Groups. Group policy filters within your organization can control each of these items. It is best to minimize the number of group policies, because they must be downloaded to each computer during startup and to each user profile during logon. (See Chapter 5, "Security Configuration Tool Set.")

The third step to plan for is the Network Logon and Authentication Strategies necessary for your organization. Will your organization utilize Kerberos logon, NTLM logon, smart card logon, or even certificate mapping? Depending on the makeup of your organization, Windows 2000 Server can operate in either mixed mode or native mode. NTLM is not available in native mode (see Chapter 4).

The fourth step is to develop Strategies for Information Security. This includes your organization's Public Key Infrastructure, use of the Encrypting File System, authentication for remote access users, IPSec utilization, secure e-mail, security for your Web site, and, if applicable, the signing of software code.

Table 1.2 is a checklist that can help you create the Network Security Plan for your organization.

Table 1.2 Checklist for the Network Security Plan

Assignment	Comments
What universal groups are necessary in the organization?	
What global groups are necessary in the organization?	
How will we utilize the built-in local groups?	
What local groups are necessary in the organization?	
What filters are necessary for group policies in the organization?	
What policies are required for Active Directory objects in the organization?	
What policies are required for the file system in the organization?	
What policies are required for registries in the organization?	

Continued

Assignment	Comments
What policies are required for system services in your organization?	
What policies are required for network accounts in the organization?	
What policies are required for local computers in the organization?	
What policies are required for Event Logs in your organization?	
What policies are required for restricted groups in your organization?	
How will we perform network logon and authentication in the organization?	
What approach do we take with smart cards in the organization?	
What approach do we take with certificate mapping in the organization?	
How do we implement Public Key Infrastructure within the organization?	
How do we implement the Encrypting File System in the organization?	
How will we provide authentication for remote access users?	
What approach do we take with IPSec in the organization?	
What approach do we take with secure e-mail in the organization?	
How do we protect the organization's Web site?	
How do implement code signing in the organization?	

How to Begin the Process

After determining the plan for network security, you need to test it in a controlled lab environment to ensure that it meets the needs of the organization before you implement the changes in a production environment. Failure to do this could result in catastrophe, both to the organization and to your job security.

The best way to test your Network Security Plan is to set up a lab that realistically mimics your existing network structure. For example, if your network consists of a Windows NT 4.0 PDC and three Windows NT 4.0 BDCs, as shown in Figure 1.3, then that is what you should strive to have in your test environment.

Figure 1.3 An example network layout to mimic for testing.

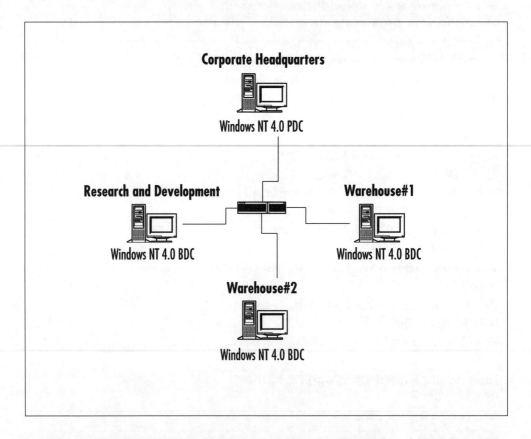

By realistically duplicating your existing network, you can easily uncover problems that may occur when you implement the upgrade for real, without any risk.

Getting Started

This procedure is applicable to both the test environment and the actual organization. Before you perform the upgrade, you must ensure that you have a good backup of each of your existing domain controllers in case something goes awry during the upgrade process. The first system that has to be upgraded in your existing environment is the primary domain controller. This is necessary so that the upgrade of the existing domain into a Windows 2000 domain can be successful. During the upgrade of the existing PDC, you must install Active Directory so that the data store, including the Kerberos authentication protocol, is installed. The existing Security Accounts Manager (SAM) is copied from the Registry to the new data store of the Active Directory. The installation process starts the Kerberos services, allowing it to process logon authentications. The domain is operating in the mixed mode of security, which means that it will honor both the Kerberos and NTLM authentication. Backup domain controllers recognize the new Windows 2000 Server as the domain master. The Windows 2000 server can synchronize security changes to the BDCs successfully.

After the PDC has been successfully upgraded, your staff can continue upgrading the rest of your BDCs until they all are Windows 2000 Servers, or they can leave the BDCs as Windows NT 4.0 systems if you want to continue operating using both operating systems. When you begin your rollout, you should continue migration for all of your BDCs to Windows 2000 Server, so that you can take full advantage of all the security features present in the operating system.

After you upgrade the domain controllers to Windows 2000 Server, you can start implementing the items in your Network Security Plan, such as group policies and the implementation of PKI.

For IT Professionals

What Happened to My Backup Domain Controllers?

In a pure Windows 2000 domain there are no longer BDCs or a PDC; there are only member servers and domain controllers. Member servers do not perform user authentication or store security policy information. Each domain controller runs Active Directory, which stores all domain account and policy information. Each domain controller in the domain has read/write capability to Active Directory, so updates can be performed at any domain controller and then replicated out to the remaining domain controllers.

Issues to Present to Your Manager

It is important that your manager be involved in the Network Security Plan, as this determines how the network will be organized in the Windows 2000 environment. Without the support of your manager, you may have a difficult time implementing the necessary security measures for your organization.

Another issue to present to your manager is the question of operating in mixed mode or native mode. If you decide to switch over to native mode, your manager needs to know these things:

- The domain controller that acts as the PDC cannot synchronize data with any remaining Windows NT BDCs.
- Domain controllers no longer support NTLM authentication.
- New Windows NT domain controllers cannot be added to the Windows 2000 domain.
- Downlevel clients cannot log on the Windows 2000 domain.

Proper Analysis

Before you implement Windows 2000 Server in your environment, you must perform a proper analysis that must take into consideration the timing, cost, and the resources necessary for the installation, especially the security features required for the organization.

Timing

Timing is very important for any new application, but especially for a network operating system. You must determine what effects it will have on the users of the network and how much time it will take to implement the new security features that are required for your organization. This is one reason it is good to begin with a controlled lab environment. This will give you a good idea of how long it will take to implement your plan in the production environment. Another issue to consider is other activity in your organization. If it is a particularly busy time of year, you may want to hold off the implementation until things calm down somewhat.

Cost

Cost analysis for upgrading to Windows 2000 Server goes well beyond the cost for the licenses. It must also include any hardware upgrades that are required, as well as the cost of training users and administrators in the use of the new features available in Windows 2000 domains, especially Active Directory and the new security features available with Distributed Security Services. You must determine whether the greater security available in Windows 2000 Server lessens the chance of downtime due to security incidents. With less downtime, the organization may experience greater productivity, which may lead to an increased return on investment.

Resources

Resources consist of both humans and hardware. Both must be analyzed to ensure that sufficient resources are available to implement and sustain the upgrade to Windows 2000 Server. Windows 2000 Server has higher minimum requirements than did previous versions of the operating system, so you may have to add new hardware or enhance the existing hardware in your organization. You also need to analyze the human resources that are available for implementing and administering the upgrade.

Summary

Windows 2000 Server adds a great number of security enhancements to those that were available in previous versions of the operating system. These enhancements include Public Key Infrastructure capabilities, the Kerberos v5 authentication protocol, smart card support, the Encrypting File System, and IPSec. These new additions to security are necessary to protect data as organizations start depending on their information technology infrastructure even more than in the past. Any vulnerability could wreak havoc on those mission-critical systems.

The Network Security Plan is vital to the upgrading of your network from Windows NT 4.0 to Windows 2000 Server. It must be thought out carefully so that your organization can take advantage of the new security features in Windows 2000 Server. If the plan is not thought out carefully, then the necessary security you desire may not be put into place. At a minimum your Network Security Plan must include security group strategies, security group policies, network logon and authentication strategies, and strategies for information security.

Before you upgrade to Windows 2000 Server in a production environment, you need to test it. The test environment should mimic the production environment so that you can obtain an accurate picture of how the implementation will affect the production environment. When you are satisfied with the results of your testing, you should carefully consider the timing of rolling out the upgrade to the production environment to ensure that there will not be an interruption during a particularly busy time for your organization.

FAQs

Q: Why do I have to upgrade my primary domain controller first?

A: The primary domain controller must be upgraded first to ensure a successful upgrade of a Windows NT domain to a Windows 2000 domain. Information from the Security Accounts Manager on the PDC is copied over to the data store of the Active Directory.

Q: Can I have Windows 9x clients on a native Windows 2000 domain?

A: No, Windows 9x clients cannot be used on a native Windows 2000 domain because Windows 9x does not support Kerberos authentication.

Q: Can I still use Windows NT 4.0 backup domain controllers in a Windows 2000 domain?

A: Yes, Windows NT 4.0 BDCs can still be used in a Windows 2000 domain. One of the Windows 2000 Server domain controllers acts as a PDC emulator, so communication can occur to/from the Windows NT 4.0 BDCs.

Chapter 2

Default Access Control Settings

Solutions in this chapter:

- Introduction
- Configuring Security During Windows 2000 Setup
- Default File System and Registry Permissions
- Default User Rights
- Default Group Membership

Introduction

One of the weaknesses in Windows NT 4.0 is inherent in the default access permissions assigned to the built-in groups for the file system and the Registry. Windows 2000 has alleviated that weakness by refining the permissions granted to these groups.

Windows 2000 Server is a member server or stand-alone server when it is first installed onto a clean system. If the server participates in a domain, it is a member server, but if it is in a workgroup, it is a stand-alone server. Active Directory is not automatically installed during a fresh installation of a system, because the setup program does not know whether you want it to be a member server or a domain controller. However, Windows 2000 Server does automatically create these groups when it is first installed:

- Administrators
- Backup Operators
- Guests
- Power Users
- Replicator
- Users

These groups are found in the "Groups" folder under Local Computer Users and Groups in the Computer Management console, as shown in Figure 2.1. These same groups, with the exception of Power Users, are also present if the system is promoted to domain controller; however, additional groups are added as domain local groups. The additional groups are:

- Account Operators
- Print Operators
- Server Operators

These groups, as well as the others, are found in the "Builtin" folder of your directory tree in the Active Directory Users and Computers console, as shown in Figure 2.2.

Figure 2.1 Built-in groups for Windows 2000 Server when it is first installed on a clean system.

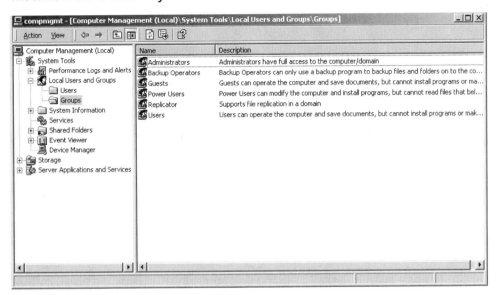

Figure 2.2 Built-in groups for a Windows 2000 Server domain controller.

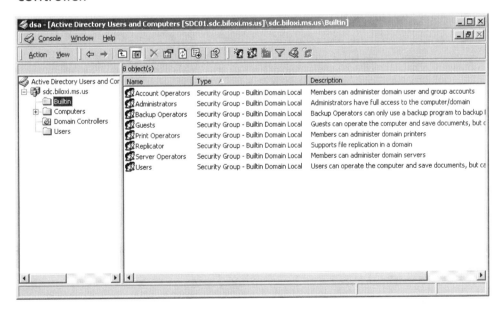

A major segment of operating system security is defined by the default access permissions granted to three groups: Administrators, Power Users, and Users.

Administrators Group

The Administrators group is the most powerful group available on the system. Members of the Administrators group can perform any function available in the operating system, and they are not restricted from access to any file system or Registry object. Members of the Administrators group should be kept to a bare minimum precisely because they do have so much power. Ideally, people who are in the Administrators group should also have another account that they normally use. They should use the account in the Administrators group only when they need to perform these functions:

- Configure system parameters such as password policy and audit functions.
- Install Service Packs and Hotfixes.
- Upgrade the operating system.
- Install hardware drivers.
- Install system services.

Users Group

The Users group is the most restrictive group available in Windows 2000. The default security settings prevent members of the Users group from modifying machine-wide registry settings, program files, and operating system files. Members of the Users group are also prevented from installing applications that can be run by other members of the Users group.

Power Users Group

The Power Users group in Windows 2000 has more system access than the Users group but less system access than the

Administrators group. Power Users can install applications to a Windows 2000 system as long as the application does not need to install any system services. Only the Administrators group can add system services. Power Users can also modify system-wide settings such as Power Configuration, Shares, Printers, and System Time. However, Power Users cannot access other users' data that is stored on NTFS partitions. Power Users can add user accounts, but they cannot modify or delete any account they did not create, nor can they add themselves to the Administrators group. Power Users can create local groups and remove users from local groups they have created. The Power Users group has much power on a system, and in Windows 2000 it is also backward compatible to the default security settings for the Users group in Windows NT 4.0.

Configuring Security During Windows 2000 Setup

The default security settings for Windows 2000 are put in place during the beginning of the GUI-mode portion of setup if the installation is a clean install, or if it is an upgrade from a Windows 95 or Windows 98 system. However, if the upgrade is being performed on an existing Windows NT system, the existing security settings are not modified. Of course, for file system settings to be applied, you must be using NTFS and not the FAT file system. To see the security settings that are applied during Windows 2000 setup, go to %windir%\Inf and locate these files:

- defltdc.inf—Domain Controller security settings
- defltsv.inf—Server security settings
- defltwk.inf—Professional security settings

Each of these files contains all the default security settings that are applied to the system, depending on the type of system that is being installed. Be warned that it does look cryptic, so you may not be able to make sense out of the settings. Here is a small portion of the security settings from the defltsv.inf file:

```
[Registry Keys]

"MACHINE\Software",2,"D:P(A;CI;GR;;;BU)(A;CI;GRGWSD;;;PU)(A;CI;
GA;;;BA)(A;CI;GA;;;SY)(A;CI;GA;;;CO)(A;CI;GRGWSD;;;S-1-5-13)"

"MACHINE\Software\Classes",2,"D:P(A;CI;GR;;;BU)(A;CI;GRGWSD;;;P
U)(A;CI;GA;;;BA)(A;CI;GA;;;SY)(A;CI;GA;;;CO)(A;CI;GRGWSD;;;S-1-
5-13)(A;CI;GR;;;WD)"

"MACHINE\SOFTWARE\Classes\helpfile",2,"D:P(A;CI;GR;;;BU)(A;CI;G
R;;;PU)(A;CI;GA;;;BA)(A;CI;GA;;;SY)(A;CI;GA;;;CO)(A;CI;GRGWSD;;
;S-1-5-13)(A;CI;GR;;;WD)"

"MACHINE\SOFTWARE\Classes\.hlp",2,"D:P(A;CI;GR;;;BU)(A;CI;GR;;;
PU)(A;CI;GA;;;BA)(A;CI;GA;;;SY)(A;CI;GA;;;CO)(A;CI;GRGWSD;;;S-
1-5-13)(A;CI;GR;;;WD)"

"MACHINE\SOFTWARE\Microsoft\Command
Processor",2,"D:P(A;CI;GR;;;BU)(A;CI;GR;;;PU)(A;CI;GA;;;BA)(A;C
I;GA;;;SY)(A;CI;GA;;;CO)"

"MACHINE\SOFTWARE\Microsoft\Cryptography\OID",2,"D:P(A;CI;GR;;;
BU)(A;CI;GR;;;PU)(A;CI;GA;;;BA)(A;CI;GA;;;SY)(A;CI;GA;;;CO)"

"MACHINE\SOFTWARE\Microsoft\Cryptography\Providers\Trust",2,"D:
P(A;CI;GR;;;BU)(A;CI;GR;;;PU)(A;CI;GA;;;BA)(A;CI;GA;;;SY)(A;CI;
GA;;;CO)"

"MACHINE\SOFTWARE\Microsoft\Cryptography\Services",2,"D:P(A;CI
;GR;;;BU)(A;CI;GR;;;PU)(A;CI;GA;;;BA)(A;CI;GA;;;SY)(A;CI;GA;;;
CO)"

"MACHINE\SOFTWARE\Microsoft\Driver
Signing",2,"D:P(A;CI;GR;;;BU)(A;CI;GR;;;PU)(A;CI;GA;;;BA)(A;CI;
GA;;;SY)(A;CI;GA;;;CO)"
```

The default security that is applied during the beginning of the GUI-mode of setup is applicable only to the core of the Windows 2000 operating system. In other words, any optional components you decide to install, such as Certificate Server or Internet

Information Server, are responsible for configuring the default security settings for their components if the security inherited by default is not sufficient.

Default File System and Registry Permissions

Default security varies for different users. For example, Administrators, System, and Creator Owner have Full Control of the registry and the file system at the beginning of the GUI-mode of setup.

However, the default permissions for Power Users and Users vary greatly from the permissions given to Administrators. Power Users do have permission to modify areas that Users cannot. For example, four areas that Power Users have the capability to use the Modify permission are:

- HKEY_LOCAL_MACHINE\Software
- Program Files
- %windir%
- %windir%\system32

Power Users can modify these four areas so that they can install existing applications. With existing applications it may be possible that Users cannot install the application, because the application may need to write to areas that Users do not have permission to modify. The Modify permission that Power Users have for %windir% and %windir%\system32 does not apply for files that were installed during the text-mode setup of Windows 2000. Power Users have read-only access to those files.

Users are limited to the areas that they are explicitly granted write access. This helps protect the system from tampering. Table 2.1 shows the only areas where Users have Write permissions. For areas not listed in the table, Users have Read-Only permission or no permissions on the rest of the system.

For IT Professionals

Windows 2000 Special Identities

Windows 2000 includes several special identities that are known by the security subsystem. Some of the special identities are:

- System
- Creator Owner
- Everyone
- Network
- Interactive

The System special identity represents the operating system of the local computer. The Creator Owner special identity is used on directories. Any users who create files or directories in a directory that has Creator Owner permissions inherit the permissions given to Creator Owner for the files or directories they create. The Everyone, Network, and Interactive groups cannot be modified; nor can you view the members of the groups. The Everyone group contains all current and future users of the network, including guests and members of other domains. The Network group consists of users who are given access to a resource over the network. The Interactive group is the opposite; it consists of users who access a resource by logging on to the resource locally. These groups are available when you assign rights and permissions to resources.

The last item in Table 2.1 states that Users may have Write permissions to the root of the hard drive. This is possible because setup does not change the existing permissions for root when Windows 2000 is installed. If you installed Windows 2000 to an NTFS partition on a clean system, the root is shared out to the

Everyone group with Full Control. This occurs when the clean system is formatted during setup. It is important that you remember that Everyone has Full Control of the root directory so that you make the changes necessary for your environment.

Table 2.1 Locations with Default Users' Write Access

Location	Access permission	Remarks
HKEY_Current_User	Full Control	Users have full control over their section of the registry.
%UserProfile%	Full Control	Users have full control over their Profile directory.
All Users\Documents	Modify	Users have Modify permission on the shared documents location.
All Users\Application Data	Modify	Users have Modify permission on the shared application data location.
%windir%\Temp	Synchronize, Traverse, Add File, Add Subdir	Users have these permissions on the per-machine temp directory so that Profiles do not have to be loaded in order for service-based applications to get the per-User temp directory of an impersonated user.
\	Not changed during setup	During setup, Windows 2000 does not change the permissions on the root directory since it would affect all objects underneath root, which is not desirable during setup.

Table 2.2 compares the default access control settings given to these two groups for objects on the file system. The permissions for directories apply to directories, subdirectories, and files unless stated otherwise in the Remarks column.

Table 2.2 File System Default Access Control Settings for Users and Power Users

File System Object	Default Users Access Control Settings	Default Power Users Access Control Settings	Remarks
boot.ini	No Permissions	Read & Execute	
ntdetect.com	No Permissions	Read & Execute	
ntldr	No Permissions	Read & Execute	
ntbootdd.sys	No Permissions	Read & Execute	
autoexec.bat	Read & Execute	Modify	
config.sys	Read & Execute	Modify	
\ProgramFiles	Read & Execute	Modify	
%windir%	Read & Execute	Modify	Power Users can write new files in this directory, but they cannot modify files that were installed during setup. All Power Users inherit Modify permission on the newly created files.
%windir%*.*	Read & Execute	Read & Execute	Only files in the %windir% directory, not any other subdirectories.

Continued

File System Object	Default Users Access Control Settings	Default Power Users Access Control Settings	Remarks
%windir%\config*.*	Read & Execute	Read & Execute	Only files in the %windir%\config directory, not any other subdirectories. Power Users can write new files in this directory, but they cannot modify files that were installed during setup. All Power Users inherit Modify permission on the newly created files.
%windir%\cursors*.*	Read & Execute	Read & Execute	Only files in the %windir%\curses directory, not any other subdirectories. Power Users can write new files in this directory, but they cannot modify files that were installed during setup. All Power Users inherit Modify permission on the newly created files.
%windir%\Temp	Synchronize, Traverse, Add File, Add Subdir	Modify	
%windir%\repair	List	Modify	
%windir%\addins	Read & Execute	Modify (Directories/Subdirectories) Read & Execute (Files)	Power Users can write new files in this directory, but other Power Users only have Read permissions for those files.

Continued

File System Object	Default Users Access Control Settings	Default Power Users Access Control Settings	Remarks
%windir%\ Connection Wizard	Read & Execute	Modify (Directories/ Subdirectories) Read & Execute (Files)	Power Users can write new files in this directory but other Power Users only have Read permissions for those files.
%windir%\ fonts*.*	Read & Execute	Read & Execute	Only files in the %windir%\fonts directory, not any other subdirectories. Power Users can write new files in this directory, but they cannot modify files that were installed during setup. All Power Users inherit Modify permission on the newly created files.
%windir%\ help*.*	Read & Execute	Read & Execute	Only files in the %windir%\help directory, not any other subdirectories. Power Users can write new files in this directory, but they cannot modify files that were installed during setup. All Power Users inherit Modify permission on the newly created files.

Continued

File System Object	Default Users Access Control Settings	Default Power Users Access Control Settings	Remarks
%windir%\ inf*.*	Read & Execute	Read & Execute	Only files in the %windir%\inf directory, not any other subdirectories. Power Users can write new files in this directory, but they cannot modify files that were installed during setup. All Power Users inherit Modify permission on the newly created files.
%windir%\java	Read & Execute	Modify (Directories/ Subdirectories) Read & Execute (Files)	Power Users can write new files in this directory, but other Power Users only have Read permissions for those files.
%windir%\ \media*.*	Read & Execute	Read & Execute	Only files in the %windir%\media directory, not any other subdirectories. Power Users can write new files in this directory, but they cannot modify files that were installed during setup. All Power Users inherit Modify permission on the newly created files.
%windir%\ msagent	Read & Execute	Modify (Directories/ Subdirectories) Read & Execute (Files)	Power Users can write new files in this directory, but other Power Users only have Read permissions for those files.
%windir%\ security	Read & Execute	Read & Execute	

Continued

File System Object	Default Users Access Control Settings	Default Power Users Access Control Settings	Remarks
%windir%\speech	Read & Execute	Modify (Directories/ Subdirectories) Read & Execute (Files)	Power Users can write new files in this directory, but other Power Users only have Read permissions for those files.
%windir%\system*.*	Read & Execute	Read & Execute	Only files in the %windir%\system directory, not any other sub-directories. Power Users can write new files in this directory, but they cannot modify files that were installed during setup. All Power Users inherit Modify permission on the newly created files.
%windir%\twain_32	Read & Execute	Modify (Directories/ Subdirectories) Read & Execute (Files)	Power Users can write new files in this directory, but other Power Users only have Read permissions for those files.
%windir%\web	Read & Execute	Modify (Directories/ Subdirectories) Read & Execute (Files)	Power Users can write new files in this directory, but other Power Users only have Read permissions for those files.
%windir%\system32\	Read & Execute	Modify	Power Users can write new files in this directory, but they cannot modify files that were installed during setup. All Power Users inherit Modify permission on the newly created files.

Continued

File System Object	Default Users Access Control Settings	Default Power Users Access Control Settings	Remarks
%windir%\ system32*.*	Read & Execute	Read & Execute	Only files in the %windir%\system32 directory, not any other subdirectories.
%windir%\ system32\ config	List	List	
%windir%\ system32\dhcp	Read & Execute	Read & Execute	
%windir%\ system32\ dllcache	No Permissions	No Permissions	
%windir%\ system32\ drivers	Read & Execute	Read & Execute	
%windir%\ system32\ catroot	Read & Execute	Modify (Directories/ Subdirectories) Read & Execute (Files)	Power Users can write new files in this directory, but other Power Users only have Read permissions for those files.
%windir%\ system32\ias	Read & Execute	Modify (Directories/ Subdirectories) Read & Execute (Files)	Power Users can write new files in this directory, but other Power Users only have Read permissions for those files.
%windir%\ system32\mui	Read & Execute	Modify (Directories/ Subdirectories) Read & Execute (Files)	Power Users can write new files in this directory, but other Power Users only have Read permissions for those files.

Continued

File System Object	Default Users Access Control Settings	Default Power Users Access Control Settings	Remarks
%windir%\system32\OS2*.*	Read & Execute	Read & Execute	Only files in the %windir%\system32\OS2 directory, not any other subdirectories. Power Users can write new files in this directory, but they cannot modify files that were installed during setup. All Power Users inherit Modify permission on the newly created files.
%windir%\system32\OS2\DLL*.*	Read & Execute	Read & Execute	Only files in the %windir%\system32\OS2\DLL directory, not any other subdirectories. Power Users can write new files in this directory, but they cannot modify files that were installed during setup. All Power Users inherit Modify permission on the newly created files.
%windir%\system32\RAS*.*	Read & Execute	Read & Execute	Only files in the %windir%\system32\RAS directory, not any other subdirectories. Power Users can write new files in this directory, but they cannot modify files that were installed during setup. All Power Users inherit Modify permission on the newly created files.

Continued

File System Object	Default Users Access Control Settings	Default Power Users Access Control Settings	Remarks
%windir%\ system32\ shellext	Read & Execute	Modify (Directories/ Subdirectories) Read & Execute (Files)	Power Users can write new files in this directory, but other Power Users only have Read permissions for those files.
%windir%\ system32\ viewers*.*	Read & Execute	Read & Execute	Only files in the %windir%\system32\viewers directory, not any other subdirectories. Power Users can write new files in this directory, but they cannot modify files that were installed during setup. All Power Users inherit Modify permission on the newly created files.
%windir%\ system32\ wbem	Read & Execute	Modify (Directories/ Subdirectories) Read & Execute (Files)	Power Users can write new files in this directory, but other Power Users only have Read permissions for those files.
%windir%\ system32\ wbem\mof	Read & Execute	Modify	
%UserProfile%	Full Control	Full Control	
All Users	Read	Modify	
All Users\ Documents	Modify	Modify	
All Users\ Application Data	Modify	Modify	

You can view permissions for the file system from Windows Explorer by right-clicking the object, choosing Properties, and then selecting the Security tab, as shown in Figure 2.3. Clicking Advanced displays the Access Control settings for the directory and the level to which the permissions apply, as shown in Figure 2.4. Selecting View/Edit shows the granular permissions available for the selected group, as shown in Figure 2.5. Other items available from the Advanced button include the Auditing and Owner tabs.

Figure 2.3 Security permissions for the %windir%\repair directory.

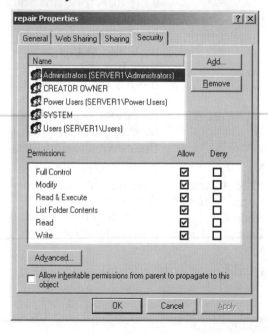

Table 2.3 shows the default access control settings for objects in the registry for Users and Power Users when Windows 2000 is installed to a clean system. Permissions apply to the object and all child objects unless the child object is listed in the table as a separate item.

Figure 2.4 Access Control settings for the %windir%\repair directory.

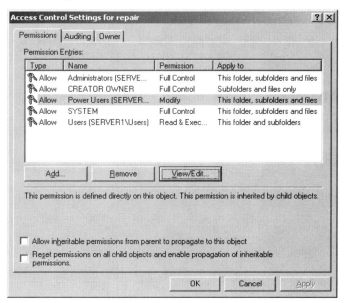

Figure 2.5 Granular permission in the %windir\repair directory for the Power Users group.

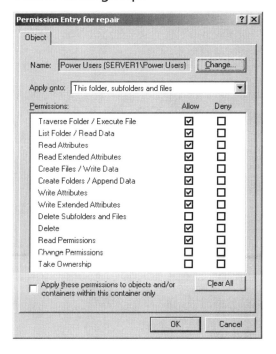

Table 2.3 Registry Default Access Control Settings for Users and Power Users

Registry object	Default Users access control settings	Default Power Users access control settings
HKEY_LOCAL_MACHINE\Software	Read	Modify
HKEY_LOCAL_MACHINE\Software\Classes\helpfile	Read	Read
HKEY_LOCAL_MACHINE\Software\Classes\.hlp	Read	Read
HKEY_LOCAL_MACHINE\Software\Microsoft\Command Processor	Read	Read
HKEY_LOCAL_MACHINE\Software\Microsoft\Cryptography\OID	Read	Read
HKEY_LOCAL_MACHINE\Software\Microsoft\Cryptography\Providers\Trust	Read	Read
HKEY_LOCAL_MACHINE\Software\Microsoft\Cryptography\Services	Read	Read
HKEY_LOCAL_MACHINE\Software\Microsoft\Driver Signing	Read	Read
HKEY_LOCAL_MACHINE\Software\Microsoft\EnterpriseCertificates	Read	Read
HKEY_LOCAL_MACHINE\Software\Microsoft\Non-Driver Signing	Read	Read
HKEY_LOCAL_MACHINE\Software\Microsoft\NetDDE	No Permissions	No permissions
HKEY_LOCAL_MACHINE\Software\Microsoft\Ole	Read	Read
HKEY_LOCAL_MACHINE\Software\Microsoft\Rpc	Read	Read
HKEY_LOCAL_MACHINE\Software\Microsoft\Secure	Read	Read
HKEY_LOCAL_MACHINE\Software\Microsoft\SystemCertificates	Read	Read
HKEY_LOCAL_MACHINE\Software\Microsoft\Windows\CurrentVersion\RunOnce	Read	Read

Continued

Registry object	Default Users access control settings	Default Power Users access control settings
HKEY_LOCAL_MACHINE\Software\Microsoft\Windows NT\CurrentVersion\DiskQuota	Read	Read
HKEY_LOCAL_MACHINE\Software\Microsoft\Windows NT\CurrentVersion\Drivers32	Read	Read
HKEY_LOCAL_MACHINE\Software\Microsoft\Windows NT\CurrentVersion\Font Drivers	Read	Read
HKEY_LOCAL_MACHINE\Software\Microsoft\Windows NT\CurrentVersion\FontMapper	Read	Read
HKEY_LOCAL_MACHINE\Software\Microsoft\Windows NT\CurrentVersion\Image File Execution Options	Read	Read
HKEY_LOCAL_MACHINE\Software\Microsoft\Windows NT\CurrentVersion\IniFileMapping	Read	Read
HKEY_LOCAL_MACHINE\Software\Microsoft\Windows NT\CurrentVersion\Perflib	Read via the Interactive special identity	Read via the Interactive special identity
HKEY_LOCAL_MACHINE\Software\Microsoft\Windows NT\CurrentVersion\SecEdit	Read	Read
HKEY_LOCAL_MACHINE\Software\Microsoft\Windows NT\CurrentVersion\Time Zones	Read	Read
HKEY_LOCAL_MACHINE\Software\Microsoft\Windows NT\CurrentVersion\Windows	Read	Read
HKEY_LOCAL_MACHINE\Software\Microsoft\Windows NT\CurrentVersion\Winlogon	Read	Read
HKEY_LOCAL_MACHINE\Software\Microsoft\Windows NT\CurrentVersion\AsrCommands	Read	Read

Continued

Registry object	Default Users access control settings	Default Power Users access control settings
HKEY_LOCAL_MACHINE\Software\ Microsoft\Windows NT\ CurrentVersion\Classes	Read	Read
HKEY_LOCAL_MACHINE\Software\ Microsoft\Windows NT\ CurrentVersion\Console	Read	Read
HKEY_LOCAL_MACHINE\Software\ Microsoft\Windows NT\ CurrentVersion\EFS	Read	Read
HKEY_LOCAL_MACHINE\Software\ Microsoft\Windows NT\ CurrentVersion\ProfileList	Read	Read
HKEY_LOCAL_MACHINE\Software\ Microsoft\Windows NT\ CurrentVersion\Svchost	Read	Read
HKEY_LOCAL_MACHINE\Software\ Policies	Read	Read
HKEY_LOCAL_MACHINE\System	Read	Read
HKEY_LOCAL_MACHINE\System\ CurentControlSet\Control\SecurePipe Servers\winreg	No Permissions	No permissions
HKEY_LOCAL_MACHINE\System\ CurentControlSet\Control\Session Manager\Executive	Read	Modify
HKEY_LOCAL_MACHINE\System\ CurentControlSet\Control\ TimeZoneInformation	Read	Modify
HKEY_LOCAL_MACHINE\System\ CurentControlSet\Control\WMI\ Security	No Permissions	No permissions
HKEY_LOCAL_MACHINE\Hardware	Read via the Everyone special identity	Read via the Everyone special identity
HKEY_LOCAL_MACHINE\SAM	Read via the Everyone special identity	Read via the Everyone special identity

Continued

Registry object	Default Users access control settings	Default Power Users access control settings
HKEY_LOCAL_MACHINE\Security	No Permissions	No permissions
HKEY_USERS\.DEFAULT	Read	Read
HKEY_USERS\.DEFAULT\Software\Microsoft\NetDDE	No Permissions	No permissions
HKEY_CURRENT_CONFIG	Permissions are equal to the permissions on HKEY_LOCAL_MACHINE\CurrentControlSet\Hardware Profiles\Current	Permissions are equal to the permissions on HKEY_LOCAL_MACHINE\CurrentControlSet\Hardware Profiles\Current
HKEY_CURRENT_USER	Full Control	Full Control
HKEY_CLASSES_ROOT	Permissions are equal to the combination of HKEY_LOCAL_MACHINE\Software\Classes and HKEY_CURRENT_USER\Software\Classes	Permissions are equal to the combination of HKEY_LOCAL_MACHINE\Software\Classes and HKEY_CURRENT_USER\Software\Classes

Security permissions for items in the registry are viewed using regedt32.exe, as shown in Figure 2.6. You cannot use regedit.exe to view security permissions. After you select a registry key, you can view and/or change the permissions for the key, as shown in Figure 2.7.

Figure 2.6 Preparation for viewing the Security Permissions for HKEY_CURRENT_USER.

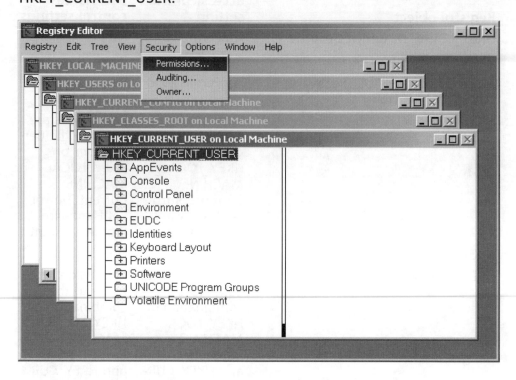

Figure 2.7 Security permissions for the EFS Registry Key.

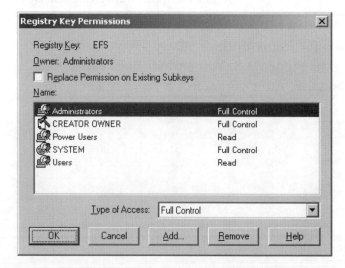

Default User Rights

The default user rights assigned to Windows 2000 vary according to the version used. Table 2.4 shows the default user rights for Windows 2000 Professional and Windows 2000 Server as member/stand-alone server and domain controller.

Table 2.4 Default User Rights for Windows 2000

User right	Default for professional	Default for member server/stand-alone server	Default for domain controller
Access this computer from network	Administrators, Backup Operators, Power Users, Users, Everyone	Administrators, Backup Operators, Power Users, Users, Everyone	Administrators, Authenticated Users, Everyone
Act as part of the operating system			
Add workstations to domain			
Back up files and directories	Administrators, Backup Operators	Administrators, Backup Operators	Administrators, Backup Operators, Server Operators
Bypass traverse checking	Administrators, Backup Operators, Power Users, Users, Everyone	Administrators, Backup Operators, Power Users, Users, Everyone	Administrators, Authenticated Users, Everyone
Change system time	Administrators, Power Users	Administrators, Power Users	Administrators, Server Operators
Create a pagefile	Administrators	Administrators	Administrators
Create a token object			
Create permanent shared objects			

Continued

User right	Default for professional	Default for member server/stand-alone server	Default for domain controller
Debug programs	Administrators	Administrators	Administrators
Deny access to this computer from network			
Deny log on as a batch job			
Deny log on as a service			
Deny log on locally			
Enable computer and user accounts to be trusted for delegation			Administrators
Force shutdown from a remote system	Administrators	Administrators	Administrators, Server Operators
Generate security audits			
Increase quotas	Administrators	Administrators	Administrators
Increase scheduling priority	Administrators	Administrators	Administrators
Load and unload device drivers	Administrators	Administrators	Administrators
Lock pages in memory			
Log on as a batch job			
Log on as a service			

Continued

User right	Default for professional	Default for member server/stand-alone server	Default for domain controller
Log on locally	Administrators, Backup Operators, Power Users, Users, Guest (if Guest is enabled)	Administrators, Backup Operators, Power Users, Users, Guest (if Guest is enabled)	Account Operators, Administrators, Backup Operators, Print Operators, Server Operators
Manage auditing and security log	Administrators	Administrators	Administrators
Modify firmware environment values	Administrators	Administrators	Administrators
Profile single process	Administrators, Power Users	Administrators, Power Users	Administrators
Profile system performance	Administrators	Administrators	Administrators
Remove computer from docking station	Administrators, Power Users, Users	Administrators, Power Users, Users	Administrators
Replace a process level token			
Restore files and directories	Administrators, Backup Operators	Administrators, Backup Operators	Administrators, Backup Operators, Server Operators
Shut down the system	Administrators, Backup Operators, Power Users, Users	Administrators, Backup Operators, Power Users	Administrators, Backup Operators, Account Operators, Server Operators, Print Operators
Synchronize directory service data			
Take ownership of files or other objects	Administrators	Administrators	Administrators

Continued

Checking or changing the default user rights in Windows 2000 is not a straightforward process, because it is not a choice on the Administrative Tools menu. Exercise 2.1 shows you how to check the user rights on your Windows 2000 Server.

Exercise 2.1

1. Click Start and choose Run.
2. Type mmc in the dialog box and click OK.
3. Select Add/Remove Snap-In from the Console menu.
4. Click Add.
5. Move the scroll bar down and highlight Group Policy as shown in Figure 2.8.

Figure 2.8 Select Group Policy from the Add Standalone snap-in window.

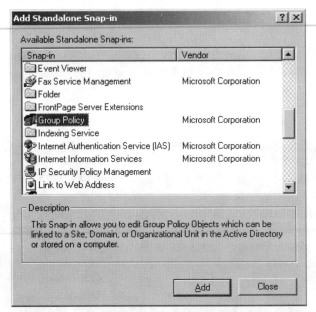

6. Click Add.
7. Click Finish to select the Local Computer as the Group Policy object. This is the default choice, but other choices are available if the Windows 2000 Server is a domain controller, as shown in Figure 2.9.

Figure 2.9 Group Policy objects available to Windows 2000 Server domain controllers.

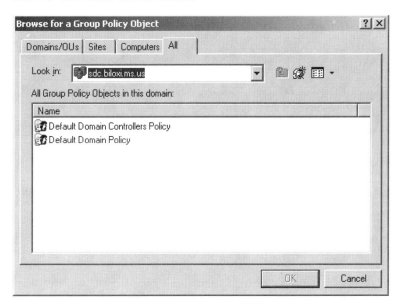

8. Click Close.

9. Click OK.

10. Double-click Local Computer Policy.

11. Double-click Computer Configuration.

12. Double-click Windows Settings.

13. Double-click Security Settings.

14. Double-click Local Policies.

15. Click User Rights Assignment. The default user rights are located in the right pane, as shown in Figure 2.10.

Additional users have rights on various items shown in Figure 2.10, because additional components are installed on the Windows 2000 Server system shown in the figure. Double-clicking any of the user rights brings up a window that displays the users who have those rights, as well as an Add button to add additional users to the right chosen. Figure 2.11 shows the Back up files and directories user rights, after the double-clicking. After you click Add, you can add additional users and/or groups to the user rights, as shown in Figure 2.12.

Figure 2.10 Default user rights for the local computer policy.

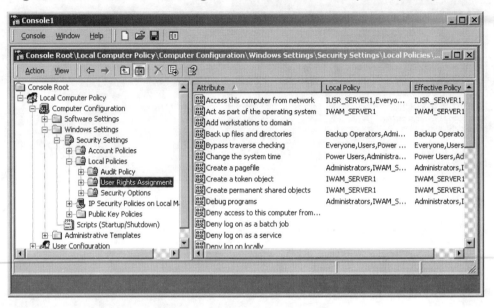

Figure 2.11 Back up files and directories user rights.

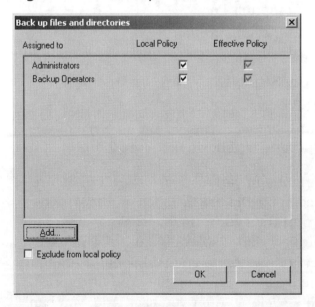

Figure 2.12 Add users or groups to the Back up files and directories user rights.

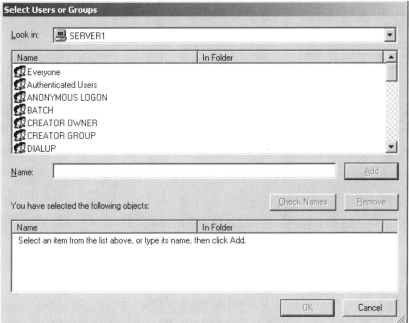

Default Group Membership

The default security settings in Windows 2000 and Windows NT 4.0 differ in the assignment of access control settings. Windows NT 4.0 depends on the Everyone group as the default group for file system access control lists, user rights, and registry access control lists. All users are automatically members of the Everyone group, and they cannot be removed by the Administrator of the system. This causes problems when more granular control is desired; the Everyone group may need to be removed and other groups added for better, more strict control.

Windows 2000 operates differently than Windows NT 4.0. The Everyone group is no longer used to assign permissions, except for maintaining backward compatibility with applications that require anonymous read access. In this case, the Everyone group is used to grant read access to some file system and registry objects. Assignment of permissions is accomplished using groups in which the administrator can control the membership. Table 2.5 lists the members of the three user groups.

Table 2.5 Default Members for Local Groups

Local group	Default professional members	Default stand-alone server members	Default domain controller members
Administrators	Administrator	Administrator	Administrator, Domain Admins, Enterprise Admins
Power Users	Interactive Users	N/A	N/A
Users	Authenticated Users	Authenticated Users	Authenticated Users, Domain Users

Table 2.5 lists the Authenticated Users group. Windows 2000 automatically creates this group during clean installations. The Authenticated Users group is similar to the Everyone group in that the operating system, not the administrator, controls the members of the group. The difference between the two groups is that the Authenticated Users group does not contain anonymous users, as the Everyone group does.

Members are added to or deleted from these three local groups in two ways, depending on whether the Windows 2000 Server is stand-alone or a domain controller. For stand-alone servers, use the Computer Management selection from the Administrative Tools menu. For domain controllers, use the Active Directory Users and Computers selection from Administrative Tools. The windows in the two systems look different from each other after you have drilled down to a particular group.

Figure 2.13 shows the General tab for the Administrators group from a Windows 2000 stand-alone server. It is the only tab available. Figure 2.14 shows the Members tab for the Administrators group from a Windows 2000 domain controller. It is one of four available tabs.

Figure 2.13 General tab for the Administrators group properties on a stand-alone server.

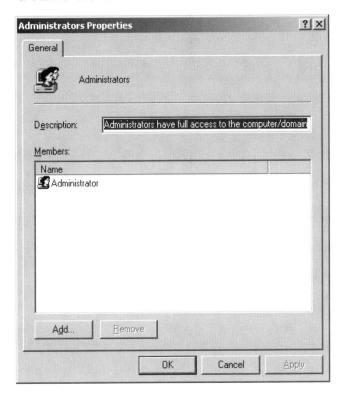

Figure 2.14 Members tab for the Administrators group properties on a domain controller.

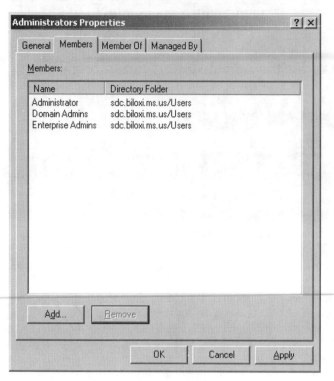

Summary

Windows 2000 has several built-in groups that are created when the operating system is first installed. Three of these groups contribute significantly to the security of Windows 2000, depending on the default access permissions granted to them. The three groups are Administrators, Power Users, and Users. Permissions vary widely from Administrators, who have complete control of the entire system, all the way down to Users, who have read-only access or no access. Power Users are in the middle of those two extremes. The Power Users group is not a built-in group on domain controllers.

Windows 2000 has refined the default file system and registry permissions given to the Users and Power Users groups to enhance the security of the operating system. An administrator can change these settings by using the Security tab in Windows Explorer for file system objects and regedt32.exe for registry objects.

Windows 2000 grants default user rights to various groups, depending on which version of the operating system is used. An administrator can change these rights by using the Group Policy snap-in for the Microsoft Management Console. The Group Policy snap-in is not available from the Administrative Tools menu by default.

Each built-in group in Windows 2000 may have a default membership assigned to it. For example, the Authenticated Users group is a default group assigned to the Users group. Authenticated Users, which is used in place of the Everyone group, does not include anonymous users, so security for the operating system is enhanced.

FAQs

Q: I installed Windows 2000 Server on my NTFS system, but I do not have the default security settings shown in the tables.

A: Default security settings are applied to a system only when Windows 2000 is installed to a clean system. When a system is upgraded to Windows 2000, the existing security settings are not modified.

Q: How can I apply the default security settings to the system I upgraded to Windows 2000?

A: You can use the secedit command to apply the default settings to your upgraded system. The secedit command is discussed in Chapter 5.

Q: Since the default security permissions have changed for the User group from Windows NT 4.0 to Windows 2000, how will my existing server-based applications function?

A: It may be necessary to change the environment in which the server-based application runs if it operated as a User in Windows NT 4.0. In Windows 2000 you will need to run the server-based application as a Power User.

Q: Why were the permissions changed for the User group?

A: The main goal was to strengthen the security for the operating system. Tighter access controls for the Users group prevent them from having access to modify the file system and the registry, except as shown in Table 2.1.

Q: Since the Users group is so strictly controlled, how are applications installed?

A: If the application supports per-user installations, members of the Users group can install it into their User's Profile directory. If the application does not support per-user installation, the user cannot install it, because Users cannot write to systemwide locations.

Chapter 3

Kerberos Server Authentication

Solutions in this chapter:

- Introduction
- Overview of the Kerberos Protocol
- Kerberos and Windows 2000
- Authorization Data

Introduction

Kerberos, version 5, is the default network authentication protocol for Windows 2000. Kerberos is not a new protocol that Microsoft invented; it has been used in the UNIX world for several years. Microsoft has chosen to implement Kerberos network authentication in Windows 2000 to enhance security because network servers and services need to know that the client requesting access is actually a valid client and so the client knows that the servers it is connecting are also valid. Kerberos is based on tickets containing client credentials encrypted with shared keys.

Authentication in Windows 2000

Windows 2000 supports five methods of authenticating the identity of users:

- Windows NT LAN Manager (NTLM)
- Kerberos v5
- Distributed Password Authentication (DPA)
- Extensible Authentication Protocol (EAP)
- Secure Channel (Schannel)

Windows 2000 uses only NTLM and Kerberos for network authentication. The other three protocols are used for authentication over dial-up connections or the Internet.

Windows NT 4.0 uses Windows NT LAN Manager (NTLM) as the default network authentication protocol. For that reason, NTLM is still available in Windows 2000 to maintain backward compatibility with previous versions of Microsoft operating systems. It is also used to authenticate logons to Windows 2000 stand-alone computers.

Kerberos is the default network authentication for Windows 2000. Kerberos is a widely used authentication protocol based on an open standard. All Windows 2000 computers use Kerberos v5 in the network environment except in these situations:

- Windows 2000 computers use NTLM when they authenticate to Windows NT 4.0 servers.

- Windows 2000 computers use NTLM when they access resources in Windows NT 4.0 domains.

DPA is an authentication protocol used on the Internet to allow users to use the same password to connect to any Internet site that belongs to the same membership organization. DPA is supported by Windows 2000 but does not come in the box. DPA must be purchased separately as an add-on product.

EAP is an extension to the Point-to-Point Protocol used for dial-up connections to the Internet. The purpose of EAP is to allow the dynamic addition of authentication plug-in modules at both the server and client ends of a connection. More information on EAP can be found in Request For Comments (RFC) 2284 "PPP Extensible Authentication Protocol (EAP)" dated March 1998. RFCs can be located at http://rfc.atc.no.

Secure channel includes four related protocols:

- Secure Sockets Layer (SSL) v2.0

- Secure Sockets Layer (SSL) v3.0

- Private Communication Technology (PCT) v1.0

- Transport Layer Security (TLS) v1.0

The primary purpose of using Schannel is to provide authentication, data integrity, and secure communication over the Internet. Secure Sockets Layer is typically used for transferring private information to/from electronic commerce sites. All four protocols in Schannel provide authentication by using digital certificates. Digital certificates are discussed in detail in Chapter 9, "Microsoft Windows 2000 Public Key Infrastructure."

Benefits of Kerberos Authentication

As the popularity and use of Windows NT 4.0 grew in the marketplace, so did hackers' interest in Windows NT systems. By adding Kerberos authentication into Windows 2000, Microsoft has increased the security capability of the operating system immensely. NTLM is provided for backward capability but should be disabled as soon as all the clients on the network can authenticate using Kerberos. As long as NTLM is available on the network, security is not at its strongest point.

Several benefits provided by Kerberos make it a better choice than NTLM for authentication. Kerberos is based on existing standards, so it allows Windows 2000 to interoperate on other networks that use Kerberos v5 as their authentication mechanism. NTLM cannot provide this functionality because it is proprietary to Microsoft operating systems. Connections to application and file servers are also faster when Kerberos authentication is used because the Kerberos server needs to examine only the credentials supplied by the client to determine whether access is allowed. The same credentials supplied by the client can be utilized for the entire network logon session. When NTLM is used, the application and file servers must contact a domain controller to determine whether access is allowed by the client. Kerberos authentication also provides authentication for both the client and server side, but NTLM provides authentication only of the client. NTLM clients do not know for sure that the server they are communicating with is not a rogue server. Kerberos is also beneficial for trusts. It is the basis for transitive domain trusts, and Windows 2000 uses transitive trusts by default with other Windows 2000 domains. A transitive trust is a two-way trust in which a shared interrealm key is created. The domains trust each other because they both have the shared key.

Standards for Kerberos Authentication

Kerberos has been around for several years. Engineers at the Massachusetts Institute of Technology (MIT) began working on Project Athena in May of 1983 and a prototype version of Kerberos was first used in Project Athena in September of 1986.

The purpose of Project Athena was to develop a new generation of campuswide client/server-based distributed computing facilities. Kerberos v4 was the first public release of the authentication protocol. Kerberos v5 adds several enhancements to the protocol, including support for forwardable, renewable, and postdatable tickets and changing the key salt algorithm to use the entire principal's name. Two of the RFCs that Kerberos v5 is defined in are RFC 1510, "The Kerberos Network Authentication Service (V5)," dated September 1993; and RFC 1964, "The Kerberos Version 5 GSS-API Mechanism," dated June 1996. (GSS—API stands for Generic Security Service—Application Program Interface.) Microsoft states that the implementation of Kerberos in Windows 2000 adheres closely to the specifications outlined in RFC 1510 for implementation of the protocol, and RFC 1964 for the mechanism and format for passing security tokens in Kerberos messages.

Extensions to the Kerberos Protocol

The version of Kerberos in Windows 2000 has been enhanced by Microsoft so that the initial authentication of users can be accomplished using public key certificates instead of the standard shared secret keys normally used by Kerberos v5. Extending Kerberos in this manner allows interactive logons to Windows 2000 using smart cards. The extensions Microsoft implemented in Kerberos for Windows 2000 are based on the draft specification "Public Key Cryptography for Initial Authentication in Kerberos," proposed to the Internet Engineering Task Force (IETF) by numerous third parties such as Digital Equipment Corporation (DEC), Novell, CyberSafe Corporation, and others.

Overview of the Kerberos Protocol

The name Kerberos (Greek spelling) or Cerberus (Latin spelling) comes from Greek mythology. Kerberos was the three-headed dog that guarded the entrance to Hades. Kerberos provides mutual authentication for both servers and clients and server to server, unlike other protocols that authenticate only the client. Kerberos operates on the assumption that the initial transactions between clients and servers are done on an unsecured network. Networks that are not secure may be easily monitored by people who want to impersonate a client or server in order to gain access to information that may help them reach their goal, whatever it may be.

Basic Concepts

A *shared secret* is shared only with those required to know the secret. It may be between two people, two computers, three servers, and so on. It is limited to the minimum entities necessary to accomplish the required task, and it allows those that know the shared secret to verify the identity of others that also know the shared secret. Kerberos depends on shared secrets to perform its authentication. Kerberos uses secret key cryptography as the mechanism for implementing shared secrets. *Symmetric encryption,* in which a single key is used for both encryption and decryption, is used for shared secrets in Kerberos. One entity encrypts information, and another entity successfully decrypts the information; this is proof of the knowledge of the shared secret between the two entities.

Authenticators

An authenticator is unique information encrypted in the shared secret. Kerberos uses timestamps so that the authenticator is unique. Authenticators are valid for only one use to minimize the possibility of someone attempting to use someone else's identity. Replay, which is an attempt to reuse the authenticator, cannot be accomplished in Kerberos v5. However, mutual authentication can occur when the recipient of the authenticator extracts a portion of the original authenticator, encrypts it in a new authenticator, and sends it to the originator of the first authenticator. A portion of the original authenticator is extracted to prove that the original authenticator was successfully decrypted. If the entire original authenticator were sent back unchanged, then the originator would not know whether the intended recipient or an impersonator sent it. Table 3.1 shows the contents of the authenticator fields.

Table 3.1 Authenticator Field Contents

Name of Field	Contents of Field
Authenticator Version Number	5
Client Realm	The name of the client's realm
Client Name	The name of the client
Checksum	The checksum of data in message authenticator
CUSEC	The millisecond portion of the client's time
Client time	The time on the client
Subkey	Key that specifies an alternate key to use instead of the session key
Sequence Number	Optional and application–specific number
Authorization data	Optional field used to include authorization data for specific applications

Key Distribution Center

Just as the Kerberos in Greek mythology had three heads, in technology Kerberos also has three parts. The Kerberos authentication protocol has a client, a server, and a trusted authority. The Key Distribution Server (KDC), the trusted authority used in Kerberos, maintains a database with all account information for principals in the Kerberos realm. A *principal* is a uniquely named entity that participates in network communication, and a *realm* is an organization that has a Kerberos server. Since the system running the KDC service contains the database with security account information, it needs to be physically secure. A portion of this security information is the secret key that is shared between a principal and the KDC. Each principal has its own secret key, and it has a long lifetime, which is why this key is also known as the *long-term key*. When the long-term key is based upon a human user's principal, it is derived from the user's password. This long-term key is symmetric in nature.

Another key used with the KDC is the *session key*, which is issued by the KDC when one principal wants to communicate with another principal. For example, if a client wants to communicate with a server, the client sends the request to the KDC, and the KDC in turn issues a session key so that the client and server can authenticate with each other. Each portion of the session key is encrypted in the respective portion of the long-term key for both the client and server. In other words, the client's long-term key includes the client's copy of the session key, and the server's long-term key includes the server's copy of the session key. The session key has a limited lifetime that is good for a single login session. After the login session is terminated, the session key is no longer valid. The next time the same client needs to contact the same server, it will have to go to the KDC for a new session key.

Session Tickets

The client receives an encrypted message from the KDC that contains both the client and server copies of the session key, as shown in Figure 3.1. The server's copy of the session key is contained in a session ticket, which also contains information about the client and

Figure 3.1 The client requests a ticket to communicate with the server.

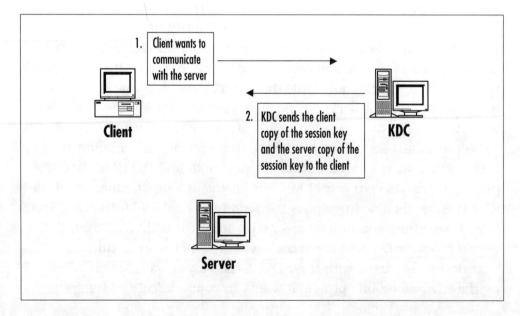

is encrypted with the shared secret of the server and KDC. The client cannot access the session ticket because it does not know the shared secret key the server and KDC share.

Now that the client has received the client session key and the servers' session ticket from the KDC, it can successfully contact the server. The client sends a message to the server that contains the session ticket and an authenticator that has been encrypted with the session key, as shown in Figure 3.2. After the server receives the credentials from the client, it decrypts the session ticket using its shared secret key (shared between the server and the KDC) and extracts the session key sent by the KDC. It then uses the session key to decrypt the authenticator sent by the client. The server believes in the stated identity of the client because the KDC, the trusted authority, told the server the identity of the client. At this point, *mutual authentication* can take place if the client has requested it, if the correct flag is set in the message the client sent.

This is one of the differences between Kerberos and other authentication mechanisms that only validate clients. If the client

Figure 3.2 The client sends its credentials to the server with which it wants to communicate.

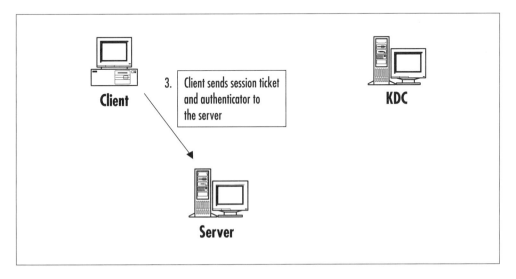

has requested mutual authentication, then the server encrypts the timestamp, including the milliseconds from the client's authenticator using its copy of the session key, and then sends it back to the client.

Session tickets can be reused for a set period of time that is determined by the Kerberos policy in the realm. The KDC places the time period in the structure of the ticket. This alleviates the principal's need to go to the KDC each time it wants to communicate to another principal. The client principal maintains the session tickets it needs to communicate to other principals in its credentials cache. On the other hand, server principals do not keep session keys in its credentials cache. It simply waits until a client principal sends it a session ticket and decrypts it, using its shared secret key.

Ticket-Granting Tickets

Session tickets are not the only tickets used in Kerberos. The KDC communicates and verifies that principals are really who they say they are by using a ticket-granting ticket (TGT). A user who logs on a Kerberos realm uses a password that is run through a one-way hashing algorithm that results in a long-term key. The results of the hashing are then sent to the KDC, which in turn retrieves a copy of the hash from its account database. When the client sends the long-term key, it also requests a session ticket and session key that it can use to communicate with the KDC during the entire length of the logon session. The ticket returned by the KDC to the client is the TGT. The TGT is encrypted in the KDC's long-term key, and the client's copy of the session key is encrypted in the client's long-term key. After the client receives the reply message from the KDC, it uses its long-term key (which is cached on the client system) to decrypt the session key. After the session key is decrypted, the long-term key is flushed from the client's cache, because it is no longer needed to communicate with the KDC for the remainder of the logon session or until the TGT expires. This session key is also known as the *logon session key*.

The client principal contacts the KDC to retrieve a session ticket to communicate with another principal such as a server. The client uses the logon session key to set up an authenticator, and then it sends off the authenticator, TGT, as well as a request for a session ticket for the server it wants to access to the KDC. When the KDC receives the message from the client, it decrypts the TGT, using its long-term key to extract the logon session key, and uses that to verify the authenticator sent by the client. Each time the client sends the TGT to the KDC, it must send a new authenticator.

Services Provided by the Key Distribution Center

The KDC separates its duties between two services, as shown in Figure 3.3. The *authentication service* (AS) is used to issue TGTs, and the *ticket-granting service* (TGS) is used to issue session tickets. This means that when a client first contacts the KDC, it is communicating with the AS, and when it needs to contact a server, it passes the ticket-granting ticket issued by the AS side of the KDC to the

Figure 3.3 These services are provided by the Key Distribution Center.

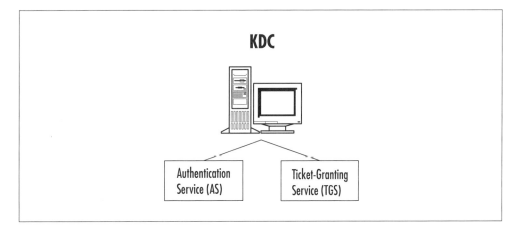

TGS side of the KDC so that it can issue a session ticket for communication to the server.

Cross-Realm Authentication

The KDC is broken down into two different services, even though one service of the KDC could perform both functions, so that Kerberos can support authentication over multiple realms. One reason multiple realms may be used in an organization is to lessen the load on a single KDC. No matter what the reason is, multiple realms can exist only if an *interrealm key* is shared between the KDCs. After the interrealm key is shared, the TGS of each realm becomes a security principal in the other's KDC.

Figure 3.4 These are the steps taken in cross-realm authentication.

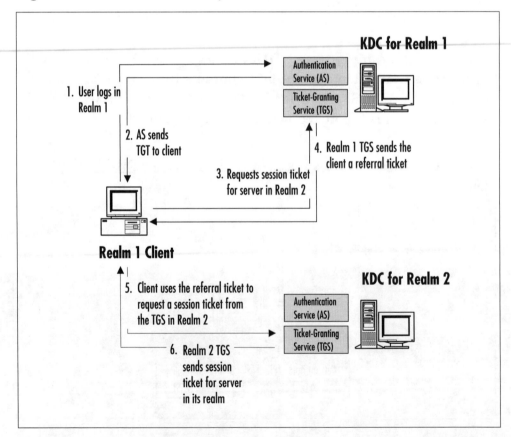

When a client in realm 1 wants to access a server that is in realm 2, it does not go straight to the KDC of realm 2. First it must log on the AS in realm 1. The AS in realm 1 sends a TGT back to the client. The client determines that it needs to contact the server in realm 2, so it requests a session ticket for the server from the TGS in realm 1. The TGS determines that the server is not in its realm, so it issues a referral ticket to the client. The referral ticket is a TGT encrypted with the interrealm key shared between realm 1 and realm 2. The client uses the referral ticket and sends a message to the TGS in realm 2. The TGS in realm 2 uses its copy of the interrealm key to decrypt the referral ticket, and if it is successful it sends a session ticket for the realm 2 server to the realm 1 client. Figure 3.4 shows the series of steps taken in cross-realm authentication.

Subprotocols

Kerberos contains three subprotocols, also known as exchanges. The three subprotocols are:

- Authentication Service (AS) Exchange
- Ticket-Granting Service (TGS) Exchange
- Client/Server (CS) Exchange

AS Exchange

The AS Exchange is the subprotocol used by the KDC to issue the client a logon session key and a TGT. When a user logs on the network, a message known as the *Kerberos Authentication Service Request* (KRB_AS_REQ) is sent to the authentication service side of the KDC. The contents of the KRB_AS_REQ message are shown in Table 3.2.

After the authentication service side of the KDC receives the KRB_AS_REQ message, it verifies the user as well as the other information contained in the message. If the verification is not successful, then the KDC generates a KDC_ERROR message and sends it

Table 3.2 Contents of the KRB_AS_REQ Message

Name of Field	Contents of Field
Protocol Version	5
Message Type	KRB_AS_REQ
Pre-Authentication Data Type	PA_AS_REQ
Pre-Authentication Data Value	Encrypted timestamp
KDC Options	Requested ticket flags
Client Name	The name of the client
Realm	The name of the realm
Server Name	The name of the KDC
From	Time to start (if postdated)
Till	The expiration time
Renew Time	The requested renew time
Nonce	A random number generated by the client
Encryption Type	Encryption algorithm to use
Addresses	Addresses from which the ticket will be valid
Encrypt Authorization Data	Not used in the KRB_AS_REQ message
Additional Tickets	Not used in the KRB_AS_REQ message

back to the client. After successful verification, the KDC creates the logon session key and the TGT and sends both back to the client in a *Kerberos Authentication Service Reply* (KRB_AS_REP) message. Table 3.3 shows the contents of the KRB_AS_REP message. The client uses the long-term key to decrypt the logon session key and the TGT and stores them in its credentials cache. The credentials cache is an area of the clients' volatile memory.

TGS Exchange

The TGS Exchange is the subprotocol used by the KDC to issue the client a server session key and a session ticket for the server.

Table 3.3 Contents of the KRB_AS_REP Message

Name of Field	Contents of Field
Protocol Version	5
Message Type	KRB_AS_REP
Pre-Authentication Data	If applicable, this data is returned from KRB_AS_REQ message
Client Realm	The name of the client's realm
Client Name	The name of the client
Ticket	TGT (ticket for TGS that is encrypted with the TGS server key)
Key	Session Key for TGS
Last Requested	Last time a ticket was requested
Nonce	Same as the nonce in the KRB_AS_REQ message
Key Expiration	The expiration time for the key
Flags	The flags set in the ticket
Authentication Time	Retrieved from the ticket showing the time it was issued
Start Time	Retrieved from the ticket showing the valid start time
End Time	Retrieved from the ticket showing the expiration time
Renew Till	Retrieved from the ticket showing the absolute expiration time
Server Realm	The requested server realm
Server Name	The requested server name
Client Address	Retrieved from the ticket showing the client address from which the ticket is valid

A client requests a session ticket for a server by sending the KDC a *Kerberos Ticket-Granting Service Request* (KRB_TGS_REQ) message. The message structure of the KRB_TGS_REQ message is the same as the one shown in Table 3.2 for the KRB_AS_REQ message, but the KRB_TGS_REQ also uses fields that were not used by the KRB_AS_REQ message. When the KDC receives the KRB_TGS_REQ message, it decrypts it, using its shared secret key. It extracts the clients' logon session key, which it uses in turn to decrypt the authenticator. If the authenticator is valid, the KDC extracts the authorization data from the ticket and then creates a session key to be shared between the client and server. The KDC encrypts a copy of the session key with the client's logon session key. Another copy of the session key is placed into a ticket along with the client's authorization data, and then the ticket is encrypted using the server's long-term key. All this data is sent back to the client in a *Kerberos Ticket-Granting Service Reply* (KRB_TGS_REP). The message structure of the KRB_TGS_REP message is the same as the one shown in Table 3.3 for the KRB_AS_REP message. Of course, contents of the fields vary according to the message type. After the client receives the KRB_TGS_REP message, it decrypts it, using its logon session key to decrypt the session key. After decrypting the session key, it stores it in its credentials cache. The client then extracts the ticket for the server and stores it in its credentials cache.

CS Exchange

The CS Exchange is the subprotocol used when the client sends the session ticket to a server. The client sends a *Kerberos Application Request* (KRB_AP_REQ) message to the server. The contents of the KRB_AP_REQ message are shown in Table 3.4.

Table 3.4 Contents of the KRB_AP_REQ Message

Name of Field	Contents of Field
Protocol Version	5
Message Type	KRB_AP_REQ
Applications Options	The two valid options are use session key or mutual authentication required
Ticket	The session ticket for the target server
Authenticator	The authenticator for the session ticket

After the server receives the ticket, it decrypts it and extracts the client's authorization data and session key. The server uses the session key to decrypt the client's authenticator. If the authenticator is valid, the server looks to see whether the mutual authentication flag is set. This flag is set by the Kerberos policy for the realm and not individually by the client. If the flag has been set, then the server uses the session key to encrypt the timestamp in the client's authenticator and send it back to the client in a *Kerberos Application Reply* (KRB_AP_REP) message. After the client receives the KRB_AP_REP message, it decrypts the server's authenticator using the session key and compares the time sent by the server with the time in the authenticator the client originally sent to the server. If the times are the same, communication continues between the client and server. Table 3.5 shows the contents of the KRB_AP_REP message.

Table 3.5 Contents of the KRB_AP_REP Message

Name of Field	Contents of Field
Protocol Version	5
Message Type	KRB_AP_REP
Client Time	The current time on the client, according to the authenticator
CUSEC	The millisecond portion of the client time, according to the authenticator
Subkey	The key to use to encrypt the client session
Sequence Number	This field to use if the sequence number is specified in the authenticator

Option Flags for KRB_AS_REQ and KRB_TGS_REQ Messages

As is shown in Table 3.2, flags for the TGT can be requested in the KDC Options field of the KRB_AS_REQ message. This same field exists in the KRB_TGS_REQ message. The field length is 32 bits, and each option corresponds to one of these bits. Table 3.6 lists the

Table 3.6 Flags Available in the KDC Options Field

Flag Bit	Flag Value	Remarks
0	Reserved	
1	Forwardable	The ticket can be forwarded to other addresses. The allowed addresses are specified in the address field of the message.
2	Forwarded	The ticket is a forwarded ticket.
3	Proxiable	The ticket can be proxied. This means that the ticket can be valid from other specified addresses instead of the client's address.
4	Proxy	The ticket is a proxy ticket.
5	Allow Postdate	The ticket can be postdated.
6	Postdated	The ticket is postdated
7	Reserved	
8	Renewable	The ticket can be renewed. Tickets are valid only for the time specified in the Kerberos realm policy. If this bit is set, they can be renewed when the maximum time for the Kerberos realm has been reached.
9–13	Reserved	
14	Request Anonymous	Creates a ticket authenticating that the user is actually anonymous.
15-25	Reserved	
26	Disable Transited Check	Disables tracking the realms a ticket has passed through.
27	Renewable OK	On the basis of this ticket, renewable tickets can be created.
28	ENC-TKT-INSKEY	Encrypts the ticket in the session key. Used in user-to-user authentication.
29	Reserved	
30	Renew	Used by the KRB_TGS_REQ message and sent with the ticket that needs to be renewed.
31	Validate	Used to validate a postdated ticket based upon the start time located in the ticket.

options available in the KDC Options field for the KRB_AS_REQ and KRB_TGS_REQ messages.

Tickets

Tickets are at the heart of the Kerberos authentication system. A variety of messages are used to request and send tickets between principals. The components that make up a ticket are similar to those in the message tables earlier in the chapter. Table 3.7 shows the contents of tickets.

Tickets contain a flag field that is 32 bits wide, just as KRB_AS_REQ and KRB_TGS_REQ messages do. Some of the fields are identical to those for the messages; others are different. Table 3.8 shows the complete list of flags available for Kerberos tickets.

Table 3.7 Contents of a Kerberos Ticket

Name of Field	Contents of Field
Ticket Version	5
Realm Name	The name of the realm
Server Name	The name of the target server
Flags	The options for the ticket
Key	The session key
Client Realm	The initial realm that performed the authentication
Client Name	The name of the client
Transited	The names of the realm that have been crossed
Authentication Time	The time the ticket was created
Start Time	The time the ticket starts being valid
End Time	The time the ticket is no longer valid
Renew Till Time	The time the ticket absolutely expires
Client Address	The valid address(es) for the client
Authorization Data	The authorization data for the client
Extensions	An optional field for the use of application-specific data

Table 3.8 Flags available in Kerberos Tickets

Flag Bit	Flag Value	Remarks
0	Reserved	
1	Forwardable	The ticket can be forwarded. This flag is applicable only to TGTs.
2	Forwarded	The ticket has been forwarded.
3	Proxiable	The ticket can be proxied.
4	Proxy	The ticket has been proxied.
5	May Postdate	In a TGT, successive tickets can be postdated.
6	Postdated	The ticket is postdated.
7	Invalid	Set for a postdated ticket and cleared by the TGS when the start time for the ticket has been validated.
8	Renewable	The ticket is renewable.
9	Initial	The ticket is the result of a KRB_AS_REQ message and not based on a TGT.
10	Preauthenticated	Specifies that preauthentication was required before the ticket was created.
11	HW-authenticated	A hardware device was used to complete preauthentication.
12	Transited Policy Checked	The KDC completed a check of all realms that the ticket has crossed to ensure that the realms were trusted.
13	OK As Delegate	The server specified in the ticket can act as a delegate for proxy or forwarded tickets.
14	Anonymous	The principal is a generic account used to distribute a session key.
15–31	Reserved	

Tickets can be used by the principal holding the ticket as many times as necessary, as long as it is within the inclusive period shown between the start time and the end time. The time for a ticket is set by the KDC and is based upon the current time unless the client has requested a different start time. Clients do not have to request a start time, but they do include the time they want the ticket to expire. The KDC consults the Kerberos realm policy and adds the time indicated in the policy to the start time. If the client has requested a specific end time, the KDC adds the requested end time to the start time. Whichever time is shorter, the time calculated using the Kerberos policy or the time calculated using the client requested time, is the time used for the end time.

If a client sends an expired session ticket to a server, then the server rejects it. It is then up to the client to go back to the KDC and request a new session ticket. However, if the client is already communicating with the server and the session ticket expires, communication continues to take place. Session tickets are used to authenticate the connection to the server. After the authentication has taken place, the session ticket can expire, but the connection will not be dropped.

Ticket-granting tickets also expire on the basis of the time set in the Kerberos realm policy. If a client attempts to use an expired TGT with the KDC, then the KDC rejects it. At that point the client must request a new TGT from the KDC, using the user's long-term key.

It is possible to renew tickets as well as flag settings. The Kerberos realm policy dictates whether tickets are renewable or not. If the policy allows tickets to be renewed, then the renewable flag is set in every ticket issued by the KDC. In this situation, the KDC places a time in the end time field and another time in the renew till time field of tickets. The time set in the renew till time field is equivalent to the time set in the start time field added to the maximum cumulative ticket life set in the Kerberos realm policy. The client must submit the ticket to the KDC prior to the original expiration time shown in the end time field. Every time the client sends a ticket back to the KDC, it must send a new authenticator also. When the KDC receives the ticket from the client, it checks the time set in the renew till time field. If the time has not already passed, then the KDC creates a new copy of the ticket that has a new time set in the end time field as well as a new session key. By issuing a new session key, the KDC helps to alleviate the possibility of compromised keys.

Proxy Tickets and Forwarded Tickets

Within tickets, the proxy and forwarded flags are used in situations in which a client connects to one server and that server connects to another server to complete the transaction for the client. This is known as delegation of authentication. Kerberos operates using tickets, so the first server must have a ticket to connect to the second server. Proxy and forwarded flags operate on different principles, and they must be specifically allowed in the Kerberos realm policy.

Proxy tickets operate on the principle that the client knows the name of the second server that will be contacted. If the policy for the Kerberos realm allows proxy tickets, then the KDC sets the proxiable flag in the TGT it sends to the client. When the client requests a ticket for server two, it sets the flag stating that it wants a proxy ticket and includes the name of server one, which is the server that will act on behalf of the client. The KDC generates the ticket for server two, sets the proxy flag, and sends it to the client. The client then sends the

Figure 3.5 These are the steps used for proxy tickets.

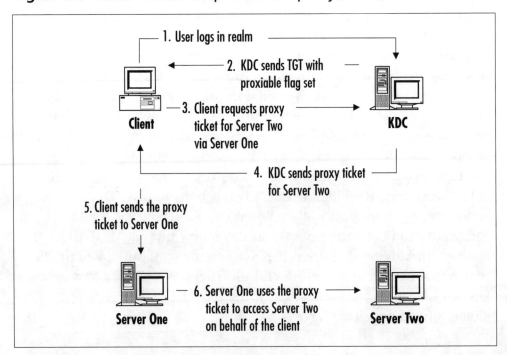

ticket to server one, which uses the ticket to access server two on behalf of the client. Figure 3.5 shows the process for proxy tickets.

If the client does not know the name of server two, it cannot request a proxy ticket. This is where forwarded tickets are used. Forwarded tickets operate on the principle that the client gives server one a TGT that it can use to request tickets for other servers when necessary. The client requests a forwardable TGT from the KDC notifying the KDC the name of the server, in this case server one, that is authorized to act on behalf of the client. The KDC generates the forwardable TGT for server one and sends it back to the client. The client then sends the forwardable TGT to server one. When server one wants to contact another server such as server two, it sends the client's TGT to the KDC. The KDC detects that the TGT is forwardable, so it creates a forwarded ticket for server two and sends the ticket to server one. Server one can then use that ticket to access server two on behalf of the client. Figure 3.6 shows the steps taken for forwarded tickets.

Figure 3.6 These are the steps used for forwarded tickets.

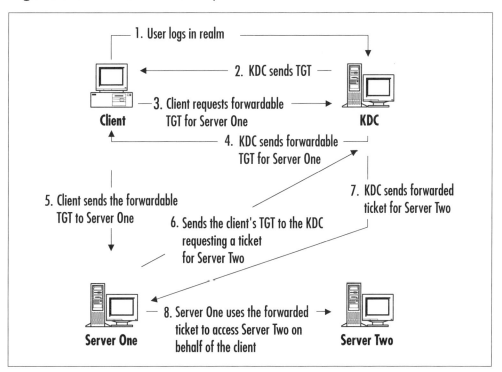

Kerberos and Windows 2000

The Kerberos implementation in Windows 2000 is called Microsoft Kerberos because Microsoft added its own extensions. Microsoft Kerberos only authenticates the identity of the user, it does not

For Managers

How Microsoft Kerberos Interoperates with Other Kerberos Implementations

A key concern for managers planning on implementing Windows 2000 into their existing networks that utilize Kerberos is the interoperability of the different flavors of Kerberos. Microsoft has tested various scenarios between Microsoft Kerberos and the Massachusetts Institute of Technology (MIT) implementation of Kerberos. Their findings are:

- Clients that are not Windows-based can authenticate to a Windows 2000 KDC.

- Windows 2000 systems can authenticate to the KDC in an MIT-based Kerberos realm.

- Windows 2000 client applications can authenticate to Kerberos services running on systems that are not Windows-based, as long as the service supports the GSS-API. Windows 2000 uses the Security Support Provider Interface that is compatible with the GSS-API.

- Client applications on Kerberos systems that do not use Windows can authenticate to services on Windows 2000 systems, as long as the client application supports the GSS-API.

- Windows 2000 domains can trust MIT-based Kerberos realms, and MIT-based Kerberos realms can trust Windows 2000 domains when everything is configured appropriately.

authorize access. After the identity of the user has been verified by Microsoft Kerberos, then the Local Security Authority (LSA) authorizes or denies access to the resource.

Key Distribution Center

The KDC is integral to the operation of Kerberos, and Windows 2000 implements the KDC as a domain service, as shown in Figure 3.7. The KDC uses Active Directory as the source of its account database (see Chapter 4,"Secure networking using Windows 2000 Distributed Security Services").

The KDC service, along with the Active Directory, is located on every Windows 2000 domain controller. This allows each domain controller to accept authentication and ticket requests instead of depending on a single KDC.

Figure 3.7 Kerberos Key Distribution Center runs as a service on Windows 2000 domain controllers.

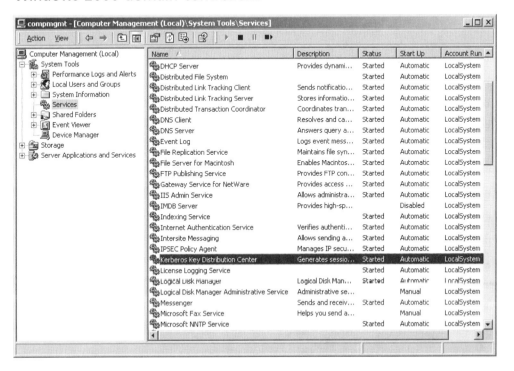

Figure 3.8 The krbtgt account is used by the Key Distribution Center.

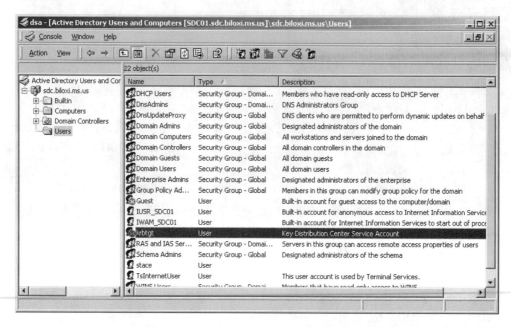

Every Kerberos KDC has its own principal name. The name used in Windows 2000 is krbtgt, which follows the guideline given in RFC 1510. When a Windows 2000 domain is created, a user account named krbtgt is created for the KDC principal, as shown in Figure 3.8. This account is a built-in account, so it cannot be deleted, renamed, or enabled for normal user use. Even though it appears that the account is disabled, in reality it is being used by the KDC. An administrator who attempts to enable the account receives the dialog box shown in Figure 3.9.

Figure 3.9 A failed attempt to enable the krbtgt account.

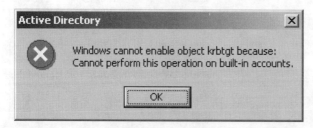

The password for the account is generated automatically by Windows 2000 and is changed automatically by the system on a regular basis. The key used by the krbtgt account is based on its password, just like a normal user's long-term key. The long-term key of krbtgt is used to encrypt and decrypt the TGTs it gives out. The krbtgt account is used by all KDCs in a domain. For example, a Windows 2000 domain may have five domain controllers, each of which has its own functioning KDC, but each of the KDCs uses the krbtgt account. This allows each KDC to encrypt and decrypt TGTs using the same long-term key. A client knows which KDC to communicate with because client computer queries the Domain Name System (DNS) for a domain controller. After the client locates a domain controller, it sends the KRB_AS_REQ message to the KDC service on that domain controller.

Kerberos Policy

Policy for Kerberos in Windows 2000 is set at the domain level. As a matter of fact, Microsoft uses the word "domain" instead of "realm" when referring to Kerberos policy. Kerberos policy is stored within Active Directory, and only members of the Domain Admins group are allowed to change the policy. Figure 3.10 shows the options available in the Kerberos policy for the domain. The settings shown are the default for Windows 2000 Release candidate 2.

The settings included in the Kerberos Domain Policy are:

- Enforce user logon restrictions
- Maximum lifetime for service ticket
- Maximum lifetime for user ticket
- Maximum lifetime for user ticket renewal
- Maximum tolerance for computer clock synchronization

Enforce user logon restrictions is enabled by default and is used to validate every request for service tickets by making sure that the client has the correct user rights for logging on the destination server.

Figure 3.10 The default Kerberos Domain Policy.

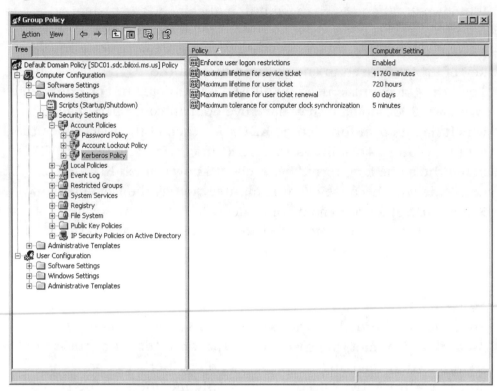

This setting can be disabled; it takes extra time to perform and may slow down network performance.

The maximum service ticket lifetime is set in minutes. Do not let the term "service ticket" confuse you; it is just the name Microsoft decided to use for session tickets. The setting for the lifetime of the service ticket cannot be more than the time specified in the maximum user ticket lifetime or less than ten minutes. A reasonable setting for this option is to make it the same as the maximum user ticket lifetime.

The maximum user ticket lifetime is set in hours. Microsoft has decided to use the term "user ticket", but in Kerberos terms it is a TGT. A reasonable setting is 10 hours for this attribute.

The maximum lifetime that a user ticket can be renewed setting is set in days. A reasonable setting is seven days for this attribute.

The maximum tolerance for synchronization of computer clocks setting determines how much difference in the clocks is

Figure 3.11 The way to change the setting for the maximum lifetime that a user ticket can be renewed attribute.

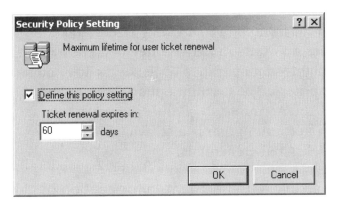

tolerated. This setting is in minutes, and five minutes is a reasonable setting.

It is easy to change an attribute by double-clicking the attribute and changing the setting, as shown in Figure 3.11.

Contents of a Microsoft Kerberos Ticket

There are additional items contained in Microsoft Kerberos tickets that are not in other Kerberos implementations tickets. Windows 2000 uses Security Identifiers (SIDs) just as in previous versions of Windows NT. SIDs are used to represent user accounts and groups. The SID for a user, along with any SIDs for the groups the user belongs to, is included in tickets used by the client and is known as the Privilege Attribute Certificate (PAC). The PAC is not the same thing as a public key certificate. The user's name, also known as User Principal Name, is added to the ticket as UPN:name@domain. For example, UPN:stace@sdc.biloxi.ms.us is placed in a ticket to identify the user Stace.

Delegation of Authentication

Kerberos supports two methods of delegation: proxiable tickets and forwardable tickets. Microsoft Kerberos provides support for forwardable tickets only, and the default Kerberos policy for Windows 2000 domains assigns this permission only to members of the Domain Admins group. It can be provided to individual users by modifying the user's account from Active Directory Users and Computers. To access user accounts in Active Directory, click Start, highlight Programs, highlight Administrative Tools, and click Active Directory Users and Computers. The account option for enabling delegation is available on the Account tab of a user's properties, as shown in Figure 3.12. An account option is also available to not allow the acceptance of delegated credentials.

Figure 3.12 The way to enable a user account for delegation of authentication.

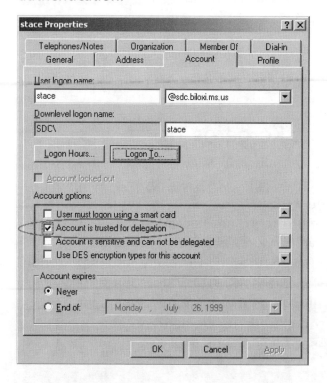

Preauthentication

In Kerberos authentication, some of the messages have a preauthentication field. Microsoft Kerberos uses preauthentication in domains by default. The data contained in this field is the encrypted timestamp of the client. If it is necessary, preauthentication can be turned off for user accounts on an individual basis, as shown in Figure 3.13. It may be necessary to turn off preauthentication if you are integrating Microsoft Kerberos with other variations of the Kerberos protocol.

Figure 3.13 The way to disable a preauthentication for a user account.

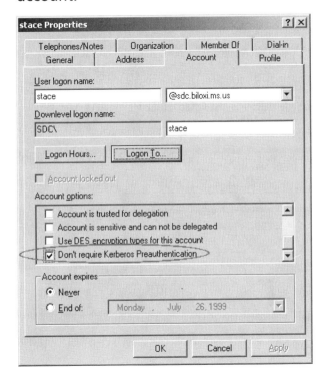

Security Support Providers

When the system is booted, Windows 2000 Server automatically starts two Security Support Providers (SSPs): the Kerberos SSP and the NTLM SSP. Both SSPs are started by the LSA, and both are available to authenticate network logons and connections between clients and servers. Windows 2000 Server defaults to using the Kerberos SSP unless the client is not capable of using Kerberos, as is the case with Windows 9x. In that case the NTLM SSP is used. The NTLM SSP is also used for Windows 2000 Servers that are configured as member servers or stand-alone servers and also for logging on a domain controller locally instead of on the domain. (Figure 3.14 outlines the process used when you log on locally.) The Kerberos SSP is used first for authentication because it is the default for Windows 2000. However, if the user is logging on locally, an error is sent to the Security Support Provider Interface (SSPI), and then the SSPI sends the logon request to the NTLM SSP.

Figure 3.14 The logon process for local logons.

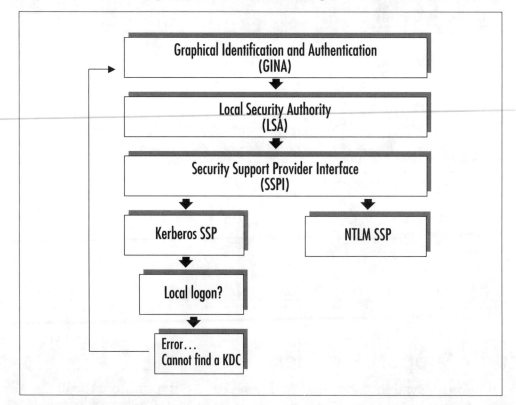

Credentials Cache

The client uses an area of volatile memory called the credentials cache. This area of memory is protected by the LSA, and it can never be put in the pagefile on the hard disk drive. When the user logs off the system, everything in the area of memory used for the credentials cache is flushed.

The Kerberos SSP controls the credentials cache and is used to attain as well as renew tickets and keys. The LSA is responsible for notifying the Kerberos SSP when these functions need to be performed.

The LSA also keeps a copy of the user's hashed password in a secure portion of the registry while the user is logged on. Once the user logs off, the hashed password is discarded. The LSA keeps a copy of the hashed password in case the TGT expires; it then gives the Kerberos SSP a method of obtaining another TGT without prompting the user to input a password. This allows this task to be smoothly accomplished in the background.

DNS Name Resolution

Microsoft Kerberos depends on the Domain Name System (DNS) to find an available KDC to send the initial authentication request. All Windows 2000 domain controllers are KDCs, and the KDC is registered as _kerberos._udp.nameofDNSdomain in the DNS service location record (SRV record). Clients can query for this SRV record to locate the IP address for computers running the KDC service. A client that cannot find the SRV record can query for a host record (A record), using the domain name.

If a Windows 2000 computer is a member of a different Kerberos realm (not a Windows 2000 domain), then it cannot look for the SRV record. In this case, the name of the KDC server is stored in the registry of the Windows 2000 computer. When the computer needs to locate the KDC, the Microsoft Kerberos SSP locates the domain name for the KDC server from the registry and then uses DNS to find out the IP address for the system.

UDP and TCP Ports

When a client sends Kerberos messages to the KDC, it defaults to using User Datagram Protocol (UDP) port 88 as long as certain criteria are met. On an Ethernet network, the Maximum Transmission Unit (MTU) that can be carried is 1500 bytes. If the Kerberos message is smaller than 1472 bytes, Microsoft Kerberos uses UDP as the transport mechanism. If the message is between 1473 bytes and 2000 bytes, IP fragments the frame over UDP on port 88. If the Kerberos message is over 2000 bytes, it is sent by the Transmission Control Protocol (TCP) on port 88. RFC 1510 states that UDP port 88 should be used for all Kerberos messages, but since Microsoft Kerberos messages may very well be more than 2000 bytes, because user and group SIDs are included, Microsoft also uses TCP port 88. A draft revision to RFC 1510 has been submitted to the Internet Engineering Task Force (IETF) proposing the use of TCP port 88, but it has not been included in the formal RFC yet. Interoperability should not be affected with other Kerberos realms; the communications are between Windows 2000 computers only.

Authorization Data

Kerberos only verifies the identity of principals; it does authorize the resources they can use. A field is available in Kerberos tickets for authorization data, but Kerberos does not control what information is placed in the field or what should be done with the information.

KDC and Authorization Data

The authorization data field in a Microsoft Kerberos ticket contains a list of SIDs for the user, including group SIDs. This information is retrieved by the KDC from the Active Directory and placed in the TGT given to the client. When the client requests a session ticket (or service ticket, in Microsoft parlance), the KDC copies the data from the authorization data field of the TGT over into the session ticket. The authorization data is signed by the KDC before the data is stored in the session ticket so that the LSA can detect whether the data has been modified. The LSA checks each session ticket to ensure that the signature is valid.

Services and Authorization Data

An access token is created after the credentials in a session ticket have been verified by the network server on which the service resides. The PAC is extracted from the session ticket and is used to construct an impersonation token that is used to access the service on the server. The impersonation token is presented to the service, and as long as the information in the PAC matches the data contained in the Access Control List (ACL) for the service, access is granted.

In Microsoft Kerberos, a session ticket is also required for access to services on local systems. The same process takes place for access to local resources; the LSA builds a local access token from the PAC contained in the session ticket.

Summary

Windows 2000 supports several authentication protocols, including Windows NT LAN Manager, Kerberos v5, Distributed Password Authentication, Extensible Authentication Protocol, and Secure Channel. The two protocols used for network authentication, for logging on locally or as an interactive user, are NTLM and Kerberos v5. Kerberos is the default authentication protocol used in Windows 2000; NTLM is provided for backward compatibility and is also used to authenticate Windows 2000 member and stand-alone servers.

Kerberos provides several advantages over NTLM, which was the authentication protocol of choice in previous versions of Windows NT. One of the advantages is that Kerberos provides mutual authentication wherein the client can also verify the identity of the server, which cannot be accomplished using NTLM. Another advantage is that Windows 2000 Kerberos domains can communicate with Kerberos realms of other implementations of Kerberos. This cannot be accomplished with NTLM, which is proprietary to Microsoft operating systems.

Kerberos is made up of several components, including the Key Distribution Center, session tickets, and ticket-granting tickets. The

Key Distribution Center is comprised of two services, the Authentication Service and the Ticket-Granting Service. Three sub-protocols used by Kerberos are the Authentication Service Exchange, the Ticket-Granting Service Exchange, and the Client/Server Exchange.

Microsoft implements its own flavor of Kerberos in Windows 2000. Microsoft Kerberos adds extensions to the Kerberos standard to meet specific requirements necessary for Windows 2000, such as the capability to use public key certificates instead of the normal shared key to log on Windows 2000 domains. Microsoft implements the KDC as a service in Windows 2000, and the service is automatically installed on all domain controllers. Microsoft Kerberos stores the Privilege Attribute Certificate in tickets. The PAC consists of the user's SID as well as group SIDs for the groups of which the user is a member. The PAC is extracted after the server authenticates the identity of the user. The server then uses the PAC to create an impersonation token for access to the service the client has requested to use.

FAQs

Q: Do I need to manually create the Kerberos settings for my Windows 2000 domain?

A: Windows 2000 Server ships with a default domain policy that includes reasonable settings for the Kerberos Policy. The only reason to change from the default settings is if the requirements for your organization differ from the default value settings.

Q: Can my Windows 9x clients authenticate using Kerberos?

A: No, Microsoft is not releasing a Kerberos add-on for Windows 9x. Windows 9x clients can only authenticate using the NTLM authentication protocol. To enhance the security of Windows 2000 domains, Microsoft recommends that you upgrade all clients to Windows 2000 so that the more secure Kerberos authentication protocol is utilized by all systems in the domain.

Q: How does a server know that a user is authorized access to a service even though it has authenticated their identity?

A: Microsoft Kerberos includes a Privilege Attribute Certificate in every ticket. The PAC includes the user's SID and the SIDs for all groups of which the user is a member. The server compares this data with the data for the Access Control List on the service to determine if access is allowed or denied. If access is allowed, the server also determines the level of access based upon information in the ACL.

Q: How does a Windows 2000 client find a Microsoft KDC?

A: It uses DNS to locate KDCs in the domain.

Q: Why are ticket-granting tickets necessary?

A: To prove to the KDC that the clients requesting a session ticket are really who they say they are. The KDC issues the TGT to the client when it first logs on the domain.

Q: How can Windows 2000 be configured to use forwardable tickets?

A: By default, members of the Domain Admins group can forward tickets. For other users, it has to be configured individually.

Chapter 4

Secure Networking Using Windows 2000 Distributed Security Services

Solutions in this chapter:

- **Introduction**

- **Windows 2000 Distributed Security Services**

- **Active Directory and Security**

- **Multiple Security Protocols**

- **Enterprise and Internet Single Sign-on**

- **Internet Security**

- **Interbusiness Access: Distributed Partners**

Introduction

Security concerns are relatively new to the PC world. In the early days of personal computing, most systems were stand-alone units that could be protected simply by locking an office door. Mainframe computers have long used high-level security technology to protect sensitive business data, but only as PCs began to be networked to one another—first within the organization, and then later connected to other networks and the global Internet—did businesses start to worry about protecting the data on their hard drives from prying eyes.

Microsoft's NT server software has made it easy for companies to join their PCs together and share all the benefits, in convenience and cost-saving, of networking. And as those networks have grown, so have concerns over the security of the data that resides on them.

The Way We Were: Security in NT

Microsoft responded to those concerns by increasing its attention to security issues in the NT operating system as the product matured (in fact, many of its service packs have addressed just that issue), but security has always been considered by many to be one of NT's less-than-strong points when compared to alternative network oper-ating systems. The NTLM security protocol used in NT, although providing a reasonable level of security for most purposes, has sev-eral drawbacks:

- It is proprietary, not an industrywide standard and not popular outside Microsoft networking.

- It does not provide mutual authentication; that is, although the server authenticates the client, there is no reciprocal authentication on the part of the client. It is just assumed that the server's credentials are valid. This has been a weak spot, leaving NT networks vulnerable to hackers and crackers whose programs, by masquerading as servers, could gain access to the system.

A Whole New World: Distributed Security in Windows 2000

Windows 2000's security protocols (note the plural; the new operating system's support for multiple protocols is one of its strongest features) are different; they are part of what is known as the distributed services. *Distributed services* is a term that pops up frequently when we discuss network operating systems, and it seems to be mentioned even more often as we familiarize ourselves with the Windows 2000 Server family. Most network administrators have a vague idea of what it means, but probably have never really sat down and tried to define it, especially in terms of security.

Distributed Services

Distributed services are those components that are spread (or distributed) throughout the network, and that are highly dependent upon one another. The high-profile member of this group of Windows 2000 subsystems is Active Directory, but the Windows 2000 security subsystem is another of the operating system's distributed services. In fact, in keeping with the interdependency of the distributed services, there is a fundamental relationship between the Active Directory service and Windows 2000's security subsystem.

Open Standards

Windows 2000 signals a big change in direction for Microsoft, away from the proprietary nature of many of NT's features, and moving toward the adoption of industry standards. This new path is demonstrated most prominently in the area of distributed services. Active Directory itself is based on the Lightweight Directory Access Protocol (LDAP), thus making it compatible with other directory services, such as Novell's NDS, which adhere to this open Internet standard.

NOTE

LDAP standards are established by working groups of the Internet
Engineering Task Force (IETF).

Active Directory is also compatible (although not fully compliant)
with the International Standards Organization's X.500 standards for
distributed directory services. With this commitment to supporting
widespread standards, Microsoft is demonstrating its serious intent to
make Windows a true enterprise-capable network operating system.

One of the primary requirements of an enterprise-level NOS in
today's security-conscious world is a way to protect the integrity
and privacy of the network's data. So it is no surprise that there
have been major, drastic changes made to the security subsystem in
the latest implementation of Windows server software.

Much as it has adopted open directory services standards,
Microsoft has incorporated into Windows 2000 support for the widely utilized and respected Kerberos security protocol developed at the
Massachusetts Institute of Technology, and the ISO's X.509 public
key security, another accepted standard. These are in addition to
the NTLM security protocol used in NT, which is included in
Windows 2000 for compatibility with downlevel (NT) domains. Figure
4.1 gives an overview of the Windows 2000 security structure.

This chapter examines Windows 2000's distributed security services in detail, with the focus on how intimately the security and
directory services are intertwined, and how Active Directory's objects
can be secured in a granular manner that was never possible in
Windows NT. It also looks at the security protocols themselves, and
the role and function of each. Finally, the chapter addresses the
special area of Internet security, and the added level of protection
from unauthorized outside access provided by the Windows 2000
distributed security subsystem.

Figure 4.1 A graphic overview of the Windows 2000 security structure.

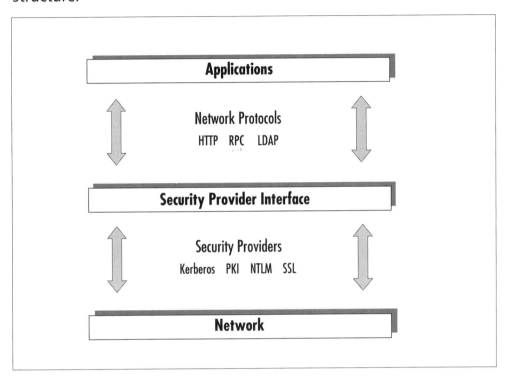

Windows 2000 Distributed Security Services

What exactly are these security services that are distributed throughout the network, and how do they work together to ensure more robust protection for user passwords and other confidential data? A number of security features, which together make up the distributed security services, are built into Windows 2000:

- **Active Directory security.** This includes the new concept of transitive trusts, which allows user account authentication to be distributed across the enterprise, as well as the granular assignment of access rights and the new ability to delegate administration below the domain level.

- **Multiple security protocols.** Windows 2000 implements the popular Kerberos security protocol, supports Public Key Infrastructure (PKI), and has backward compatibility with NT through the use of NTLM.

- **Security Support Provider Interface (SSPI).** This component of the security subsystem reduces the amount of code needed at the application level to support multiple security protocols by providing a generic interface for the authentication mechanisms that are based on shared-secret or public key protocols (see Chapter 9, "The Security Support Provider Interface," for a more detailed explanation of these protocols).

- **Secure Socket Layer (SSL).** This protocol is used by Internet browsers and servers, and is designed to provide for secure communications over the Internet by using a combination of public and secret key technology.

- **Microsoft Certificate Services.** This service was included with IIS 4.0 in the NT 4.0 Option Pack and has been upgraded and made a part of Windows 2000 Server. It is used to issue and manage the certificates for applications that use public key cryptography to provide secure communications over the Internet, as well as within the company's intranet.

- **CryptoAPI (CAPI).** As its name indicates, this is an application programming interface that allows applications to encrypt data using independent modules known as cryptographic service providers (CSPs), and protects the user's private key data during the process.

- **Single Sign-On (SSO).** This is a key feature of Windows 2000 authentication, which allows a user to log on the domain just one time, using a single password, and authenticate to any computer in the domain, thus reducing user confusion and improving efficiency, and at the same time decreasing the need for administrative support.

As a network administrator, you are probably not most concerned with the intricacies of how the various cryptographic algorithms work (although that can be an interesting sideline course of study, especially if you are mathematically inclined). This jumble of acronyms can be used to keep your organization's sensitive data secure. This chapter emphasizes just that—combining the distributed security services of Windows 2000 in a way that balances security and ease of accessibility in your enterprise network.

Active Directory and Security

It should come as no surprise, given the amount of time and care Microsoft has put into developing its directory services for Windows 2000, that a great deal of attention was paid to making Active Directory a feature-rich service that will be able to compete with other established directory services in the marketplace. After extensive study of what network administrators out in the field want and need in a directory service, Active Directory was designed with security as a high priority item.

These are some of the important components of Active Directory's security functions:

- Storage of security credentials for users and computers in Active Directory, and the authentication of computers on the network when the network is started.

- The transitive trust model, in which all other domains in the domain tree accept security credentials that are valid for one domain.

- Secure single sign-on to the enterprise (because security credentials are stored in Active Directory, making them available to domain controllers throughout the network).

- Replication of all Active Directory objects to every domain controller in a domain.

- Management and accessibility of user and computer accounts, policies, and resources at the "nearest" (in terms of network connectivity) domain controller.

- Inheritance of Active Directory object properties from parent objects.

- Creation of account and policy properties at the group level, which can then be applied to all new and existing members.

- Delegation of specific administrative responsibilities to specific users or groups.

- Ability of servers to authenticate on behalf of clients.

All these features work together, as part of Active Directory and the security subsystem. Compared to Windows NT, this is a whole new (and better) way of doing things.

Active Directory can be of benefit for managing user and computer accounts in the enterprise.

Advantages of Active Directory Account Management

Windows NT, as it came out of the box, was not a particularly secure operating system. There are several reasons for this. First, during the timeframe in which NT was initially developed, security was not as big a concern in the corporate environment as it has become in the past several years. Second, security is not traditionally as crucial in smaller network environments as in large ones, and NT was not in widespread use in large-enterprise situations. Finally, Microsoft's focus in designing NT was ease of use; there will always be a trade-off between security level and accessibility. With Windows 2000, security is built right into Active Directory.

Active Directory will support a much larger number of user objects (more than a million) with better performance than the NT Registry-based domain model. Maximum domain size is no longer limited by the performance of the security account repository. A domain tree can support much larger, complex organizational structures, making Windows truly suitable for enterprise networking.

Since account management is the foundation of any NT or Windows 2000 security plan, it stands to reason that the easier and more specific management of user accounts is, the better it will be for security purposes.

Account management is an important issue. Every user initially enters the network through a user account; this is the beginning point for assignment of user rights and permissions to access resources, individually or (as Microsoft recommends) through membership in security groups (see Figure 4.2).

Figure 4.2 The user account is the entry point to the network and the basis for security.

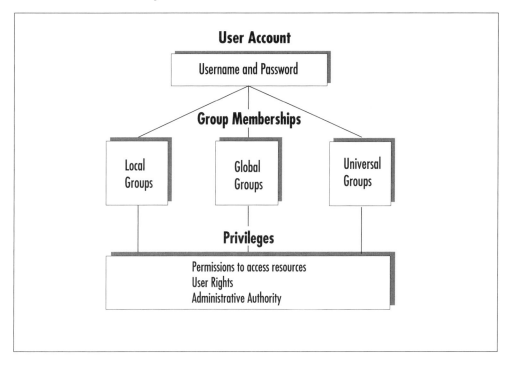

In Windows NT 4.0 Server, user accounts were administered from the User Manager for Domains and computer accounts were managed via Server Manager. In a Windows 2000 domain, both types of accounts are managed from a single point, the Active Directory Users and Computers MMC snap-in. To access this tool, follow this path: Start menu|Programs|Administrative Tools|Active Directory Users and Computers.

Figure 4.3 shows the separate folders for computers and users (showing the Users folder expanded).

Figure 4.3 Accounts can be managed with the Active Directory Users and Computers snap-in.

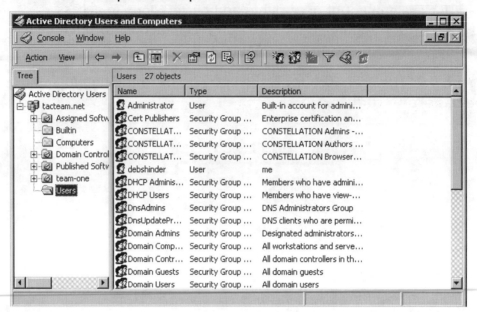

TIP

Group names, as well as individual user accounts, are included in the Users folder.

This one-stop account management setup makes it easier for the network administrator to address the issues that arise in connection with the security-oriented administration of users, computers, and resources.

Managing Security via Object Properties

In Active Directory, everything is an object, and every object has properties, also called attributes. The attributes of a user account include security-related information. In the case of a user account, this would include memberships in security groups and password and authentication requirements. Windows 2000 makes it easy for the administrator to access the attributes of an object (and allows for the recording of much more information than was possible with NT). Figure 4.4 shows the Account property sheet of a user account and some of the optional settings that can be applied.

Figure 4.4 The user account properties sheet (Account tab).

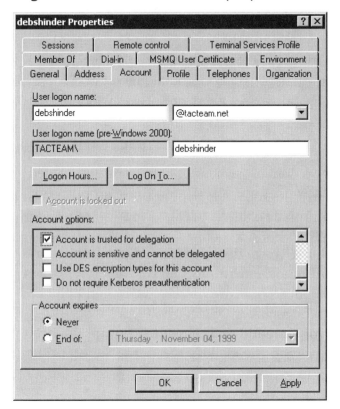

It is possible to specify the use of DES encryption or no require-ment for Kerberos preauthentication, along with other security crite-ria for this user account, simply by clicking on a check box. The same is true of trusting the account for delegation or prohibiting the account from being delegated. Other options that can be selected here (not shown in the figure, but available by scrolling up the list) include:

- Requirement that the user change the password at next logon
- Prohibition on the user's changing the password
- Specification that the password is never to expire
- Specification that the password is to be stored using reversible encryption

Some of the settings in the user account properties sheet (such as password expiration properties and logon hours) could be set in NT through the User Manager for Domains. Others are new to Windows 2000.

Managing Security via Group Memberships

In most cases, in a Windows domain, access to resources is assigned to groups, and then user accounts are placed into those groups. This makes access permissions much easier to handle, especially in a large and constantly changing network.

Assigning and maintaining group memberships is another important aspect of user account management, and Active Directory makes this easy as well. Group memberships are managed through another tab on the property sheet, the Member Of tab (see Figure 4.5).

As the figure shows, you can add or remove the groups associated with this user's account with the click of a mouse.

Active Directory Object Permissions

Permissions can be applied to any object in Active Directory, but the majority of permissions should be granted to groups, rather than to individual users. This eases the task of managing permissions on objects.

You can assign permissions for objects to:

- Groups, users, and special identities in the domain
- Groups and users in that domain and any trusted domains
- Local groups and users on the computer where the object resides

To assign Active Directory permissions to a directory object, do one of these things:

1. Open the Active Directory Domains and Trusts tool by following this path: Start|Programs|Administrative Tools|Active Directory Domains and Trusts. Right-click the selected domain and choose Manage.

2. Open the Active Directory Users and Computers tool directly, and expand the tree for the domain you wish to manage.

3. In the View menu, be sure Advanced Features is checked (see Figure 4.6).

WARNING

If the Advanced Features selection is not checked, you will not see the Security tab in the next step.

Figure 4.6 The Advanced Features option on the View menu must be selected in order to set Active Directory permissions on an object.

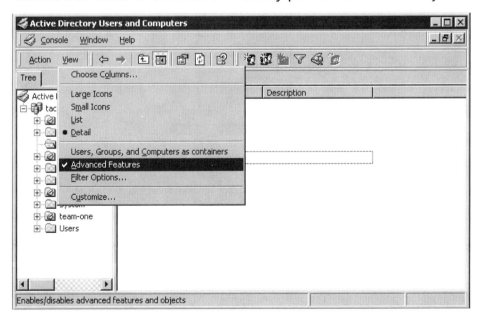

4. Now choose an Active Directory object and right-click it, then select Properties. The Security tab (see Figure 4.7) will provide you with the available permissions for this type of object. In the example, we've selected a computer object named Excelsior.

Figure 4.7 Active Directory permissions are assigned in the Security section of the Properties sheet.

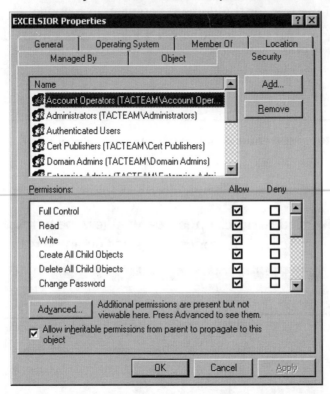

5. To view additional special permissions that may be set on this object, click the Advanced button at the bottom left of the dialog box. Figure 4.8 shows that the resultant dialog box allows you to choose permissions entries to view or edit.

Figure 4.8 The Access Control Settings dialog box.

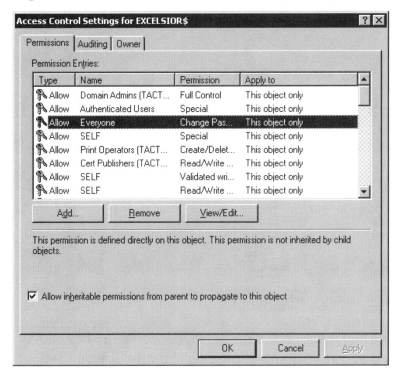

6. Now select the entry that you wish to view, and click View/Edit. The special permissions are shown in Figure 4.9.

7. Finally, to view the permissions for specific attributes, click the Properties tab (see Figure 4.10).

Active Directory permissions can be fine-tuned to an extraordinary degree. But remember, especially as you begin to deploy your security plan using Windows 2000's new features, that just because you *can* do something does not mean you *should* do it.

Figure 4.9 Special permissions for an Active Directory object.

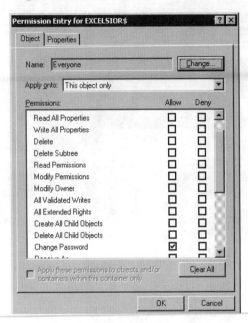

Figure 4.10 The Properties tab on the Permission Entry box shows permissions that can be granted for specific property attributes.

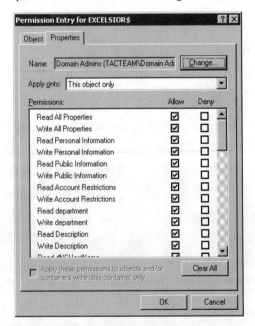

Although Windows 2000 gives you the ability to assign Active Directory permissions not only to objects themselves but to their individual attributes, Microsoft recommends in general that you should not grant permissions for specific object attributes, because this can complicate administrative tasks and disrupt normal operations.

WARNING

You should use these powerful features only when absolutely necessary, and only when you are absolutely sure of the effects your actions will have.

Relationship between Directory and Security Services

Every object in Active Directory has a unique security descriptor that defines the access permissions that are required in order to read or update the object properties. Active Directory uses Windows 2000 access verification to determine whether an Active Directory client can read or update a particular object. Because of this, LDAP client requests to the directory require that the operating system enforce access control, instead of having Active Directory make the access-control decisions.

In Windows 2000, security is directly integrated with the directory services. This differs from the NT model. In NT 4.0, the SAM (Security Accounts Manager) database and the characteristics of the NTLM trust relationship combined to limit security to three levels within the domain: global and local groups, and individual users. With Active Directory, the database is distributed throughout the enterprise.

The result is that security can be administered with much more granularity and flexibility. One example is the ability to delegate administrative authority at the OU level. In NT, assignment of administrative privileges made that user an administrator through-out the entire domain.

Windows 2000 Distributed Security Services use Active Directory as the central repository for account information and domain security policy. This is a big improvement over the registry-based implementation in terms of both performance and scalability. It is also easier to manage. Active Directory provides replication and availability of account information to multiple Domain Controllers, and can be administered remotely.

In addition, Windows 2000 employs a new domain model that uses Active Directory to support a multilevel hierarchy tree of domains. Managing the trust relationships between domains has been enormously simplified by the treewide transitive trust model that extends throughout the domain tree.

Windows 2000's trusts work differently from those in NT, and this affects security issues and administration in the Active Directory environment.

Domain Trust Relationships

The Kerberos security protocol is the basis for the trust relationships between domains in a Windows 2000 network. Chapter 3, "Kerberos Server Authentication," is devoted to the details of how Kerberos works; for purposes of this chapter, it is important to understand that Kerberos is what makes the two-way, transitive trusts of Windows 2000 work.

For an Active Directory namespace, when the first Windows 2000 Server computer in a network is promoted to domain controller, this creates the internal root domain for your organization. It will have a hierarchical name, like mycompany.com.

NOTE

Microsoft calls this the *root domain*. I use the term *internal root domain* to distinguish it from the Internet root domain, which is represented by a dot. On the Internet, mycompany.com, although referred to as a "second-level" domain, resides below both the Internet root and the external "top-level" domain "com."

When additional domains are created in your company's network (by promoting other Windows 2000 servers to domain controllers and designating them as DCs for the new domains), there are two options:

- They can be created as children of the internal root domain, if they include the internal root's namespace in their own; for instance, sales.mycompany.com is a child domain of mycompany.com.

- They can be created as root domains for new domain trees in the forest, if they use an unrelated namespace (also called a noncontiguous namespace); for example, the creation of a domain named yourcompany.com would start a new domain tree that can exist in the same forest as the tree for which mycompany.com is the root.

Figure 4.11 illustrates the relationships of parent and child domains within a tree, and trees within a forest.

Figure 4.11 The relationships of domains within a tree and trees within a forest.

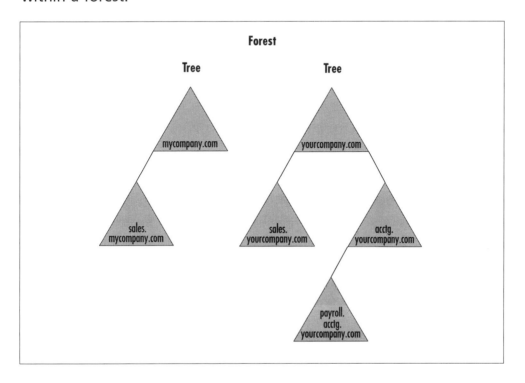

In the figure, two domain trees exist in the forest. The internal root domains are mycompany.com and yourcompany.com; each has one or more child domains that include the parents' namespace, and as you can see, the child domains can have children of their own (to continue the analogy, these would be the grandchildren of the internal root domain).

The Great Link: Kerberos Trusts between Domains

In NT networks, every domain was an island. In order for users in one domain to access resources in another, administrators of the two domains had to set up an explicit trust relationship. Moreover, these trusts were one-way; if the administrators wanted a reciprocal relationship, two separate trusts had to be created, because these trusts were based on the NTLM security protocol, which does not include mutual authentication.

In Windows 2000 networks, that has been changed. With the Kerberos protocol, all trust relationships are two-way, and an implicit, automatic trust exists between every parent and child domain; it is not necessary for administrators to create them. Finally, these trusts are transitive, which means that if the first domain trusts the second domain, and the second domain trusts the third domain, the first domain will trust the third domain, and so on. This comes about through the use of the Kerberos referral, and as a result every domain in a tree implicitly trusts every other domain in that tree.

All this would be cause enough for celebration for those administrators who have struggled with the trust nightmares inherent in the NT way of doing things, but there is one final benefit. The root domains in a forest of domain trees also have an implicit two-way transitive trust relationship with each other. By traversing the trees, then, every domain in the forest trusts every other domain. As long as a user's account has the appropriate permissions, the user has access to resources anywhere on the network, without worrying about the domain in which those resources reside.

For practical purposes, as is shown in Figure 4.11, a user in the payroll.acctg.yourcompany.com domain who needs to access a file or printer in the sales.mycompany.com domain can do so (provided the user's account has the appropriate permissions). The user's domain, payroll.acctg.yourcompany.com, trusts its parent, acctg.yourcompany.com, which in turn trusts its own parent, yourcompany.com. Since yourcompany.com is an internal root domain in the same forest as mycompany.com, those two domains have an implicit two-way transitive trust; thus mycompany.com trusts sales.mycompany.com—and the chain of Kerberos referrals has gone up one tree and down the other to demonstrate the path of the trust that exists between payroll.acctg.yourcompany.com and sales.mycompany.com.

On the other hand, these Kerberos trusts apply only to Windows 2000 domains. If the network includes downlevel (NT) domains, they must still use the old NTLM one-way, explicit trusts in order to share resources to or from the Windows 2000 domains.

NOTE

Despite the transitive trust relationships between domains in a Windows 2000 network, administrative authority is *not* transitive; the domain is still an administrative boundary.

Taking a Shortcut

This process requires many referrals, which is why shortcut trusts are useful. Shortcut trusts are two-way transitive trusts that allow you to shorten the path in a complex forest. They must be explicitly created by the administrators, to create a direct trust relationship between Windows 2000 domains in the same forest. A shortcut trust is used to optimize performance optimization and shorten the trust path that Windows 2000 security must take for authentication purposes. The most effective use of shortcut trusts is between two domain trees in a forest. For instance, in the domain trust example, a shortcut trust could be established between the two domains, payroll.acctg.yourcompany.com and sales.mycompany.com.

Shortcut trusts are one of the two types of explicit domain trees that can be established in Windows 2000; the other is the external trust used to establish a trust relationship with domains that are not part of the forest. The external trust is one-way and nontransitive, as in NT 4.0 domain models. However, as with NT, two one-way trusts can be established if a two-way relationship is desired.

TIP

Windows 2000 explicit trusts are created using the Active Directory Domains and Trusts administrative tool.

Delegation of Administration

One of Active Directory's strongest points, and one most attractive to administrators in a large, complex enterprise network, is the ability it confers on you to delegate administrative authority all the way down to the lowest levels of the organization. It does this by creating an OU tree, in which organizational units can be nested inside one another and administrative responsibility for any part of the OU subtree can be assigned to specific groups or users, without giving them administrative control over any other part of the domain. This was not possible in NT networks, where administrative authority was assigned only on a domain-wide basis.

You will still have an Administrator account and a Domain Administrators group with administrative authority over the entire domain, but you can reserve these accounts for occasional use by a limited number of highly trusted administrators.

TIP

Because logging on routinely with an Administrator account can pose a security risk, even trusted administrative personnel should normally use a nonadministrative account for daily business.

Windows 2000 provides the secondary logon service, which allows you to use the run as command to run programs that require administrative privileges while you are logged on a nonadministrative account.

The delegation of administration responsibilities can be defined in three ways:

- Permissions can be delegated to change properties on a particular container.
- Permissions can be delegated to create and delete child objects of a specific type beneath an OU.
- Permissions can be delegated to update specific properties on child objects of a specific type beneath an OU.

You can delegate administrative control to any level of a domain tree by creating organizational units within the domain and delegating administrative control for specific organizational units to particular users or groups. This lets you define the most appropriate administrative scope for a particular person, whether that includes an entire domain, all the organizational units within a domain, or just a single organizational unit.

Microsoft has made it easy for you to use this newfound power to delegate by providing a Delegation of Control Wizard that walks you through the steps (see Figure 4.12).

To access the wizard, open Active Directory Users and Computers, double-click the domain node in the console tree, right-click the folder for which you want to delegate administrative authority, and select Delegate control. This will start the wizard.

Figure 4.12 Assign administrative authority with the Delegation of Control Wizard.

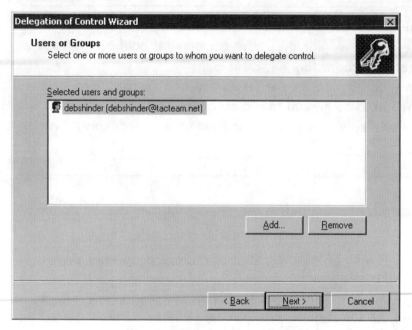

After you have chosen the users or groups to whom you wish to delegate authority, you will be able to choose exactly the administrative tasks you wish to delegate to them (see Figure 4.13).

This gives you a great deal of flexibility and control over the delegation process. You can even create a customized task to delegate.

You will be shown a summary of your actions and informed of the successful completion of the wizard (see Figure 4.14).

You should carefully review the summary to make certain you have assigned control over the objects and tasks to which you intended to delegate authority. Then click Finish, and the process is complete.

Figure 4.13 Select specific administrative tasks to be delegated.

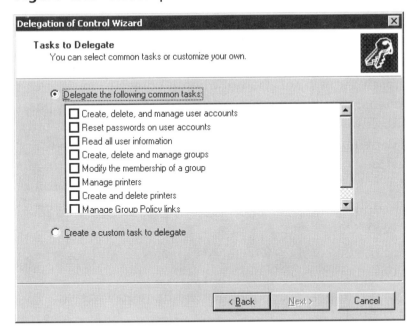

Figure 4.14 Finish the Delegation of Control process.

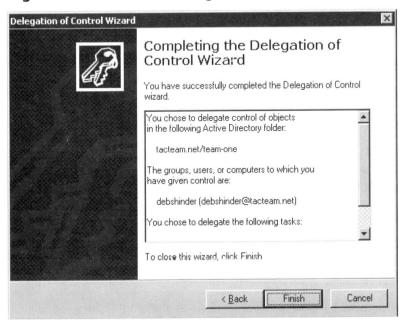

Fine-Grain Access Rights

Access can be controlled in a much more granular fashion than NT allowed. Instead of the familiar set of a few file and directory permissions that were available then, Windows 2000 provides an almost embarrassing wealth of choices when it comes to assigning access permissions, and then goes a step further by making it possible not only to grant each permission on an individual basis, but to specifically deny particular permissions as well.

The Access Control List (ACL) in the security descriptor of an Active Directory object is a list of entries that grant or deny specific access rights to individuals or groups. Access rights can be defined on any of these levels:

- Apply to the object as a whole (this applies to all properties of the object).

- Apply to a group of properties defined by property sets within the object.

- Apply to an individual property of the object.

Inheritance of Access Rights

Microsoft defines two basic models for the implementation of inherited access rights:

- **Dynamic inheritance.** The effective access rights to an object are determined by an evaluation of the permissions defined explicitly on the object along with permissions defined for all parent objects in the directory. This gives you the ability to change access control on parts of the directory tree by making changes to a specific container that will then automatically affect all subcontainers and objects within those subcontainers.

- **Static inheritance** (also referred to as **Create Time inheritance**). Access control information that flows down to child objects of the container can be specifically defined. When a child object is created, the inherited rights from the container are merged with default access rights on the new object. Any changes to inherited access rights at higher levels in the tree must be propagated down to all affected child objects. New inherited access rights are propagated by Active Directory to objects for which they apply, on the basis of the options available for defining the new rights.

When you assign permissions, you can choose to allow inheritable permissions from the parent object to propagate to its child object (which is the default setting), or you can prevent inheritance by unchecking the inheritable permissions check box (see Figure 4.15).

Figure 4.15 You can allow inheritable permissions from the parent object to propagate.

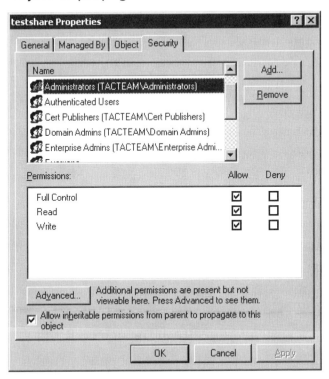

When you choose to prevent inheritance, the only permissions that will be assigned to the object will be those you explicitly assign.

Effect of Moving Objects on Security

It is easy to move an object from one OU to another in Active Directory. You simply select the object, choose Move from the Action menu, and choose a container into which you want to move the object (see Figure 4.16). You can even move more than one object at a time by selecting multiple objects (hold down the Control key while you make your selections).

Figure 4.16 The way to move an object in Active Directory.

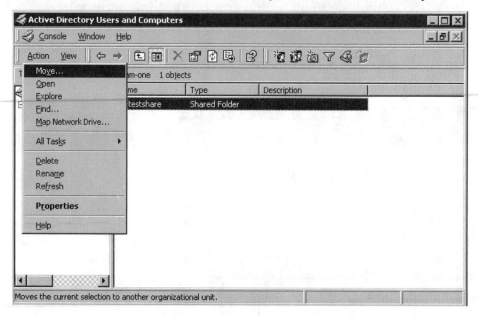

What happens to the permissions that have been set on those objects (or that were inherited from their former parent object) when you move them?

The rules are pretty simple:

- If permissions were assigned directly to the object, it will retain those permissions.

- If the permissions were inherited from the old container, they will no longer be in effect.

- The objects will inherit permissions from the new container.

It is a good idea, after you move an object, to check its security properties to be certain the permissions are assigned as you desired and expected them to be.

Multiple Security Protocols

The three basic security protocols used by Windows 2000 are NTLM, Kerberos, and PKI (Public Key Infrastructure, which is also referred to as Private/Public Key Pairs). NTLM was used in Windows NT and is supported in Windows 2000 to provide compatibility with NT 3.51 and 4.0 domains. Kerberos and PKI are based on popular non-vendor-specific Internet standards. Kerberos is the default protocol, but PKI can be used to grant access to users outside the network who are unable to use Kerberos.

As a network administrator, you will need to understand the basics of all three, when each is used, and how they work.

NTLM Credentials

NTLM, or NT LAN Manager security, is the mainstay of Windows NT and was considered a relatively powerful protocol in its heyday. However, NTLM suffers in comparison to Kerberos for several reasons:

- Authentication with NTLM is slower than with Kerberos.

- NTLM performs one-way authentication only, which allows server spoofing.

- NTLM trusts are one-way and nontransitive, and thus harder to manage.

- NTLM is proprietary, and not compatible with non-Microsoft networks.

However, NTLM is necessary for establishing trusts with NT domains, and for authenticating downlevel clients. By default, Windows 2000 is installed in mixed mode, meaning it can use any combination of Windows NT 4.0 and Windows 2000.

If you do not have a mixed-mode network (that is, if you have upgraded the network to a pure Windows 2000 environment), you can disable NTLM authentication by switching to native mode at a domain controller.

Kerberos Credentials

Kerberos is both powerful and complex. It is widely used in UNIX and other networking environments and is the default authentication protocol for Windows 2000.

Kerberos is a private key (also called secret key) encryption protocol. In private key cryptography, the same key, called a shared secret, is used for both encryption and decryption of data.

Windows 2000 domain controllers run the Kerberos server service (and Windows 2000 client computers run the Kerberos client service). Kerberos passwords (called keys) and identities are stored in Active Directory, reinforcing security/directory services integration. Kerberos includes these elements:

- **KDC.** The Key Distribution Center stores and distributes Kerberos tickets. The KDC runs on Windows 2000 domain controllers and uses Active Directory for secure storage.

- **Tickets.** Just as you do at the movies, you use a ticket to get in (in this case, to get into the domain itself or a network resource that you want to access). The process is a little more complex than at the theater, though, because with Kerberos you have to have a ticket to get a ticket; after authenticating a client, the KDC issues a ticket granting ticket (TGT) for this purpose.

- **Hash.** This one has nothing to do with corned beef, but is a fixed-size numerical result that is generated when a one-way mathematical formula is applied to a string of text (the formula is called the hash algorithm).

Getting a Ticket to Ride

Kerberos logon authentication follows this procedure: A user at a Windows 2000 client machine types in a username and password to log on the network. The user's password is hashed and bundled, and this little package (called an Authentication Service request) goes to the KDC.

The KDC has its own copy of the user key, which it hashes and compares to the hash in the AS request. If they match, the KDC issues a TGT to the client, which can be used to get service tickets to access network services within the domain.

Now when the client attempts to access a network resource, the TGT is sent back to the KDC, along with a ticket-granting service request (TGS). The TGT is checked, as are the user's access permissions, and if all is in order, the KDC issues a session ticket, which is used to access the requested service.

Cross-domain authentication is dependent on yet another ticket type, the referral ticket, which is the basis for the transitive trust model.

Kerberos provides tight security for network resources with relatively low overhead, which helps explain why Microsoft made it Windows 2000's primary security protocol.

NOTE

Kerberos works only between Windows 2000 clients and servers, so if you have a mixed-mode environment, NTLM will be used to interact with NT systems.

Private/Public Key Pairs and Certificates

PKI, or Public Key Infrastructure security, is familiar to many Internet administrators as the technology behind Pretty Good

Privacy (PGP), an encryption method that has been popular, especially for protecting Internet e-mail, for quite some time.

Public key cryptography differs from Kerberos and other private-key varieties in that it uses a pair of keys; one is public and available to everyone, and the other is private. In general, one of these keys is used to encrypt the message and the other is used to decrypt it.

This is similar to the act of opening a safety deposit box at the bank. You have a key to the box, and the bank officer has a key, and it takes both keys to open the box. You might think of the bank's key as the public key because it is used for all the boxes, while yours, specific to your box only, is analogous to the private key.

The two keys together are known as a private/public key pair. Windows 2000 uses a certificate authority to store the public and private keys. Digital certificates are used to verify that the public key really belongs to the user to whom it is supposed to belong. The certificate is issued by a trusted third party—in this case, Microsoft Certificate Services running on the Windows 2000 server—and guarantees that the public key you are using is valid.

Windows 2000's Public Key Infrastructure support is based on the X.509 standard, first established in 1995 to specify the syntax and format of digital certificates, and the certificates are called X.509 v3 digital certificates.

NOTE

The X.509 standards were established by the International Telecommunication Union, an international organization responsible for standardization of global telecommunications networks and services.

Other Supported Protocols

Windows 2000 also supports Distributed Password Authentication (DPA). This is an authentication protocol that is used by several online services, such as MSN.

For Managers

What About Smart Cards?

This term is used in reference to credit-card-sized plastic instruments that come in several different flavors, depending on just how "smart" they really are. They range from relatively simple stored-value cards to those that include integrated circuits and are essentially tiny computers (with limited processing and storage capacity).

Microsoft has made smart card technology support a key component of the Windows 2000 operating system, through its Public Key Infrastructure.

Smart cards can be used to store private keys and other personal information, and are used in conjunction with Kerberos and Active Directory to provide for secure logon authentication in one of three ways:

- Interactive logon
- Client authentication
- Remote logon

With interactive logon, the user puts the smart card into a smart card reader, and in return Windows 2000 prompts the user for a PIN (Personal Identification Number), which is used to authenticate to the smart card. Then a public key certificate, which is stored on the card, authenticates to the domain via Kerberos.

With client authentication, smart cards can be used in conjunction with SSL and TLS protocols. These protocols do not even have to be smart card aware, since Windows 2000's smart card support is integrated with CryptoAPI. The private key that corresponds to the public key is stored on the smart card, and the user must authenticate both to the card and to the domain, making for tighter security.

With remote logon, two separate authentication processes take place. One is to the remote server, and the other is to

Continued

the network. Windows 2000's remote access service (RAS) supports smart card authentication through a built-in smart card module. The authentication to the domain uses EAP (Extensible Authentication Protocol) over TLS. This is similar to SSL authentication, but the public key certificate is required to include a UPN (the "friendly name" such as johndoe@mycompany.com) that matches an Active Directory account.

Since smart cards provide increased security for networks using Kerberos, Active Directory, and PKI, it will benefit many organizations to consider their deployment.

For additional information on smart card support in Windows 2000, and useful instructions for deploying and managing their use, see the Microsoft Smart Card Logon White Paper or visit www.microsoft.com/security for the latest updates on Windows security technologies, and refer to Chapter 8, "Smart Cards," of this book.

Enterprise and Internet Single Sign-on

Single sign-on (SSO) allows a user to log on with one username and password and access multiple computers. There are obvious benefits to this:

- It is easier for users to remember one password.
- It saves time in the authentication process.
- It decreases the amount of administrative support required.

There are two parts to the single sign-on process in a Windows 2000 domain:

- **Interactive logon.** The user logs on the network with a password (or a smart card), using single sign-on credentials that are stored in Active Directory. Windows 2000 uses Kerberos V5 for authentication (with certificates, if a smart card is used to log on).

- **Network authentication.** The Windows 2000 security system supports many different authentication mechanisms, including Kerberos V5, Secure Socket Layer/Transport Layer Security (SSL/TLS), and NTLM. Which is used is dependent on what operating system is being used and whether the user is logging on over the Internet or via the local network.

The single sign-on feature can potentially increase productivity and improve security. Microsoft's ultimate goal is to implement SSO in mixed-platform networks through a combination of SSL and Kerberos, so that a user can be authenticated just once to access both Windows and non-Windows systems within the enterprise. This is even expected to include mainframe computing environments, through the next version of Microsoft's SNA (Systems Network Architecture) Server.

This ambitious strategy would allow for interoperability with Apple MacIntosh, UNIX, Solaris, and Novell environments via Kerberos, IBM mainframes via SNA, Windows downlevel systems via NTLM, and Web clients from a variety of vendors via SSL (see Figure 4.17).

Figure 4.17 Windows 2000 can set up a secure communication with multiple vendors via SSO.

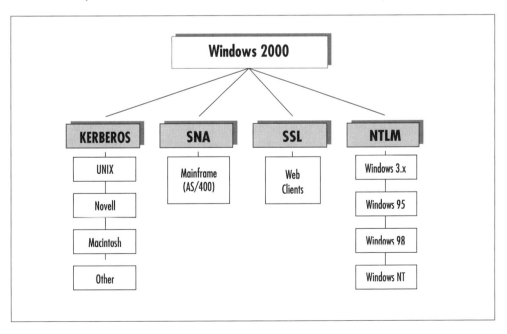

Security Support Provider Interface

The Security Support Provider Interface defines the security APIs for network authentication. It is the architectural layer of Windows 2000 that provides a generic Win32 system API, so that security providers can use various authentication services and account information stores.

A security provider is a dynamic-link library that implements the Security Support Provider Interface and makes one or more security packages available to applications. A security package maps the SSPI functions to an implementation of the security protocol that is specific to that package, such as NTLM, Kerberos, or SSL.

In other words, SSPI provides a common interface between transport-level applications, such as Microsoft RPC or a file system redirector, and security providers. Using SSPI, a distributed application can call one of several security providers to obtain an authenticated connection without knowledge of the details of the security protocol.

Internet Security for Windows 2000

Microsoft's Windows 2000 Internet security infrastructure is based on industry standards for public key security. This includes support for RSA Public-key Cipher, X.509 certificate formats, and Public Key Cryptography Standards (PKCS).

These Internet security technologies include client authentication with SSL/TLS protocols, the Microsoft Certificate Services, and the CryptoAPI components for certificate management and administration.

Microsoft's Web browser software, Internet Explorer (MSIE), and Internet Information Services (IIS), its Web server software, use many of these Internet security components.

Client Authentication with SSL 3.0

Secure Socket Layer and Transport Layer Security (SSL/TLS) are public-key-based security protocols, which are used by Web browsers and servers for mutual authentication, message integrity, and confidentiality.

Typically, the server's certificate is presented as part of the SSL/TLS secure channel establishment. The client program (in this case, Internet Explorer) accepts the server's certificate by verifying the cryptographic signatures on the certificate, a known or config- ured root certificate authority. Client authentication is also support- ed, using public key certificates as part of the secure channel establishment. Authentication of the client by the server is basically the same process as server authentication.

Windows 2000 uses Active Directory to map certificate informa- tion to existing Windows accounts. Client authentication directly integrates public key certificates with the Windows 2000 security architecture. This means there is no requirement for a separate database to define the access rights associated with public key cer- tificates. Instead, access control information is part of the group membership information stored in Active Directory.

Authentication of External Users

Another benefit of Windows 2000's support for public key certificate authentication is that it allows users who do not have domain accounts to be authenticated. These are known as external users. Any user who is authenticated via a public key certificate that was issued by a trusted CA can access resources in the Windows 2000 domain. This makes it easy to allow chosen users from other organi- zations to access your domain's resources, without your having to create domain accounts for them in Windows 2000.

Microsoft Certificate Services

The Microsoft Certificate Services included with Windows 2000 Server is an upgraded version of the Certificate Server software included in the NT 4.0 Option Pack with IIS 4.0. It includes enhanced capabilities such as a customizable policy module and integration with EFS (Encrypting File System). This service allows you to issue and manage certificates using public key encryption, allowing you to provide more secure communications across the Internet or within your company's intranet.

MCS gives an administrator great flexibility to customize policies, set optional properties of the certificates it issues, and add elements to the Certificate Revocation List (CRL), which can be published regularly. Certificate Services can also generate server certificates used by IIS and other Web servers to provide server authentication to assure clients (browsers) that they are communicating with the intended entity.

Microsoft's Certificate Services adheres to the X.509 standards.

CryptoAPI

Microsoft's CryptoAPI is an application programming interface that first appeared in NT 4.0. It can be used by applications to easily encrypt and decrypt messages and files, and consists of a set of functions that allow applications to encrypt or digitally sign data in a flexible manner, while at the same time providing protection for the user's private key data.

The actual cryptographic operations are performed by independent modules that are known as cryptographic service providers (CSPs). The API is used to isolate the application from the CSP modules, allowing use of different CSPs.

The encryption algorithms that are available to an application depend on the cryptographic service provider that is being used, but all data encryption using CryptoAPI is performed with a symmetric algorithm, no matter which CSP is installed.

Microsoft signs the CSPs to guarantee the integrity of the CSP to the operating system. Every CSP must be digitally signed by Microsoft in order to be recognized by the operating system. The signature is validated on a periodic basis by the operating system to ensure that the CSP has not been tampered with.

Interbusiness Access: Distributed Partners

Everywhere you look, you see the Internet. E-commerce, doing business on the World Wide Web, is the latest and greatest thing in the corporate world. Many large and small companies are already conducting business with their customers and business partners over the Internet. More and more, employees in the field use local access to public networks, such as an Internet service provider, and then connect to remote corporate networks via Virtual Private Networking. Windows 2000 is designed to support this growing and ever-changing area of distributed partnership and interbusiness access.

Security technologies are changing all the time as well. Windows 2000 supports multiple security protocols, and provides for a migration path to new technologies as they become available.

By integrating Windows 2000's security subsystem with Active Directory, Microsoft makes administration of external users easier. For instance, organizational units can be created for users outside the organization who need access.

VPNs, using PPTP or L2TP (Point-to-Point Tunneling Protocol and Layer 2 Tunneling Protocol), both supported by Windows 2000, can be established through which users can establish a secure connection to the company LAN from a remote location.

Active Directory's domain trust model is another mechanism that is useful in setting up interbusiness relationships. The hierarchical structure of the Active Directory domain tree and the namespace integration with DNS make it easier to route information between separate domains in an enterprise network.

Finally, Windows 2000's support of industrywide security protocol standards such as Kerberos, SSL, and X.509v3 certificates simplify the establishment of interbusiness communications over the Internet.

Summary

Computer security is of major concern to organizations today, due to many factors; greater levels of accessibility and connectivity makes companies vulnerable. This is exacerbated by an increasing number of persons with a combination of the technical knowledge, the motive, and the opportunity to break into corporate networks.

In response, the security services in the new Windows 2000 operating system have been drastically revamped and include many significant improvements over those of Windows NT.

The foundation of Windows 2000's security subsystem is its role as one of many distributed services and its interaction and integration with the directory services. By storing security information and policies in Active Directory, Microsoft has made them more granular, easier to manage, and more fault-tolerant through AD replication.

Windows 2000, unlike NT, supports a multiplicity of security protocols. These include Microsoft's proprietary NTLM for backward compatibility, as well as industry-standard specifications such as the popular Kerberos protocol and Public Key Infrastructure with X.509v3 certificates.

Microsoft has provided many security-related services and components with Windows 2000 Server, such as Microsoft Certificate Services and the CryptoAPI.

Finally, because security threats can come either from within the organization or across the global Internet to which most modern corporations are connected, Microsoft has designed Windows 2000 with a dual focus, to withstand both internal and external attacks. The growing phenomenon of interbusiness computer communications has also been taken into account, and provisions made for creating an environment that allows remote access that is both convenient and safe.

The goals of high security—to protect against unauthorized access and to provide easy accessibility for those who are authorized—will always be at odds. In designing Windows 2000, Microsoft has attempted to balance these two conflicting needs in a way that will provide companies with options that can be easily customized to fit their individual situations and desires.

As networks grow, the role of security in the enterprise will become an even bigger issue. Windows 2000's modular design is intended to allow for adaptation in an ever-changing and increasingly connected world.

FAQs

Q: What are the security advantages of upgrading the entire domain to Windows 2000?

A: When the NT domain controllers and clients have been replaced by Windows 2000 machines, the domain can be run in native mode (as opposed to mixed mode), and all systems will use Kerberos as the default authentication protocol; support for NTLM can be discontinued.

Q: If Kerberos is so good, why does Windows 2000 include support for other security protocols like PKI and SSL?

A: Kerberos security is used by many vendors, but not all systems support it. Windows 2000 supports multiple security protocols in order to provide the widest possible compatibility and the broadest scope of secure connectivity to other platforms.

Q: What is the difference between private key security and private/public key security?

A: Briefly, private key protocols use a shared secret (key, or password) that both sides know, for both encryption and decryption purposes. With private/public (also sometimes just called public key cryptography), there are two keys: a public key that is accessible to everyone, and a private key that is not shared with anyone. One is used to encrypt but cannot decrypt; the other is used to decrypt but cannot be used for encryption. The public key's authenticity may also be validated by a certificate issued by a trusted certificate authority.

Q: How does Windows 2000's hierarchical domain structure affect security and access within the enterprise?

A: The domain tree and forest concept provides for a flow of trust relationships down the tree. Because Active Directory uses Kerberos for authentication, trusts between connected domains are implicit, two-way, and transitive. This means that, with proper permissions, users in all domains have access to resources in all other domains.

Q: What exactly is single sign-on and why is it desirable in the enterprise network?

A: Single sign-on (SSO) provides a way for a user to access all needed resources, both internally and across the Internet, by logging on with one valid username and password. This is more convenient for the users and enhances their productivity, and reduces administrators' support time as well.

Chapter 5

Security Configuration Tool Set

Solutions in this chapter:

- Introduction
- Configuring Security
- Analyzing Security
- Group Policy Integration
- Using the Tools

Introduction

This chapter introduces the functions and uses of the Windows 2000 Security Configuration Tool Set. The Tool Set is a response to systems administrators' need for a central, easy-to-use program that will allow configuration of domain, organizational unit, and local security. In Windows NT 4.0, configuration of various security parameters required using multiple tools, such as User Manager, User Manager for Domains, TCP/IP protocol properties, direct registry edits, the RAS administrator, and more. The Tool Set makes it possible to configure and manage these security services from a single, centralized interface.

In addition to conveniently bringing together formerly widely disparate programs into a single interface, the Security Configuration and Analysis snap-in allows the administrator to analyze a local machine's current configuration. This analysis can be performed against security templates so that the network manager can compare the present configuration to a proposed ideal configuration, which can then be applied with a couple of simple clicks of the mouse.

The Security Configuration Tool Set comes at an opportune time. Never before has a Microsoft operating system offered the degree of airtight security that Windows 2000 offers. Neither has security been so configurable at such a granular level. The Tool Set allows the administrator to get a handle on the configuration and management of the Windows 2000 security scheme.

Security Configuration Tool Set Overview

The Security Configuration Tool Set is a collection of security configuration and management programs included in Windows 2000. The primary goal of each of these components is to make management of enterprisewide security parameters easier. The administrator can group the Tool Set components together into a single Microsoft Management Console (MMC) and manage security for the entire enterprise from a central location.

Each component of the Security Configuration Tool Set is integrated into the security infrastructure of Windows 2000. The new Distributed Security Services model as defined in Windows 2000 requires a central interface to manage an enterprise's complex security requirements. The Tool Set components interact with Active Directory, Kerberos Authentication mechanisms, and Windows 2000 Public Key Infrastructure.

Security Configuration Tool Set Components

The four main components of the Security Configuration Tool Set are:

- Security Configuration and Analysis snap-in
- Security Settings Extension to Group Policy
- The command line tool, secedit.exe
- Security Templates snap-in

Security Configuration and Analysis Snap-in

The Security Configuration and Analysis snap-in is a security tool that allows you to create, test, and apply a variety of security scenarios. From within the Security Configuration and Analysis snap-in you can create text-based files that contain security settings that can be transported and applied to any Windows 2000 computer. The text files are saved with the .inf extension, and can be easily edited with basic text editors such as Notepad. When you manipulate security configuration, you should use the graphical interface to minimize mishaps.

Information about different security scenarios is saved to a personal database that the administrator creates for personal use. Use the Security Configuration and Analysis snap-in to import other security configurations that have been saved as security templates. You can create multiple security templates and merge them into a single security database. Each personal database contains a scenario based on the security templates that have been imported into the database.

After creating a security scenario, the administrator can test the scenario against the current security configuration on that machine. After the analysis, the Security Configuration and Analysis snap-in will report what current settings deviate from the scenario stored in the database.

An administrator who is pleased with the scenario results can then use a simple point-and-click procedure to update the local machine's own security configuration to match that of the scenario stored in the database.

Security Setting Extensions to Group Policy

A security scenario can be saved using the Security Configuration and Analysis snap-in and then applied to the local computer. An administrator can export security scenarios as text-based template files that can be imported into the group policy of a domain or organizational unit. This provides a tremendous degree of flexibility for the administrator who wishes to obtain granular control over the security infrastructure of an enterprise.

The ability to save security settings in a template file, which can be saved and backed up, provides a high degree of fault tolerance for the organization's security plan. If an administrative misadventure causes complex alterations to the domain security policy, the administrator can restore the original security policy by importing and applying a template.

Security Templates

Microsoft provides a full set of templates that conform to a number of common security scenarios. These security templates can be broken down into two general categories: Default and Incremental. The Default or Basic templates are applied by the operating system when a clean install has been performed. They are not applied if an upgrade installation has been done. The incremental templates should be applied after the Basic security templates have been applied. The four types of incremental templates are: Compatible, Secure, Highly Secure, and Dedicated Domain Controller. Table 5.1 describes the function of these provided templates.

The administrator can save time and effort during an initial roll-out by applying these templates to workstations, domain controllers, and member and stand-alone servers. Then, as time allows, the administrator can customize and fine-tune security settings for local computers, organizational units, or an entire domain.

Table 5.1 Default and Incremental Security Templates

Template Security Level	Description
Basic	These include the basic*.inf templates. Use these to correct configuration. These Basic or Default templates allow the administrator to roll back security to the original installation defaults.
Compatible	These are the compat*.inf templates. By default, all users are Power Users on Windows 2000 professional. If you do not want your users to have Power User rights, the Compatible configuration alters the default permissions for the Users group so that legacy applications can run properly. Many applications required that a user have an elevated level of permissions in order to run properly. This is not a secure environment.
Secure	These are the secure*.inf templates. The Secure templates will increase the level of security for Account Policy, certain Registry keys, and Auditing. Permissions to file system objects are not affected with this configuration.

Continued

Template Security Level	Description
Highly Secure	These include the hisec*.inf templates. Highly Secure configurations add security to network communications. IPSec will be configured for these machines, and will be required for communications. Downlevel clients will not be able to communicate
Dedicated Domain Controller	The dedica*.inf templates. These templates optimize security for local users on domain controller that do not run other server applications (which is the preferred configuration for domain controllers).

The secedit.exe Command Line Tool

The secedit.exe Command Line tool offers much of the functionality of the Security Configuration and Analysis snap-in from the command line. This allows the administrator to script security analyses for many machines across the enterprise, and save the results for later analysis.

The reporting capabilities of the secedit.exe tool are limited. Although you can perform a security analysis from the command line, you cannot view the results of the analysis with secedit.exe. You must view the results of the analysis from the graphic Security Configuration and Analysis snap-in interface.

Security Configurations

One limitation of the security templates, at this time, is that you cannot test security configurations defined in the database against current domain or organizational unit security configurations. This functionality will probably be included with future releases. Figure 5.1 shows the Security Configuration and Analysis snap-in together with the Security Templates snap-in to create a central security console for managing security policy throughout the organization.

By using the provided security templates, the administrator can implement well thought out and tested security constructions to a

Figure 5.1 The Security Configuration and Analysis snap-in Security Console.

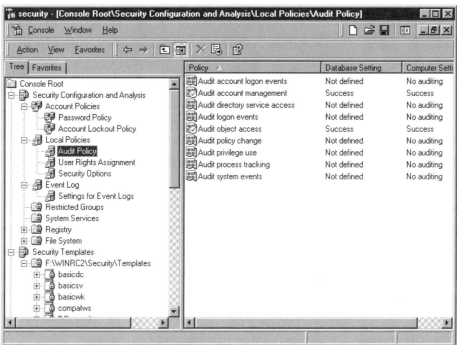

new domain rollout without having to reinvent the wheel. Customizations to the provided security templates can be made at the network manager's convenience as time and experience allow.

Security Configuration and Analysis Database

The Security Configuration and Analysis snap-in database contains all the existing security properties available for Windows 2000 computers. It does not add any additional settings or extend the security capabilities of the operating system. The Security Configuration and Analysis snap-in database contains the administrator's security preferences. The database is populated with entries derived from security templates. You have the choice to import multiple templates and merge the contents of those templates, or you can import templates in their entirety after the previous database entries have been cleared.

The database is central in the security analysis process. The administrator can initiate a security analysis after configuring the entries in the database to meet the organization's perceived needs. The security analysis will compare the settings in the database with the actual settings implemented on the local computer. Individual security settings will be flagged by an icon that will change, depending on whether the actual security settings are the same or different from those included in the database. You will also be informed if there are settings that have not been configured at all, and thus may require the administrator's attention.

Figure 5.2 shows the results of a security analysis. Prior to the security analysis, the administrator configured the preferred security settings into the database. After the database had been populated with an ideal security scenario, it was tested against the current machine settings. A green check mark indicates that the current machine settings are the same as those set in the database; a red

Figure 5.2 The results of a Security Analysis in the Security Configuration and Analysis snap-in.

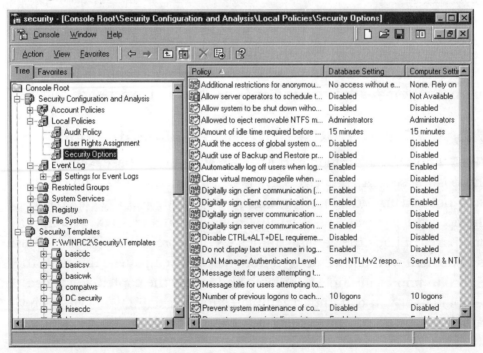

"x" indicates that there is a conflict, and a generic icon indicates that the setting was not defined in the database.

After the analysis has been performed, the administrator can then make changes to the database as desired and rerun the analysis. When the database matches the precise security configuration required, the administrator can then apply the settings in the database to the local machine's security policy.

The formulation of a well thought out security policy is a time-consuming process. To add a measure of fault tolerance, the database entries can be exported to a text file template, which can be saved for later use on the same machine, or can be applied to another machine, domain, or organizational unit.

The procedure used to export the template to be saved is simple; just right-click on the Security Configuration and Analysis snap-in node and choose Export Template, as shown in Figure 5.3.

Figure 5.3 Export the Security Database entries into a portable template.

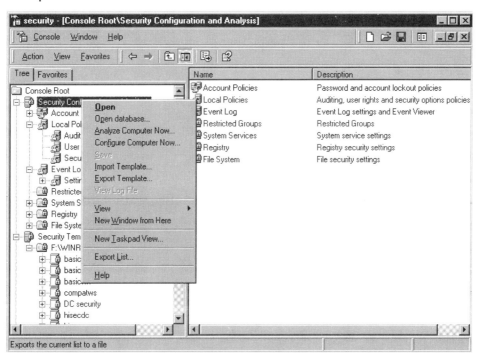

The exported template is saved as an .inf file, and can be imported to other computers, domains, and organizational units. In this way the security parameters can be reproduced exactly from one machine to another.

Security Configuration and Analysis Areas

The Security Configuration and Analysis snap-in brings together in a single workspace security configuration components that were formerly spread throughout many different programs in NT 4.0. The areas of analysis are shown in Figure 5.4.

Figure 5.4 The areas of Security Configuration and Analysis.

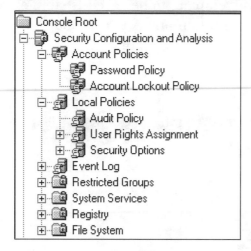

Account Policies

The Account Policies node includes those configuration variables that you formerly manipulated in the User Manager for Domains applet in NT 4.0. The two subnodes of the Account Policies node include the Password Policy node and the Account Lockout Policy node. In the Password Policy node, you can set the minimum and maximum password ages and password lengths. The Account Lockout Policy allows you to set lockout durations and reset options.

Local Policies

Local policies apply to the local machine. Subnodes of the Local Polices node include the Audit Policy, User Rights Assignment, and the Security Options. Audit and User rights policies look familiar to users of NT 4.0.

The Security Options node offers the administrator many options that formerly were available only by the manipulation of the Windows NT 4.0 registry. Examples include the ability to set the message text and message title during logon, restricting the use of the floppy disk, and the Do not display last username at logon.

Event Log

The Event Log node allows you to configure security settings for the Event Log. These include maximum log sizes, configuring guest access to the Event Log, and whether or not the computer should shut down when the security log is full.

Restricted Groups

You can centrally control the members of groups. There are times when an administrator will add someone temporarily to a group, such as the backup operators group, and then neglect to remove that user when the user no longer needs to be a member of that group. These lapses represent a potential hole in network security. You can configure a group membership list in the Restricted Groups node, and then configure an approved list of members by reapplying the security template you have created.

System Services

The Security parameters of all system services can be defined in the database via the System Services node. You can define whether a service startup should be automatic, manual, or disabled. You also can configure what user accounts have access to each service.

Registry

The Registry node allows you to set access restrictions on individual registry keys.

File System

The File System node allows you to set folder and file permissions. This is a great aid to the administrator who may have been experimenting with access permissions on a large number of files or folders, and then later cannot recall what the original settings were. A security template can be applied to restore all file and folder permissions to their original settings.

Security Configuration Tool Set User Interfaces

There are two user interfaces available to configuration system security settings: the graphical interface and the secedit.exe command line interface.

You should do most of your work from the graphical interface. From the graphical interface you will design your security scenarios, test them against extant security settings, and then apply scenarios stored in the security database after testing. After security scenarios are customized to the administrator's needs, the scenario can be exported in a plaintext file, which can be saved for later use.

The exported text file can be edited by hand using any available text editor. However, Microsoft recommends that users confine themselves to the graphical interface so as to not introduce random elements into the structure of the file and inadvertently corrupt its contents.

Your interfaces with the Security Tools set will be via these interfaces:

- Security Configuration and Analysis snap-in
- The secedit.exe command line tool
- Security Extensions to the Group Policy Editor

Security Configuration and Analysis Snap-in

You use the Security Configuration and Analysis snap-in to control local machine security policies. You cannot directly affect domain or organizational unit security policies from the Security Configuration and Analysis snap-in. This limits the use of the Security Configuration and Analysis snap-in somewhat, since you cannot use it to test different scenarios against the prevailing domain or organizational unit's security configuration.

Nonetheless, the Security Configuration and Analysis snap-in remains a powerful tool. To get started, you must first create an MMC that will allow you to work with the Tool Set. To make your Security Configuration Tool Set Console:

1. From the Run command enter "mmc" into the text box and click OK.

2. From the MMC menu, click Add/remove snap-in, and then click the Add button.

3. Select and add:

   ■ Security Configuration and Analysis

   ■ Security Templates

   ■ Group Policy

After adding these, save your MMC as Security Tool Set or any other name you wish.

You now need to open an existing database, or create a new one. It is against these entries in the database that you will test your present security configuration. You can also apply the settings saved in the database to the computer itself, thus updating the local machine's security configuration.

1. Right-click Security Configuration and Analysis and select Open Database (see Figure 5.5).

2. If there is already an existing database, you can open that one. If there are no databases currently defined, you can create a new one by entering the name of the database in the filename box. Click Open.

Figure 5.5 The Open database dialog box.

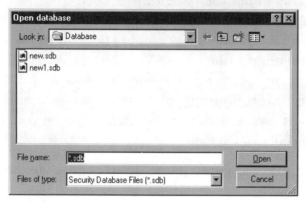

3. After you click Open, the Import Template dialog box appears. You need to populate the database with security configuration entries. The templates contain this information. Select the template that contains the information that most closely represents the level of security you are interested in, and then click Open.

4. In the right pane, you will see instructions on how to Analyze or Configure your computer. Right-click the Security Configuration and Analysis node and select either Configure or Analyze. Be careful; if you select Configure, it will apply the settings that you have imported into the database to the active security configuration of the computer.

After the database has been created, you can test your configuration. You have two options. You can merge settings from another template file into your working database, or you can clear the working database so that it will contain only entries from the new template being imported. Merging templates allows the administrator a great deal of flexibility in analysis and in the application of different security scenarios.

In order to merge or replace the entries in the database:

1. Right-click Security Configuration and Analysis and select Import Template. You will see the Import Template dialog box as it appears in Figure 5.6.

Figure 5.6 The Import Template dialog box.

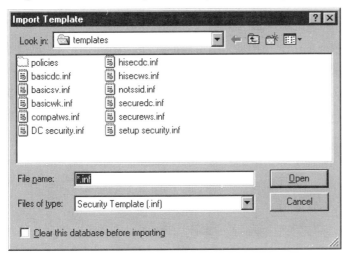

2. You have two choices at this point. You may select a template and then click Open. By doing this, you will merge the entries from the template with those already in the database. However, if you would prefer to start with a "clean" database by clearing the entries in the database before you import the new entries, you can select Clear this database before importing by putting a check in the box. Then click Open.

The Security Settings Extension to the Group Policy Editor

The Security Configuration and Analysis snap-in allows you to configure local machine policies easily. However, for the configuration of security structure of an entire domain or organizational unit, you need to use the Security Settings Extension to the Group Policy editor.

You cannot use the Security Configuration and Analysis snap-in to configure the security settings of a domain or organizational unit. To apply a security configuration to an organizational unit:

1. Open the Active Directory Users and Computers console from the Administrative Tools menu. Right-click an organizational unit and select Properties.

2. The Organizational Unit's properties box appears. Click the Group Policy tab (see Figure 5.7).

Figure 5.7 The Group Policy tab in the Organizational Unit's Properties sheet.

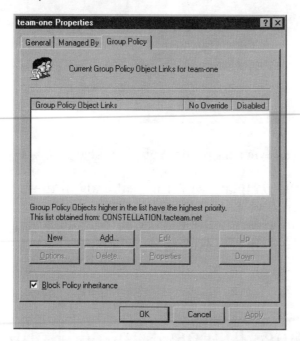

3. Click New. Type a name for the group policy object. Make sure the new object is selected, then click Edit.

4. Expand Computer Configuration, then expand Windows Settings. There are two subnodes of Windows Settings: Scripts and Security Templates. Select the Security Templates node (see Figure 5.8).

5. Right-click the Security Settings node, and select Import
    Policy. Notice that the policies are template files with the .inf
    extension. You have the option of merging the template's
    entries into the present organizational unit's security setup,
    or you can clear the present OU's security settings and have
    them replaced by the settings in the imported template.
    Click Open to enact the new policy.

You are not given the option to test the template settings against
the present OU's security configuration. The settings are enabled
after you import the policy via the .inf file.

Figure 5.8 Group Policy Security Settings.

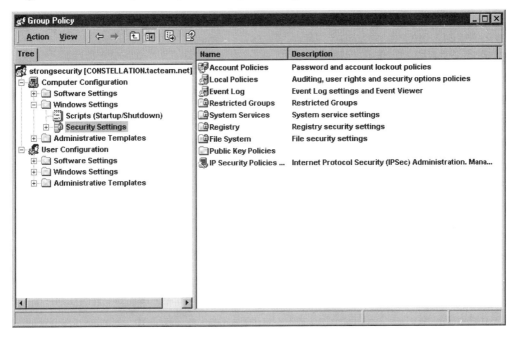

The secedit.exe Command Line Tool

The secedit.exe Command Line Tool allows the administrator to:

- Analyze System Security
- Configure System Security
- Refresh Security Settings
- Export Security Settings
- Validate the syntax of a Security Template

secedit Switches for Security Analysis

`secedit /analyze`

The analyze switch is used to initiate a security analysis. Additional parameters include:

`/DB filename`

This informs secedit.exe what database to apply the security analysis results to.

`/CFG filename`

This points to the location of the template that will be imported into the database for analysis.

`/log logpath`

This is the location of the logfile that will be created from the analysis; the default file is used.

`/verbose`

This provides additional screen and log output when analysis is carried out.

`/quiet`

This provides little screen or log output.

secedit.exe Switches Used to Configure System Security

```
secedit /configure
```

Secedit will apply a template by using the configure switch. Additional parameters include:

```
/DB filename
```

This informs secedit.exe what database to apply the security analysis results to.

```
/CFG filename
```

This points to the location of the template that will be applied to the database.

```
/overwrite
```

This switch will cause the current template in the database to be overwritten rather than appended.

```
/area area1 area2...
```

This allows you to specify a specific security "area" to be configured. The default is "all areas."

```
/log logpath
```

This is the location of the logfile that will be created with details of the security configuration.

```
/verbose
```

Provides additional screen and log output.

```
/quiet
```

Suppresses screen and log output.

Refresh Security Settings

```
secedit /refreshpolicy
```

This command updates the system security policy after changes have been made.

Additional parameters include:

`machine_policy`

This updates the security settings for the local computer.

`user_policy`

This updates the security settings for the currently logged in local user account.

`/enforce`

This refreshes security settings, even if there have been no changes to the group policy object settings.

Export Security Settings

`secedit /export`

Use the export switch to export the template stored in the database to an .inf file.
Additional parameters include:

`/DB filename`

This informs secedit.exe what database to extract the template from.

`/CFG filename`

This is the name and location of the file for the newly exported template.

`/area area1 area2...`

This allows you to specify a specific security "area" to be configured. The default is "all areas."

`/log logpath`

This is the location of the logfile that will be created with details of the security configuration.

`/verbose`

This provides additional screen and log output.

`/quiet`

This suppresses screen and log output.

For Managers

Testing Your System Configurations

The Security Configuration and Analysis snap-in, Security Templates, secedit.exe command line tool, and Security Extensions to the Group Policy Editor are powerful and efficient tools that allow you to manage and control the security infrastructure of your organization. However, as with all the new tools and capabilities of Windows 2000, you should use appropriate caution before employing these tools in a live environment. Be sure to test your security configurations in a lab environment that resembles your live environment as closely as possible.

The secedit.exe command line tool will allow you to schedule regular security audits of local policies on the machines in any domain and organizational unit. By running scripts that call on the secedit.exe program, you can update each computer's personal database with the results of your security analysis. You can then later use the Security

Continued

Configuration and Analysis snap-in to analyze the results of your automated analysis. Always watch for the effective policy, as this can differ from the policy that you applied to the local machine. Any existing domain or organizational unit security polices that apply to the machine will overwrite local machine policy.

There is a workaround for the present lack of template saving functionality seen in domain and organizational unit security configurations. You can get around this problem if you always change security configuration by using only templates, and then keep track of what templates are applied when. You must not make changes to the security configuration of the computer in any other way. In this way, you can always roll back to a previous configuration.

Configuring Security

The administrator can configure the entries in the security database via each of the nodes in the Security Configuration and Analysis and Security Templates snap-ins. You cannot define new security attributes. Only modification of existing Windows 2000 security elements are configurable. Microsoft or third parties may include extensions to the security attributes in the future.

Account Policies

Account Policies define aspects of security relating primarily to passwords. The Password Policy contains entries related to password aging and password length. Account Lockout Policy determines how many bad tries a person gets before the account is locked out. Kerberos Policy applies only to domain controllers, since local logons do not use Kerberos. Entries include maximum lifetimes for various tickets, such as user tickets and user renewal. Figure 5.9 shows some entries for the Account Policies nodes.

Figure 5.9 Account Policies.

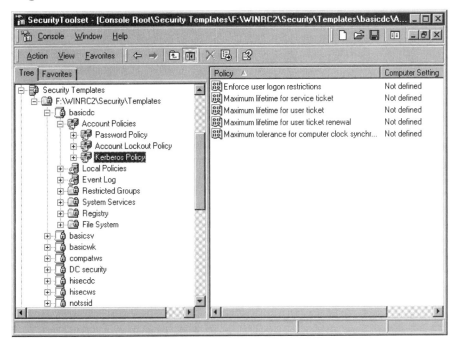

In Windows NT 4.0, Account Policies were configured in User Manager for Domains.

Local Policies and Event Log

Local Policies include the Audit Policy, User Rights Assignment, and Security Options. Some Audit Policy selections include auditing logon events, use of user privileges, systems events, and object access. The User Rights Assignment node includes granting or denying user rights such as the right to add workstations to the domain, changing the system time, logging on locally, and accessing the computer from the network.

The most profound improvements are represented in the Security Options node, where you can make changes that could be made only via direct registry edits in Windows NT 4.0. Examples of such Security Options include: clearing the pagefile when the system shuts down, message text during logon, number of previous logons kept in cache, and shut down system immediately if unable to log security audits. Figure 5.10 shows some of the entries seen in the Local Policies node.

Figure 5.10 Local policies.

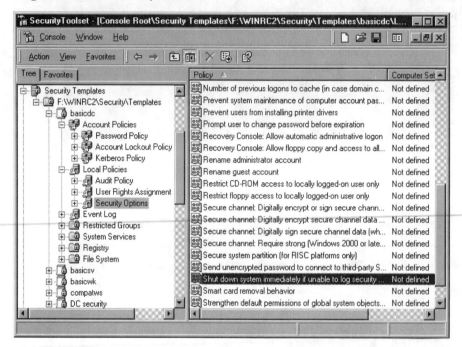

The improvements in local policy management are numerous with the addition of the configurable objects available in the Security Options node.

Event Log

The Event Log node allows you to configure settings specifically for event logs, as shown in Figure 5.11.

Event Log Configuration settings allow you to configure the length of time logs are retained as well as the size of the event logs. You can also configure that the system should shut down if the security log becomes full.

Figure 5.11 The Event Log Configuration node.

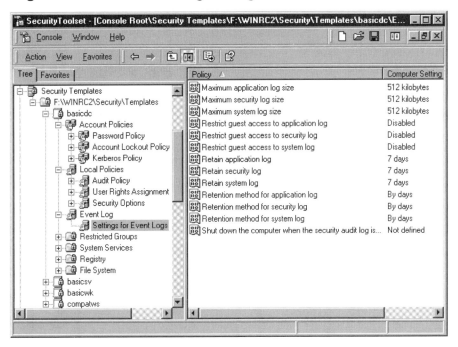

Restricted Groups

The Restricted Groups node lends something new to the security configuration options available in Windows 2000. You can define, as part of security policy, the members of a group. There are times when the administrator needs to temporarily add users to groups with a higher classification than the users' typical group membership. This might be the case when an administrator goes on vacation and another member of the team is assigned full administrative rights. However, often the "temporary" promotion ends up being an inadvertently permanent one, and the user remains in the Administrators group. Groups may also become members of other groups, when this is not part of the company security plan. By defining Restricted Group membership rules, you can return group membership to that defined by security policy. Figure 5.12 shows the Restricted Groups node entries.

You can add users to restricted groups by double-clicking on the group in the results pane and adding new members from there. You can also restrict what groups the group itself can be a member of (a type of recursive checking), using the nested group capabilities now available in Windows 2000.

Figure 5.12 The Restricted Groups node.

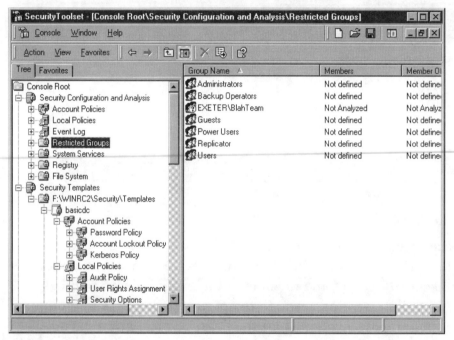

Registry Security

Registry keys can be protected by policy. You can define a security policy for a registry key or value in the database, and then customize the propagation of the setting using the Key properties dialog box. Figure 5.13 demonstrates how to control propagation of security settings.

Figure 5.14 illustrates the results of configuring Registry Key security.

Figure 5.13 The way to configure Registry Key security.

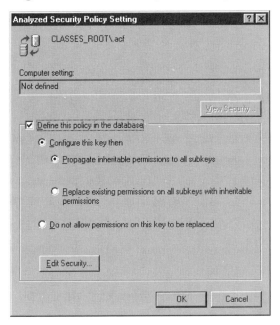

Figure 5.14 Entries in the Registry node.

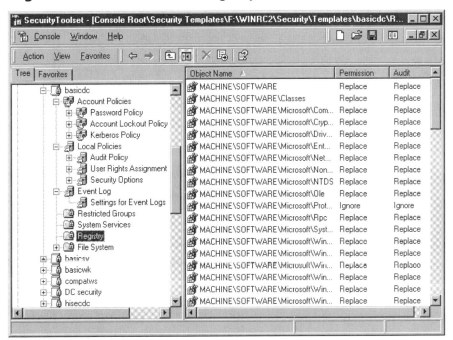

This approach is much easier and less error-prone than controlling the security of registry entries via the Registry editor.

File System Security

The File System Security node allows you to configure NTFS permission for all local drives. It is common for a number of different administrators to get into the Explorer and customize the NTFS permissions on file and folders through the file system. File and folder security should be part of a well thought out and implemented security plan. This security plan can be realized by setting File System Policy in the templates (seen in Figure 5.15). You can then periodically audit the status of the file system to look for inconsistencies between the plan and the actual state of NTFS permissions in the local environment.

Figure 5.15 File System Security settings.

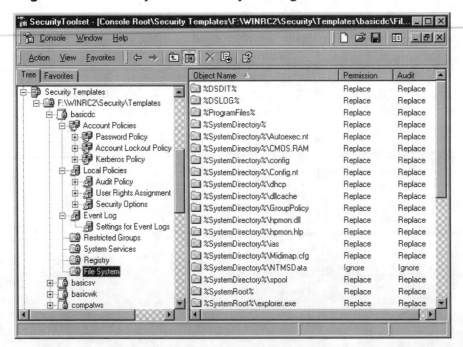

In the template, the volume letters are not assigned. You can do this by right-clicking on the File System node, and then picking the volumes that you would like to include in the template.

System Services Security

The System Services node allows you to control security and startup policy on all the services defined in the template. Controlling the startup behavior of system services can save the administrator many headaches over time. Consider the situation of users starting up their own RAS services or DHCP services haphazardly. This type of situation creates a large security risk for any network. You can set restrictive networking services startup properties, and assign all computers that require certain services to an OU that does have the right to start up particular networking services.

Figure 5.16 shows some of the content of the Services node.

Figure 5.16 The System Services node.

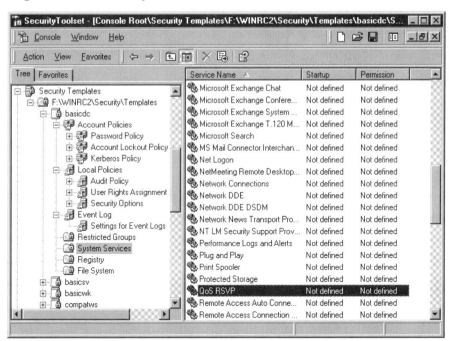

Analyzing Security

One of the most useful features of the Security Configuration and Analysis snap-in is the ability to compare the desired security policies as they are set up in the template with the actual state of the local machine. The administrator is able to glean a tremendous amount of insight regarding the current security configuration of the machine by using the Analyze feature of the Security Configuration and Analysis snap-in.

Running the analysis is easy. After you import the security settings from the appropriate templates, all you need to do is right-click on the Security Configuration and Analysis node and select the Analyze Computer Now command. The machine will run an analysis and show you its progress, as shown in Figure 5.17.

Security analyses can be run against various selected templates.

Figure 5.17 Run the analysis.

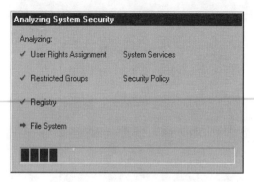

Account and Local Policies

Figure 5.18 shows the results of an analysis on the local audit policy.

Icons with a green check mark indicate that the database setting and the machine settings are the same. Icons with the red "x" indicate that there is a discrepancy between the entry in the database and that of the actual configuration. The generic icon means that no setting for that security parameter was set in the database.

Restricted Group Management

Figure 5.19 shows the results of an analysis of the Restricted Group Management Policy.

The columns in this analysis show an OK status for the Members and Members Of columns. The same icon indicators apply to this analysis as well.

Figure 5.18 The results of the Audit Policy analysis.

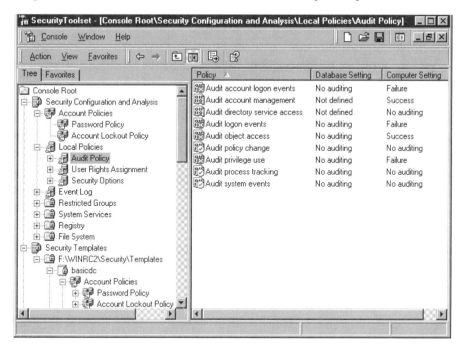

Figure 5.19 Restricted Group Management Policy analysis results.

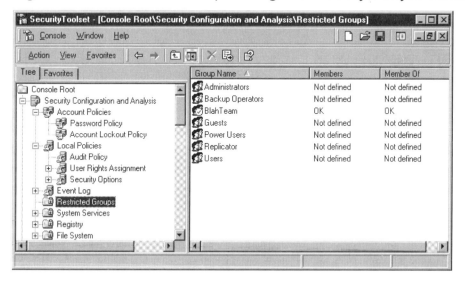

Registry Security

Figure 5.20 shows the results of a Registry Policy analysis. After the Registry analysis, you can zoom in on specific keys and values to assess the consistency between the database and the actual registry security attributes.

Figure 5.20 The results of a Registry Policy analysis.

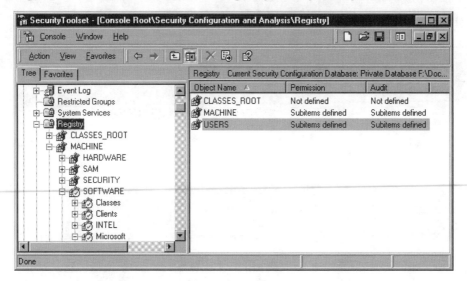

File System Security

Figure 5.21.shows the results of a File System Security analysis. The results of the analysis show whether permissions or audit policies have been set on volumes, folders, or individual files. The same icon schema applies in this instance. In Figure 5.21, the Program Files and WINRC2 folders have permissions and auditing configured. The database settings and the actual settings match in both instances.

System Services Security

Figure 5.22 shows the results of a System Service Policy analysis. The results show the status of Startup and Permissions options and their consistency with the database.

Figure 5.21 The results of a File System Security analysis.

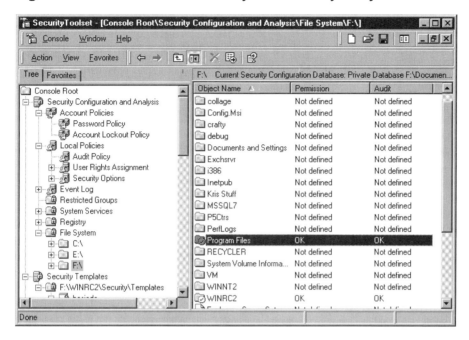

Figure 5.22 The results of a System Service Policy analysis.

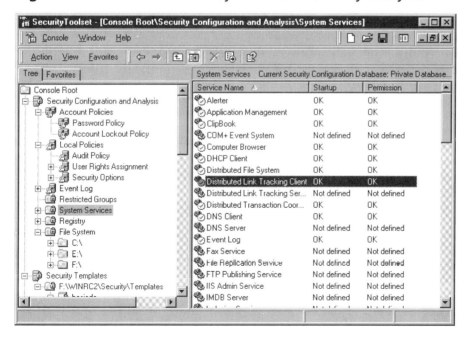

Group Policy Integration

You can use the features of the Security Configuration Tool Set to configure group policies. This is important to the administrator who is interested in configuring the security of an entire domain or organizational unit. By extending the group policy capabilities of the Security Configuration Tool Set to the group policy objects of choice, the network manager is able to speed deployment of uniform policy through many computers in the domain.

Security Configuration in Group Policy Objects

The Security Configuration Tool Set allows for the configuration of security policy, which is one aspect of group policy. Security policies designed and tested using the Security Configuration and Analysis snap-in can be exported and applied to domains and organizational units.

A significant limitation at this time is the inability to export security configuration parameters from a domain or organizational unit. This limits the full functionality of the Security Configuration and Analysis snap-in to analyzing security parameters of the local machine only. You cannot, at this time, export the domain or organizational unit's security policy for analysis. However, you can import a security policy that has been saved as an .inf file.

Security policy can be edited in the group policy object. These include all Windows 2000 security configuration objects.

Additional Security Policies

- **IPSec Policy.**
  IPSec security policies can be configured and analyzed in the Security Configuration and Analysis snap-in. For more information on IPSec, see Chapter 7, "IP Security for Microsoft Windows 2000 Server."

- **Public Key Policies.**
  Included in the public key policies are the encrypted data recovery agents, Root certificates, and certificate trust lists. These topics are covered in detail in Chapter 9, "Microsoft Windows 2000 Public Key Infrastructure" and Chapter 6, "Encrypting File System for Windows 2000."

Using the Tools

Let's put what we have covered into practice. In this section we will walk through using both the Security Configuration and Analysis snap-in and the Security Settings Extension to the Group Policy Editor.

Using the Security Configuration and Analysis Snap-in

It is possible to configure a Security console that includes both the Security Configuration and Analysis snap-in and the Security Templates. That console can be used to configure a new security template, and then configure the new security template with a policy that restricts membership to the administrator's local group.

1. Start the Security Tool Set console that you created.

2. Expand the Security Templates node. Right-click on the basicsv node and select Save As. In the Save As dialog box, type "practicebasicsv" and press Enter.

3. Expand the "practicebasicsv" node and select the Restricted Groups node. Right-click that node and select the Add Group command. Click Browse.

4. In the Select Groups dialog box, click the down arrow in the Look in box, and select the name of your computer. Then select Administrators, click Add, and then click OK. Click OK again to close the Add Group dialog box.

5. In the results pane you should see the Administrators Group listed. Right-click on the Administrators Group, and select the Security command (see Figure 5.23).

Figure 5.23 Configure Membership Policy for the Administrators Group.

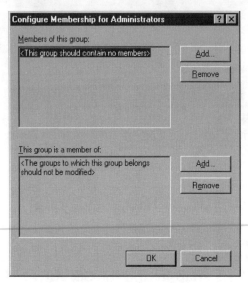

6. Click Add for the Members of this group: text box. Next, click Browse in the Add Member dialog box. This brings up the Select Users or Groups dialog box. In the Look in box, make sure the local machine is selected. Then select the Administrator account and click Add. Click OK, and then click OK again. Click OK one more time to close the Configure Membership for Administrators dialog box. Right-click the practicebasicsv node and click Save to save the changes you have made to the template.

7. Now the template is properly configured. The next step is to open or create a new database to import the security entries from the template. Right-click the Security Configuration and Analysis node, and select the Open database command.

8. In the Open Database dialog box, type "practice," and then click Open. You are now asked what template you want to use to populate the database. Select the practicebasicsv template and click Open. The entries in the template are imported into the practice.sdb database.

9. Right-click the Security Configuration and Analysis node and select the Analyze Computer Now command. A dialog box appears where the log file is stored that contains the results of the analysis. Click OK. You will see a progress bar that informs you how far the analysis has progressed. You can now check the results of the analysis by clicking on the Restricted Groups node.

Using Security Settings Extension to Group Policy Editor

To use the Security Settings Extension to the Group Policy Editor:

1. At the Run command type "mmc" to start an empty console.

2. Click the Console menu, and then select the Add/Remove Snap-in command.

3. Click Add, and then select Group Policy from the list of Standalone snap-ins. Click Add.

4. In the Select Group Policy dialog box, click Browse and select the Default Domain Policy, then click OK. Click Finish, click Close, and then click OK.

5. Expand the Default Domain Policy node, expand the Computer Configuration node, expand the Windows Settings node, and then expand the Security Settings node.

6. Double-click the Account Policies node and select the Password Policy node.

7. Double-click the Minimum Password Age entry and change the valuc to 14.

You have successfully changed the domain password age policy.

Summary

The Security Configuration Tool Set introduces a new and more efficient way to manage security parameters in Windows 2000. Using this new set of configuration and management tools, the administrator can configure and manage the security policies for a single machine, or an entire domain or organizational unit.

The Tool Set includes the Security Configuration and Analysis snap-in, Security Templates, the secedit.exe command line tool, and the Security Settings Extensions to the Group Policy Editor. Together, you can use these tools to create and configure security policies for local machines, domains, or organizational units.

The Security Configuration and Analysis snap-in allows the administrator to create a database with security configuration entries. These security configuration entries can be used to test against the existing security configuration of a local machine. After the security analysis is complete, the network manager can save the database entries into a text file, which is saved with the .inf extension. This text file, which is a template consisting of security configuration entries, can be saved or imported in order to define the security definition of another local machine, a domain, or an organizational unit.

The security variables in the database can also be applied to the local machine, replacing the current security configuration. The new configuration is applied after the analysis has been completed.

Security configuration can be saved as templates, which are text files that contain security configuration information. These templates are imported into the Security Configuration and Analysis snap-in database for analysis and application.

The Security Configuration and Analysis snap-in cannot be used to configure or analyze security configurations of a domain or organizational unit. At the present time, there is no way to export extant domain or organizational unit security configurations. However, you can configure the security of a domain or organizational unit via the Security Settings Group Policy Extensions.

The secedit.exe command line tool allows the administrator to script security analyses, security configurations, security updates, and export of templates. Its functionality is almost equal to that of the Security Configuration and Analysis snap-in, except that you must review the results of a security analysis performed by secedit.exe via the graphical interface.

An administrator can use the Security Settings Group Policy Extensions to configure domain or OU security policy. In addition, you can import security templates directly into the domain or organizational unit. You should do this with great caution if you have already customized the security settings for a domain or OU. At the present time, you cannot export the previous settings into a template that might be restored later. However, if the administrator always reconfigures the security parameters of a domain or OU by using templates, such templates can always be restored in the future.

FAQs

Q: Can I use the Security Configuration and Analysis snap-in to analyze the security configuration of a domain or organizational unit?

A: Not at this time. This capability should be added in the future. However, at present, you can test scenarios against the current configuration for the local machine.

Q: I would like to analyze a number of computers in my domain using scripts. What tool would I use to accomplish this?

A: The secedit.exe command line tool allows the administrator to analyze a number of machines by creating scripts that can be automated. You can then view the results of the analysis by opening up the database file that the analysis was run against.

Q: Why have the changes I made to the Security Policy on the local computer not taken effect?

A: Effective policy depends on whether a computer is a member of a domain or an organizational unit. Policy precedence flows in the order that policies are applied. First the local policy is applied, then domain policy is applied, and finally organizational unit policy is applied. If there are conflicts among the policies, the last one applied prevails.

Q: Can I migrate my Windows NT 4.0 Policies to Windows 2000?

A: No. The NT policies were stored in a .pol file, which included things such as group memberships. There is no way for the Windows 2000 Group Policy Model, which is centered about Active Directory, to interpret the entries in the .pol file. Microsoft recommends configuring the settings in the old .pol files in Active Directory. You can do this easily using the Security Settings Extension to the Group Policy Editor. The Windows NT 4.0 .pol files were created by the System Policy Editor, which used .adm files as templates for the options configured in system policy. These files are compatible with Windows 2000 .adm files. However, you should not import these templates, because you might damage the registries of client machines. This means that after a registry setting is set using Windows NT 4.0 .adm files, the setting will persist until the specified policy is reversed or the registry itself is edited directly.

Q: How do I reverse the changes I made after applying a security policy?

A: There is no direct mechanism, such as an Undo button, that will allow you to reverse the changes. Before you enact any changes to the local computer policy, back up the present configuration by exporting the current settings to an .inf file. Then you can restore your system to its previous state by importing the .inf file into the database, and reapplying the changes.

Chapter 6

Encrypting File System for Windows 2000

Solutions in this chapter:

- Introduction

- Using an Encrypting File System

- User Operations

- EFS Architecture

Introduction

Windows 2000 provides a new security feature by supporting file encryption. It will no longer be necessary to locate a third-party product to use as you had to do in your Windows NT environment for data encryption. As computers in general are more widely used, and laptop use is at an all-time high, the concern for data security increases for everyone, not just the system administrator. The fact that you have implemented a firewall, and that the Windows NT operating system includes mandatory logon and access control for files, does not guarantee that your data is protected from unauthorized eyes. To keep your data from being viewed and/or modified by any unauthorized user, technology has now turned to the process of file encryption, which replaces physical security.

If thieves want your data, there are many ways they can achieve their goal. Tools are available on other operating systems that can access NTFS volumes while bypassing the access control supplied by NTFS. The lack of physical security allows laptops to be stolen easily. Laptops now come with removable hard drives. This is great for the thief, since there is less to conceal. The laptop still appears on the desk, so the thief has more time to exit the building before any alarms go off. The desktop's second hard drive can be missing by the next morning.

The protection of data by physical security would be very easily implemented if all the rooms where equipment is used were locked and nothing were ever allowed to leave the room. Of course this approach to data security has a tremendous negative side; portability comes to a screaming halt. Physical security is not really a solution in today's world; the technological solution is file encryption.

Many file encryption products currently offered on the market by third-party vendors are designed around password keys. This kind of encryption is not very secure, because the encrypted file can be hacked quickly by brute force. Security products that were available before Windows 2000 required the user to encrypt and decrypt files manually with each usage. Most users do not have the time to back up their hard drive daily, and it is just as difficult to make the time to encrypt/decrypt files.

On occasion, users encrypt a file and then forget the password. The third-party product can handle this major problem in one of two ways: the product can provide data recovery, or it can not provide recovery. The more secure encryption software at the application level will not provide data recovery. The downside of this becomes evident when a person is authorized, needs to get to the data, and has forgotten the password. If the vendor did provide some form of data recovery, security is weakened, and the recovery code is now the system's weak point.

Some of the Windows 2000 Encrypting File System code runs down in protected mode. The kernel mode must not be available to users, or the operating system will crash. Microsoft has built encryption into the operating system, making encrypted data more secure than ever before. The new feature of Encrypting File System on Windows 2000 provides an element of security that Windows NT and third-party encryption software never approached in the past.

Using an Encrypting File System

The Encrypting File System that is supported in Windows 2000 is a new piece of security in the NTFS file system. Both public key encryption and secret key encryption are implemented within the complete process, so data gets encrypted quickly and in such a way that it can stand up against an attack from any cryptoanalysts. U.S. customers who purchase Windows 2000 will receive a 56-bit standard DES algorithm for implementation, but they can also obtain a 128-bit encryption DES algorithm. Until export approval is received, Microsoft will also have a 40-bit DES algorithm for all international customers.

The encrypted file can be read by anyone with a private key that can decrypt the File Encryption Key. If a user leaves the company, or if a user's private key becomes corrupted or is accidentally deleted, Windows 2000 can implement data recovery. This may sound like a security weak spot, but data recovery in Windows 2000 is not a security weakness. Microsoft has written code to establish an Encrypted Data Recovery Policy (EDRP), which controls who can recover the data if the owner's private key is lost or if the employee leaves the organization. In the Workgroup environment, Windows 2000 automatically sets up the EDRP on the local machine. In the domain environment, the EDRP is set up in the domain policy by the system administrator, and computers belonging to the domain will receive the EDRP from that location.

Encryption Fundamentals

Encryption is the process of taking a plaintext file and processing it so that the original data is in a new ciphertext format. Typically the encryption process uses an algorithm and a secret value that is referred to as the key.

Public key cryptography is designed so that each person has two keys, a public and a private key. Table 6.1 identifies the differences between them.

Table 6.1 Public and Private Keys

Key	Description	Used
Private	Never made known to anyone else	Decryption
Public	Known worldwide	Encryption

Public key cryptography is also known as asymmetric cryptography, since different keys are used by different users to encrypt and decrypt a file. Public-key-based algorithms usually are very high at the security level, but they are considered to be a slow process. The basic process of public key encryption and decryption is illustrated in Figure 6.1.

Instead of the key pair, symmetric cryptography uses a single secret key. One popular method of symmetric cryptography is Data

Figure 6.1 A public key encryption.

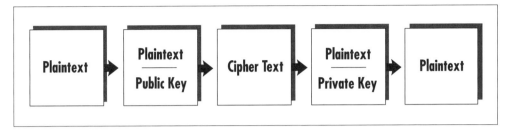

Encryption Standard (DES), which was defined in 1977 by the National Bureau of Standards for commercial and nonclassified use. Developed by a team of IBM engineers, who used their Lucifer cipher and input from the National Security Agency, DES is an encryption algorithm using a 56-bit binary number key.

Secret key algorithms are implemented quickly. Because the DES algorithm is the key that is used for both encrypting and decrypting data, this security mechanism is weak in its design. Figure 6.2 illustrates the secret key algorithm method.

Figure 6.2 A secret key algorithm.

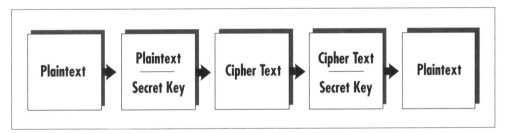

One major difference between symmetric and asymmetric algorithms is the number of keys that are used in the process. Public key algorithms use a key pair, but secret key algorithms use a single key. This major difference can clearly be seen in Figures 6.1 and 6.2. What the figures do not show is the difference between the two algorithms in the amount of time needed to process fully the encrypting/decrypting of the file. At one end of the spectrum, the symmetric algorithms are useful for large amounts of data; at the other end, asymmetric algorithms are useful for small amounts of data. Public key encryption is a slower process method than secret key encryption, so each should be implemented appropriately.

How EFS Works

Microsoft implements both secret key encryption, which is a fast and less secure process, along with public key encryption, which is slow but more secure. When a request is received to encrypt a file, Microsoft has the Encrypting File System generate a random number for the file, and this random number is known as the file's File Encryption Key. With this File Encryption Key, a modified DES algorithm, called DESX, is used to generate the encrypted file and store it on disk. The secret key algorithm is being implemented at this point.

The Windows 2000 operating system encryption process can be illustrated with this diagram:

Plaintext ➡ FEK and DESX ➡ Ciphertext

When a file needs to be decrypted, the File Encryption Key is used again. If we store the File Encryption Key on disk with the file, we have the FEK available for decryption at any time later on. Anyone who needs to decrypt the file and who has access to it also has access to the file's File Encryption Key.

Keeping sensitive data secure is the most important concern. The File Encryption Key is stored on disk and is available whenever it is needed, so that result is achieved, but anyone who can get to the file will have available the one thing needed for decrypting the file. What has been overlooked here is the security of the File Encryption Key. Secret key encryption is weak here, but public key encryption is most useful. To tighten the security of the File Encryption Key, we will encrypt it also. When a user encrypts a file, the Encrypting File System uses the user's public key to encrypt the File Encryption Key. This Windows 2000 design prevents users from sharing the same decryption key. The public key encryption method is used only on the small File Encryption Key, so there is no impact on the system's performance. What is stored with the encrypted file is the ciphered File Encryption Key. Only the user, with that user's private key, can decrypt the ciphered File Encryption Key, which is needed to decrypt the actual file. At this point both the sensitive data and the File Encryption Key have been secured. The slow method of public key algorithm is not used on the large file. The final design of file encryption for Windows 2000 allows us to get the best from both encryption worlds.

Now it is time to pull all these loose ends into one clear precise picture. Figure 6.3 demonstrates the encrypting process on a non-technical level.

Figure 6.3 A nontechnical view of the encrypting process.

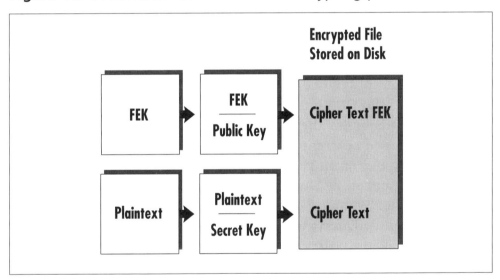

User Operations

The Encrypting File System adds more security than ever before in the Windows operating system. This built-in encryption allows any user to protect sensitive data against unauthorized use. This much-needed security feature can be used immediately after the installation of the operating system. The only requirement for the Encrypting File System is an NTFS partition. No new administrative tasks involving installation and configuration of the Encrypting File System need to be completed in order for it to work.

These are the user operations that use file encryption:

- Encrypting a file
- Accessing an encrypted file
- Copying an encrypted file
- Moving and renaming an encrypted file
- Decrypting a file
- Directory encryption
- Recovery operations

File Encryption

The Encrypting File System uses a public key pair and a secret key in the encryption/decryption process. When a user tries to encrypt a file, the EFS must determine first whether a user key pair is in existence for the user or whether it must be created. If a key pair needs to be created, the generation will occur on a domain controller or on the local computer, depending on the environment, unnoticed by the user. Other tasks completed by the Encrypting File System include creating the actual ciphered file, ciphering the File Encryption Key, creating a log, creating a backup file, and deleting the log and backup file used in the encryption process. There is much activity in the background, but the user is unaware of it.

In order to manage encrypted file resources, the user must first identify what data needs to be protected and then use either the Windows Explorer interface or the Cipher command utility to let the operating system know where Encrypting File System should be implemented.

Any folder or file, as long as it is stored on a NTFS volume, can be encrypted by the owner. The easiest way to maintain encrypted files is to first create an encrypted folder where you plan to store all sensitive data. Marking the directory for encryption does not have any effect on the listing of the files in the directory when you use the Explorer interface.

When the folder is created, the user will go to the Advanced Properties and there check Encrypt contents to secure data, as shown in Figure 6.4.

Figure 6.4 A directory marked for encryption.

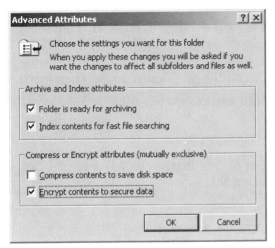

Once this bit is set, the directory is marked for encryption. Any newly created file or subdirectory stored in the marked directory from this point on will be automatically encrypted. If the directory is marked for encryption and it already contains existing files and sub-directories, the user will receive a message explaining how far down in the directory structure encryption should be set.

Any compressed or read-only file cannot be encrypted under Windows 2000. With the Windows 2000 operating system, you should not encrypt the files needed for booting. Much in the same way that stripe sets are not available under Windows NT until the system is fully booted up, encryption will not be available under Windows 2000 until the boot process is completed, which is efficient, considering the complexity of the encryption/decryption process. Never try to encrypt the files the system uses in order to boot up. Microsoft wrote the Encrypting File System code to prevent the accidental encrypting of system files.

The Encrypting File System process will fail if you try to encrypt a file that has the system bit set. Encrypting File System also will fail if you try to encrypt a file on the root. An attempt to encrypt a system file—that is, a file in which the system attribute is set—produces the message "An error occurred applying attributes to the file. Access is denied." The safeguard seems to be in place and currently working.

Encryption can be implemented at both the directory level and the file level. To encrypt a single file on a NTFS partition, follow these steps:

1. Using the Explorer, select the file you want to be encrypted.
2. Right-click to bring up the Context menu and then select Properties.
3. Click Advanced on the General tab.
4. In the Advanced Attributes dialog box, select the check box Encrypt contents to secure data.
5. Click OK.
6. On the General tab click OK or Apply to mark the file as encrypted.

Assessing an Encrypted File

Assessing an encrypted file involves no special action by the user. When the Windows 2000 operating system verifies that the user has an acceptable private key, it decrypts the file so the user can read and/or modify it. The stored file is still encrypted on the disk. As the bytes are moved from the disk into the user's working set, the bytes go through the decryption process. Using the Windows NT operating system and a third-party product, each encrypted file has to be manually decrypted before its contents can be read. This added user task was definitely a reason to forget about protecting sensitive data through encryption on Windows NT.

It is important to back up encrypted files. In the Windows 2000 operating system, just as in earlier versions of Windows NT, the owner of a file can control access to the file. If owners want to remove all access except for their own, they can do so through the NTFS permissions. The fact that only the owner has access to a file does not prevent the file from being backed up on a regular basis by the system administrators. Any user who belongs to the Backup Operators group has the ability to execute the Backup Utility and back up the file. The Backup Operators group is tied to the Backup Files and Directories Right which, when it runs the Backup Utility, allows the file to be opened and read. The Backup Files and Directories Right contains written code that will bypass the normal access control list.

The Encrypting File System also provides Backup Utilities with the ability to back up and restore files in ciphertext format. The backup process will not be able to decrypt the sensitive information; nor will it have to decrypt and encrypt during the backing-up operation.

The ADVAPI32.DLL library will provide the EFS APIs necessary for access to the encrypted data.

Windows 2000 backs up encrypted files in much the same way. No special configuration is needed. Members of the Backup Operators group will not have a private key, so there no chance of their reading the sensitive data that you have encrypted. Encrypted data is backed up during a backup operation as it exists on disk. The Backup Utility reads the Ciphertext file and records the Ciphertext file without decryption occurring.

Copying an Encrypted File

The COPY command will be extended, with two new switches, to export and import an encrypted file. When an encrypted file is copied, that encryption always take precedence. If either the file you want to copy or the destination directory is encrypted, then the resulting new file will be encrypted. Table 6.2 lists various situations and the status of the resulting created file.

Table 6.2 Copying Encrypted Files

Starting encryption	Copy	New file
Both the directory and file encrypted	Directory that is not encrypted	Encrypted
Both the directory and file encrypted	Directory that is encrypted	Encrypted
The directory encrypted but not the file	Directory that is encrypted	Encrypted
The directory encrypted but not the file	Directory that is not encrypted	Unencrypted
Both the directory and file unencrypted	Directory that is encrypted	Encrypted
Both the directory and file unencrypted	Directory that is unencrypted	Unencrypted

When the COPY command is used without the /E or /I switch, Windows 2000 will first decrypt the file and then make a copy in plaintext. The original encrypted file is still encrypted on the hard drive.

COPY Command

The Windows 2000 operating system adds to the COPY command by including two new switches. The /E switch is used for an Export function, and the /I is used to do the converse, which is to Import.

The /E can be added to the COPY command to export a ciphertext file as a ciphertext file. This means that the newly created file is still protecting the sensitive data. If the new file is accessed without having the encryption bit set, it will display the ciphertext created from the encryption process. The security of the Windows 2000 Encrypting File System means that a cryptanalyst would have to break both the public key encryption and the secret key encryption in order to see the sensitive data in plaintext.

The /I switch should be used to import a ciphertext file onto a NFTS partition as a ciphertext file. The newly created file from the import operation is marked as encrypted. When access to the file occurs, the NTFS driver knows the file is encrypted and will decrypt the file before displaying the contents. This decryption will occur only if the user making the request has the proper private key.

Unlike the Backup Utility of older Windows NT systems, which limited the media that could be used for backup operations, the Windows 2000 COPY command can copy the ciphertext to any file structure on any media. That means it is now possible to export the sensitive file to a floppy that uses FAT as a file system and then later, at a different location in the domain, to import the file and use it.

Moving or Renaming an Encrypted File

Renaming an encrypted file is no different from renaming a compressed file. The operating system changes the file name but does not make any modification to any other fields in the file's header. The fact that the file is encrypted sets an encryption bit in the file's header. Renaming will change the file's name but does not touch the encryption attribute.

When an encrypted file is moved, it retains its encrypted status regardless of the destination folder. When an encrypted file is moved on the same partition, there is no difference to the file other than the resident directory of the file. When the encrypted file is moved to a different NTFS partition, the file will first be decrypted and then encrypted before being stored at the new location.

Decrypting a File

Decryption is never a necessary request by the user after the file is encrypted as long as only that user needs to access the file. That does not mean that the decryption process will never occur on Windows 2000. The decryption process does occur in two instances: The Windows 2000 Encrypting File System will go through the decryption process when the file is accessed and also when the owner decides that the added security method is no longer needed.

When the user wants to read and/or modify the contents of the encrypted file, the Windows 2000 operating system decrypts the file as it is moved from the hard drive into physical memory. The decryption of the file for use is transparent to the user, and the ciphered file is still stored on the hard drive. The user does not have to decrypt the file manually before each use. The Encrypting File System must have the user's private key in order to decrypt the file. The user will work with their encrypted files just as with normal unencrypted files. If the user does not have a valid private key to the file, the system message "Access is denied" will appear, just as when the user does not have the proper permission.

Decryption must also occur when the user decides that the information is no longer sensitive and therefore does not have to be encrypted. When the information stored in a secretive fashion is no longer needed, the user can implement the decryption process at the file or the directory level. The user can use the Windows Explorer interface to clear the encryption bit, or the user can use the Cipher Utility and execute the appropriate command. When an individual file is selected for decryption, only that file is affected. When the user at the directory level requests decryption, a message will appear in the Explorer asking whether the user wishes to decrypt all files and subdirectories found within this directory, as shown in Figure 6.5.

Figure 6.5 The Confirm Attribute Changes dialog box.

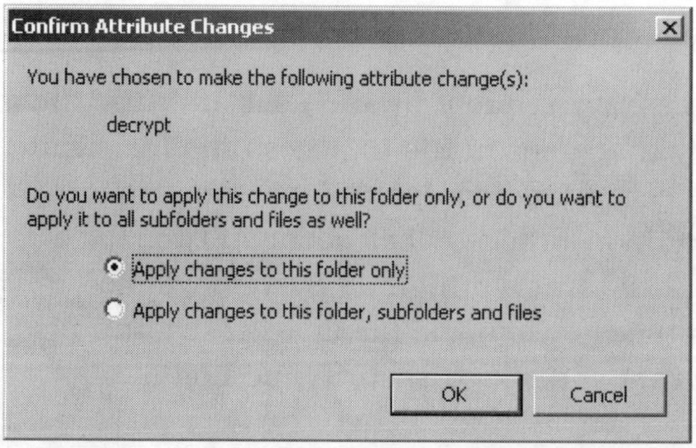

This decryption process at the directory level is exactly like the process for changing permissions at the directory level. Use these steps to decrypt a file:

1. Using the Explorer, select the file you want to be stored unencrypted.
2. Right-click to bring up the Context menu and select Properties.
3. Click Advanced on the General tab.
4. In the Advanced Attributes dialog box, clear the check box to Encrypt contents to secure data.
5. Click OK.
6. On the General tab, click OK or Apply to mark the file as unencrypted.

Cipher Utility

Windows 2000 allows users to use file encryption from the command prompt. The general format of the Cipher Utility is:

>cipher [/e] [/d] [/s [dir]] [/i] [/f] [/q] [filename]

When the cipher command is executed without any switches or filename, the result will be a display of the encryption status of the current directory and any files in that directory. Table 6.3 identifies each switch of the cipher command.

Table 6.3 Cipher Command Switches

Switch	Function
/e	Encrypts the specified files. The directory is marked for encryption so any files/subdirectories created and placed here will be encrypted.
/d	Decrypts the specified files. The directory will be cleared of the encryption attribute so that files added here will not be encrypted.

Continued

Switch	Function
/s	Performs the specified operation on the files in the directory and on all subdirectories.
/i	Continues to perform the cipher command even if errors occur, overriding the default behavior of the cipher command stopping if an error occurs.
/f	Forces encryption to occur on all specified files, even those that are already encrypted, overriding the default behavior of not encrypting already encrypted files.
/q	Reports only the most essential information.

The filename can be replaced with a filename or directory. The filename specification allows for wildcard usage, thus allowing multiple listings to be affected with a single command execution.

Figure 6.6 shows a cipher command that was executed without any switches at the root level of the directory structure. Every existing directory is listed, and it is possible to see whether or not the directory is marked for encryption.

Figure 6.7 shows the result of executing the cipher command at the directory level. The directory is marked for encryption, and any new objects stored here will be encrypted. All files and subdirectories are shown, along with their current encryption status.

Figure 6.6 A cipher command is executed.

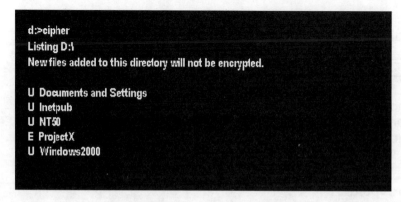

```
d:>cipher
Listing D:\
New files added to this directory will not be encrypted.

U Documents and Settings
U Inetpub
U NT50
E ProjectX
U Windows2000
```

Figure 6.7 The result of executing the cipher command.

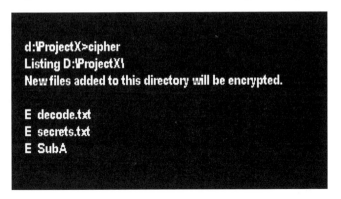

```
d:\ProjectX>cipher
Listing D:\ProjectX\
New files added to this directory will be encrypted.

E  decode.txt
E  secrets.txt
E  SubA
```

Directory Encryption

The Windows 2000 Encrypting File System allows encryption to be set at the directory and file level. When the directory is selected for encryption, what really happens is that any new object placed in this directory, including files and subdirectories, is encrypted. Any current existing file and subdirectory will not be encrypted unless the owner manually sets the encryption bit on the existing object. It is best to create a directory, to mark it for encryption, and then to store all sensitive data in that directory when you work with the Encrypting File System.

When you modify a directory's attribute to include encryption, the directory itself is not technically encrypted; rather, the directory is marked for encryption. This encryption mark controls all the new objects becoming encrypted.

Recovery Operations

Windows 2000 contains an Encrypted Data Recovery Policy (EDRP), which is part of the local security policy in a Workgroup environment or part of the domain security policy for Windows NT domains. The Security Subsystem in user mode is responsible for the enforcement of this policy. So that users can use file encryption offline, the Security Subsystem is responsible for caching the Encrypting File System policy much as logon information is cached on the local machine.

The Recovery Policy must first be set up by the system administrator. The Windows 2000 operating system contains a Recovery Agent Wizard, in which Recovery Agents are assigned along with their corresponding key pairs. The Microsoft Base Cryptographic Provider is used to create a Data Recovery File for each Recovery Agent.

The recommended steps in the recovery of an encrypted file that the owner cannot manipulate are:

1. The person who will be doing the recovery—that is, the Recovery Agent—should use a Backup utility and restore a copy of the user's ciphertext file on the computer that has the recovery certificates.

2. Using the Explorer, the encrypted file's Properties should be displayed.

3. On the General tab, the Recovery Agent needs to click Advanced.

4. The clearing of the Encrypt contents to secure date check box will use the Recovery Agent's private key and decrypt the file.

5. The decrypted file should now be backed up and restored to the user.

The Windows 2000 operating system also provides a command line utility that can be used to recover an encrypted file. If you decide to use the EfsRecvr utility, the same steps should be applied in order to back up the file and restore it on the computer that contains the recovery keys.

The EfsRecvr command line utility uses this general format:

EFSRECVR [/S [:dir]] [/I] [/Q] [filename [...]]

Table 6.4 summarizes each of the items in the EfsRecvr command line.

Table 6.4 EfsRecvr Command Line

Item	Function
/S	Recovers the files in the given directory and all subdirectories. The default directory is the current directory.
/I	The recovery process will continue even if an error occurs. The default behavior is to immediately stop the recovery process should an error occur.
/Q	Limits the reporting of only essential information needed to load the appropriate keys.
Filename	Specifies a file, directory, or pattern.

EFS Architecture

The Encrypting File System components and the encryption process, along with the Encrypting File System File Information and the decryption process, are involved in file encryption on Windows 2000.

EFS Components

In order to understand the entire encryption/decryption process, you need to look at the architecture of the Windows 2000 operating system. Keeping the same structure as previous releases of Windows NT, the Windows 2000 structure contains both the user mode and the kernel mode. When they developed the data encryption process, the designers had to decide where the encryption code should run. If data encryption were left in user mode, temporary files that were not encrypted would be created, which would provides no security at all. On Windows 2000, when the Encrypting File System is implemented, some of the activity will occur in each of these two modes.

In earlier versions of the Windows NT operating system, the Local Security Authority Subsystem (LSASS) was in user mode. With Windows 2000, this subsystem takes on additional tasks and includes some additional functions for the Local Security Authority Server in order for the Encrypted File System to work properly. The functions are grouped as EFS functions. Applications still run in user mode, so when a user requests encryption by using the Explorer or the Cipher Utility, the activity will start here.

The NTFS driver, which was first introduced in Windows NT 3.1, is in the kernel mode. Since users can protect sensitive data only on a NTFS partition, this driver has an active role in the overall encryption process. Figure 6.8 shows both old and new components.

Figure 6.8 The EFS components.

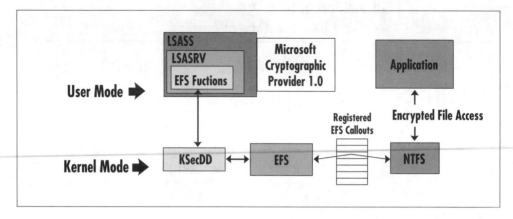

These are new key components of the Encrypting File System:

- **EFS Driver.** EFS is really a device driver connected with the NTFS driver, both of which run in Windows 2000's kernel mode. Whenever a user needs encryption or decryption to occur, the EFS driver works with the cryptography services in Windows 2000's user mode. The EFS communicates with the KsecDD (security device driver) to request many of the required key management services. When the NTFS needs to complete an impossible encryption task, the EFS driver takes on that responsibility.

- **EFS Callouts.** These are functions that the EFS driver can handle for the NTFS driver. When the EFS driver initializes, it registers these functions with the NTFS driver. The EFS Callouts are in the protected environment of the kernel mode, so the EFS Callouts are not available for direct user access.

- **KsecDD.** This takes the EFS request and talks with the Security Subsystem on behalf of the EFS driver. The KsecDD acts as a connection between the needed LPC calls and the Local Security Authority Subsystem in user mode.

- **EFS Services**. These are in the Local Security Authority Server, which is part of the Local Security Authority Subsystem. In user mode, the Encrypting File System

For Managers

Callback Functions

When the EFS driver initializes, it registers seven EFS Callback functions with the NTFS driver. These are the current Callback functions:

- **EfsOpenFile.** When an application opens an existing file having EFS attributes, the NTFS driver invokes the EFS Callback function EfsOpenFile.

- **EfsFilePostCreate.** After an NTFS file has created or opened a file for an application, the NTFS driver needs the help of the EfsFilePostCreate EFS Callback function.

- **EfsFileControl and EfsFsControl.** When a user modifies the file's encryption settings, the NTFS driver makes a request for the EFS Callback functions, EfsFileControl and EfsFsControl.

- **EfsRead.** When NTFS retrieves data for an application, it petitions EFS for the function named EfsRead.

- **EfsWrite.** When the user writes information in an encrypted file, the NTFS driver invokes the EFS Callback function known as EfsWrite, because NTFS cannot encrypt the data itself.

- **EfsFreeContext.** For the sake of security, which is what encrypting sensitive data is all about, the NTFS driver invokes the EFS Callback function EfsFreeContext, when the context data buffer is no longer required.

Services interface with the Microsoft Base Cryptographic Provider 1.0 to provide File Encryption Keys and to generate the needed Data Decryption Fields (DDF) and Data Recovery Fields (DRF). The Encrypting File System Service is used to obtain and enforce the Encryption Data Recovery Process and to locate the user's key pair when it is needed.

- **Cryptographic Provider.** For file encryption on Windows 2000, this is the Microsoft Base Cryptographic Provider 1.0. In the future releases of Windows 2000, support will be added so that third-party vendors can write their own Cryptographic Providers and have them tied to the Encrypting File System functions. One role of the Cryptographic Provider currently is to provide RSA encryption operations.

The Encryption Process

Before any encryption can be used on Windows 2000, the EFS device driver must be installed. When the EFS driver initializes, it notifies the NTFS driver of its existence, and it also registers seven related functions at that time. In the registration of these functions, the EFS driver seems to be telling the NTFS driver, "Here is a list of things I can do for you." (See the sidebar for the list of the EFS Callback functions.)

When the NTFS driver receives a request for EFS, it looks into the table of EFS Callback functions and invokes the function that the EFS driver must execute. The EFS driver will not communicate directly with the Local Security Authority Subsystem (LSASS), which runs in unprotected user mode. The EFS driver sends a request to encrypt or decrypt a file to the LSASS, but an additional driver intercepts this request in kernel mode. The driver used to send the actual LPC message to Local Security Authority Subsystem, KsecDD, resides in kernel mode. The Local Security Authority Server, which is part of the LSASS, listens for these LPCs. When the LSASRV receives a call from the FEClient (File Encryption Client DLL) to encrypt a file, it invokes the internal function EfsRpcEncryptFileSrv.

EfsRpcEncryptFileSrv handles these tasks in the early stages of a file encryption request:

- Impersonates the user making the encryption request
- Creates a log file that is used by LSASRV to keep a record of the encryption process from start to finish
- Loads the impersonated user's profile into the Registry
- Makes a call to the internal function EncryptFileSrv

There is a reason that impersonation occurs. The System account has always been used by the Local Security Authority Subsystem by default. If this account were used for the encryption process, the System's private key would be needed to decrypt the file. The objective of the Encrypting File System is to encrypt the file and then require a unique private key belonging to the user for any future usage. By impersonating the user, the proper private key is used in the manipulation of the file.

The log file that is created when an encrypt file request is received is used to record the events in the encrypting process. The log file is on the same drive as the encrypted file in the System Volume Information subdirectory. The name of the log file is EFS0.LOG. If an EFS0.LOG file already exists, the name of the log file is generated by incrementing the numeric value by one digit.

This need exists despite the fact that the user's profile has already been loaded into the Registry because logging on the system is mandatory. In most circumstances, the profile would already be loaded, but software engineers cannot leave anything to chance, especially when it comes to security. If the user executed the new Run As command of the Windows 2000 operating system, which allows the logged-on user to take on a different identity, the loaded profile would be the result of logging on the system, not the profile of the user making the encryption request.

When control is passed to the EncryptFileSrv function, an entirely new list of tasks must be performed. EncryptFileSrv is in user mode, and the EncryptFileSrv function will take on the remaining tasks in the encryption process. This function is responsible for these tasks:

- Queries the NTFS driver about the data stream being used in the file
- Calls the GenerateFEK function
- Constructs the EFS information that is stored with the encrypted file
- Creates a backup file
- Initializes the log file
- Sends an encrypted command to the NTFS driver to encrypt the file

In order for the EncryptFileSrv function to generate a File Encryption Key, another function called GenerateFek is used. The GenerateFek initiates a session with the Microsoft Base Cryptographic Provider and requests to use the RSA encryption algorithm. When it has established the session, GenerateFek calls another function to have the provider in fact generate the File Encrytion Key. After the File Encryption Key is created, the session with the Microsoft Base Cryptographic Provider is closed, and control is returned to the internal EncryptFileSrv function.

EncryptFileSrv uses the File Encryption Key and the user's key pair to create the EFS File Information. At this point in the encryption process, a key is created for a user who does not have one. The system can easily identify a user's lack of a key pair by the absence of the CertificateHash value found in the Registry for the current user.

After the EFS File Information is built, a backup file named EFS0.TMP is created for the original plaintext file. The security descriptor for this backup file is set up so that only the system account will have access to the file.

EncryptFileSrv now sends an encrypted control command to the NTFS driver to add the recently constructed EFS File Information to the original file. The NTFS driver understands an encrypted command in this way: At boot time, the Encrypting File System receives from the Local Security Authority Subsystem a session key that is used to decrypt any control command received from User Mode. When the NTFS driver receives the encrypted control command, the driver makes a request to the EFS Callback function, EfsFileControl. The EFS driver applies the session key to decrypt the control command and adds the EFS File Information to the original file. The EFS driver also creates the $EFS NTFS meta data attribute. This is a new attribute added to the Windows 2000 operating system that contains the EFS File Information.

After the EFS File Information is added to the file, the activity is once again handed back to the EncryptFileSrv internal function. EncryptFileSrv performs these tasks:

- Records in the log file that the backup file was created
- Sends another encrypted control command to the NTFS driver to encrypt the file at this time

When the NTFS receives the encrypted control command, it makes a request to the EFS Callback function, EfsWrite. The Callback function EfsWrite uses the unencrypted File Encryption Key to do secret key encryption of the file one sector at a time. The data is encrypted before the NTFS driver writes the data to disk. In the United States, the Encrypting File System uses a 56-bit standard DESX encryption key.

When the file is completely written to disk in ciphertext form, EncryptFileSrv is handed control once again. The EncryptFileSrv function completes the encryption process by doing these tasks:

- Records in the log file that the encryption process was successfully completed without errors
- Deletes the backup copy of the original file
- Deletes the log file
- Passes control back to the user

These tasks draw together the built-in fault-tolerant side of the encryption process. A backup copy of the original file is always available until the encryption process is completed successfully. If there is a system crash or other fatal error, the log file indicates where the encryption process stopped, and the original copy of the file can be used to redo the entire process.

The EFS File Information

After the File Encryption Key has been created, the EFS File Information can be constructed. The LSASRV function called EncryptFileSrv has the control of the creation of the EFS File Information that is stored with the file. The user's key pair is needed to supply the necessary information in the encrypted file's header. The function CryptoAPI is called to get a handle to the needed key pair. If the user does not have a key pair, because this is the first file to be encrypted, a key pair has to be created. The function GenerateUserKey is used in creating the key pair and returns the signed certificate for the pair. The generation of the key pair will happen on a domain controller or on the local machine on the basis of the computer's environment. When the signed certificate is received, it is stored in the Registry in the subkey HKEY_CURRENT_USER\Software\Microsoft\WindowsNT\CurrentVersion\EFS\CurrentKeys\CertificateHash.

Now that EncryptFileSrv has the user's key pair, a function is used to obtain information about the provider that was used to generate the key pair. In Windows 2000, that provider is the Microsoft Base Cryptographic Provider 1.0. The information about the user that is needed at this point is the provider's name and the container used to store the key pair, which in fact is nothing more than a file specification.

An example of a container would be:

```
D:\Documents and Settings\Administrator\Application Data\
Microsoft\SystemCertificates\My\Certificates\
1612DAFAD20E037F2DBACD4113FC755BC23B6711
```

EFS now uses the function CryptAcquireContext to set up a cryptographic session with the provider, using the provider's name, container's name, and the fact that it desires to use the RSA encryption service of the Windows 2000 operating system. The provider's name must be identified at this point because the Windows 2000 operating system will allow software vendors to write their own providers and implement them if they want to. RSA is the public key encryption algorithm that was written by Rivest, Shamir, and Adleman. The provider will create 128 bits of random data that will become the file's File Encryption Key, and then a function is called to close the session with the Microsoft Base Cryptographic Provider.

Now that EncryptFileSrv has a File Encryption Key, the EFS File Information can be constructed and stored with the file. The function GetCurrentKey is used to read the Registry information and get a handle to the user's public key. A Local Security Authority Server function will use the public key to store the EFS information with the file. Figure 6.9 identifies the components that make up the EFS File Information.

The Data Decryption Field contains entries for each user who has access to the encrypted file. Each individual entry is referred to as a DDF Key Entry. The components of the Data Decryption Field Key Entry provide information to represent a user's public key. The user's SID is a component of the Key Entry. Also included in the

Figure 6.9 The EFS File Information.

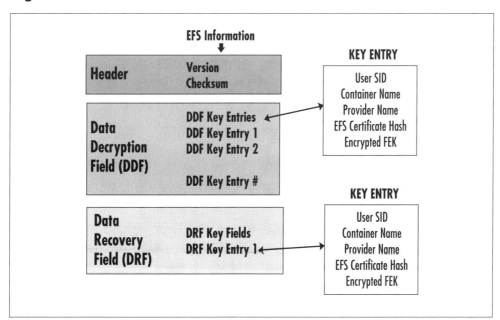

Key Entry is the provider name and container name, the public/private key pair certificate hash, and the encrypted File Encryption Key. Any collection of multiple key entries in the EFS File Information is called a key ring.

The EFS File Information component of the Encrypting File System is not yet completed. There is no entry that will provide recovery if the user's private key somehow becomes corrupted.

The EFS creates another key ring that contains recovery key entries. All information tied to the recovery process is in the file's Data Recovery Field. Figure 6.9 shows that the information in the Data Recovery Field entries uses the same format as the Data Decryption Field entries. The number of entries created here is determined by the Recovery Agents previously defined using the Recovery Agent Wizard. That means that Local Security Authority Server will have to read the recovery policy at boot time or when it receives notification of policy changes so the correct Data Recovery Field entries can be created. The EFS will use the same provider, the Microsoft Base Cryptographic Provider 1.0, in creating a Data Recovery Field entry key for each Recovery Agent.

The EFS adds Recovery Agent entries to the DRF section of the EFS File Information for each recovery key pair on the system. The system administrator can create any number of Recovery Agents by assigning their account access to an EFS recovery key pair. The number of Recovery Agents should be kept to a minimum.

The final step in building all this EFS information is to calculate a checksum value for the DDF and DRF. EFS will store the checksum value with the other header information. This checksum is tied to the decryption process. In order to guarantee that the EFS File Information has not been changed, the checksum is used for verification during the decryption process.

The information that is saved with the encrypted file as the EFS File Information must always be current; otherwise users who are issued new certificates will be unable to access their protected encrypted files. To compensate for this, when the key field that can successfully decrypt the FEK is located, a function is used to compare the SID, provider name, container name, and certificate hash value to the properties of the user's current EFS cryptographic key pair. If any of the information in the key field does not match the current registry values, the key field will be updated in the EFS File Information. If the key field needs to be updated, a new key field is created containing the new matching information, and then the old key field is deleted.

The Decryption Process

When a user accesses an encrypted file, the decryption process begins. Once again, this lengthy process is transparent to the user. As is the case when any file on an NTFS volume is accessed, the NTFS driver looks at the file's attributes. If the file is indeed encrypted, the NTFS driver invokes the EFS Callback function, EfsOpenFile, which the Encrypting File System registered at the time it initialized. The task of reading the EFS attribute is now handed over to the EFS driver.

The EFS Callback function, EfsOpenFile, now performs these tasks:

- Opens the Encrypting File System attribute
- Calls the NTFS function NtOfsQueryLength to determine the attribute's length
- Allocates this much buffer space
- Copies the EFS attribute to the buffer

If the Encrypting File System attribute fails to open for any reason, the user receives an error message. If the Encrypting File System attribute successfully opens, the NTFS driver again invokes a registered EFS Callback function, this time named EfsFilePostCreate.

If all has gone smoothly, the job of the EfsFilePostCreate is now to make sure the user requesting to open the file has access to the file's encrypted data. In order for the user to have access to an encrypted file's data, the user needs a private key to decrypt the File Encryption Key, which in turn is used to decrypt the file itself.

The actual decryption of the File Encryption Key is handled by Local Security Authority Server, which resides in user mode. To perform the decryption of the File Encryption Key, the EfsFilePostCreate sends a LPC message to the LSASRV by way of KSecDD. The Microsoft Base Cryptographic Provider is used to encrypt/decrypt. This Cryptographic Provider functions in User Mode and is attached to the Local Security Authority Subsystem. Much as is the case with the encryption process, impersonation must occur in the Local Security Authority Subsystem process when the user opens the file, because the LSASS executes using the System account. This impersonation must be set up before the KSecDD sends the Local Procedure Call (LPC) message to LSASRV and is handled by the EfsFilePostCreate EFS Callback function.

When the LSASRV receives the LPC message from KsecDD, a function call is used to load the user's profile into the Registry, if it is not already there. A second function call named DecryptFek is called to perform the actual file decryption.

This DecryptFek has some legwork to complete before it actually decrypts the file. The DecryptFek must use the Encrypting File System Certificate Hash, stored as a component of the Key Entry, to identify the private key to be used. DecryptFek uses the user's private key to try to decrypt the ciphered FEK in each key entry in both the Data Decryption and the Data Recovery Fields of the EFS File Information.

When every DDF and DRF entry has been tried and the result is that the entry's File Encryption Key cannot be decrypted, the user is denied access to the file, but if a private key can decrypt the File Encryption Key, a cryptographic session with the Microsoft Base Cryptographic Provider is established. Much as is the case with the encryption process, to establish a session with the Microsoft Base Cryptographic Provider the container name and the provider name must be known. This time the information is known by the key fields of the EFS File Information.

Once the session with the provider is created, the decryption of File Encryption Key is completed by using the user's private key. Just as an added security step, the hashing of the EFS attribute and the decrypted File Encryption Key takes place and is compared with the checksum value located in the header information. Any different values seen here will indicate that the file has been compromised in some way, and an error will result. Windows 2000 will now establish another session with the Microsoft Base Cryptographic Provider. This session will use the plaintext File Encryption Key and the RSA algorithm to completely decrypt the file.

Summary

Windows 2000 now supplies the user with the ability to encrypt files that contain sensitive information. The Encrypting File System can be set both at the directory and file level. This new security feature is efficient in that the encryption/decryption process is totally transparent to the user, once the files are marked for encryption.

Basic file encryption is accomplished using two methods. Secret key encryption uses the same key for encrypting and decrypting data, so it is not considered very secure. The secret key algorithm is relatively fast and therefore is appropriate for encrypting a large amount of data.

Public Key Cryptography uses a key pair. The public key is used for encryption, and the private key is used to decrypt the file. This method of encryption provides more security, because only a private key can unscramble the ciphertext back into plaintext. The price you must pay for better security is that the process is slow; it should be used only on a small amount of data.

Windows 2000 uses both methods of encryption. The file is encrypted using a secret key called a File Encryption Key, along with the DESX algorithm. To protect the File Encryption Key from dishonest people, the File Encryption Key is then encrypted by the owner's public key.

When it comes to the user actually working with sensitive data, no additional configuration steps are needed. When the file or directory is marked for encryption, the whole encrypting/decrypting process is transparent to the user. The user can identify for the Windows 2000 operating system what files are to be encrypted through either the Windows Explorer interface or a command line utility called Cipher.

The basic COPY command has been extended with two new switches that allow the exporting and importing of a cipher-text object. The /E switch exports an encrypted file in ciphertext without setting the EFS bit. This file can only then be read by using the COPY command again with the /I switch, which copies the cipher-text file and marks the encryption bit.

The encryption of files does not modify the normal file operations of renaming or moving. When you move an encrypted file on the same partition, the pointer in the directory is changed, but nothing in the encryption fields is modified. A rename operation on an encrypted file will change only the filename, once again not modifying any field tied to the encryption process.

The new Cipher Utility allows users to encrypt/decrypt files or directories at the command prompt. The included switches for this utility allow the user to indicate whether the requested operation should be performed on all files and subdirectories, and whether the operation is to continue in the event an error has occurred, thus forcing encryption of already encrypted files.

The EfsRecvr Utility can be used to recover an encrypted file if the owner's private key is corrupted or lost. This EfsRecvr utility has switches that are similar to the Cipher Utility in that the Recovery Agent can indicate how much of the directory structure is to be recovered and whether the process should continue even if an error has occurred.

The Encrypting File System follows the Windows NT operating system model. Some of the encryption activity is handled down in the protected mode, known as the kernel mode, while other tasks are performed in user mode. Windows 2000 has added in kernel mode the Encrypting File System driver, which, at initialization time, registers seven EFS Callout functions with the NTFS driver. When the NTFS driver needs to do any Encrypting File System operation, the NTFS makes a call to one of the appropriate callout functions. The other component employed in kernel mode is known as the KSecDD driver. The role of the KSecDD driver in the encryption process is to send the Local Procedure Call messages from the Encrypting File System driver to the Local Security Authority Subsystem.

Windows 2000 has added to the Local Security Authority Subsystem, which runs in user mode, a series of internal functions for encryption/decryption operations. In the encryption process, the internal function EncryptFileSrv plays a major role. Also located in user mode is a Cryptographic Provider, which currently is the Microsoft Base Cryptographic Provider 1.0. One major responsibility of this Cryptographic Provider is to provide the RSA encryption operation after a session has been established.

The EFS File Information is created by the EncryptFileSrv function call. The information includes a checksum, the Data Decryption Field, and the Data Recovery Field. The checksum is used at decryption time to verify the integrity of the EFS File Information. The DDF is a list of owner key entries, and the DRF is a list of Recovery Agents' key entries. This EFS File Information is used with every occurrence of decryption.

FAQs

Q: Do encrypted files have be stored on the local hard drive, which would result in users having to be responsible for backing up their hard drive daily?

A: The Encrypting File System is not limited in design to storage only on the local hard drive. The encrypted file can be stored on any file server located on the network. The EFS is responsible for file encryption and is not assigned the additional task of securing packets on the network. The functionality of packet security on the network is part of SSL.

Q: Our corporation is an international company. Can I use the 128-bit encryption at some locations and not at others, without having encryption problems?

A: By default, EFS provides standard 56-bit encryption to its U.S. customers. For security reasons, they can obtain the 128-bit encryption by ordering the Enhanced CryptoPAK from Microsoft. The files encrypted with the Enhanced CryptoPAK cannot be decrypted, accessed, or recovered on a system that supports 56-bit encryption only.

Q: How would you summarize the basic steps that occur on Windows 2000 when a file is encrypted?

A: The basic steps are:

1. When a user executes an encryption request, the NTFS driver makes a request to the appropriate EFS Callout function.

2. The requester's user profile is loaded into the Registry, if it is not already there.

3. A log file is created that records events as they occur during the encryption process.

4. The EFS identifies the user's key pair and then uses the public key to create an entry in the Data Decryption Field for the user.

5. Entries are created in the Data Recovery Field for each Recovery Agent.

6. A backup file is created and used to guarantee a fault-tolerant Encrypting File System.

7. All entries in the DDF and DRF are added to the file's header.

8. Encryption of the file occurs.

9. The log file and the backup file are deleted at the end of the encryption process.

10. The requester's profile is unloaded from the Registry, if needed.

Q: Many applications work through the use of temporary files. Is this a weak security area in the Windows 2000 Encrypting File System?

A: Current applications do create temporary files, and they are not encrypted. To keep the sensitive data secure, Windows 2000 includes setting encryption at the directory level. For any applications that work with temporary files, the user should make sure that the directory, where the temporary files will be stored, is marked for encryption.

Q: How much training is needed for users of sensitive data that requires encryption?

A: Windows 2000's Encrypting File System is transparent to the user after the file or the directory is marked for encryption. Minimum training may be needed to introduce the Windows Explorer interface and the new switches for the COPY command, and to introduce the Cipher Utility.

Q: What happens to the data if during the encryption process the system should crash?

A: The Encrypting File System is designed to be fault-tolerant. Throughout the entire encryption process, a log file keeps track of certain operations as they are completed. If the system crashes before the file is completely encrypted, the Local Security Authority Server looks for log files at boot time. If the LSASRV locates any Encryption log file, the contents are read. Usually the LSASRV copies the backup file over the original semiencrypted file and then deletes the backup and log files. If the LSASRV finds that the original file has not been modified, it deletes the backup and log files.

Q: When does encryption actually occur, on the reading or writing to an encrypted file?

A: The NTFS driver calls the EFS Callback function, EfsRead, when an encrypted file needs to be read. The data is decrypted as the NTFS driver reads it from the hard drive and before it is placed in the file system cache. When an application writes to an encrypted file, the data in the file system cache is in plaintext. When the application or the Cache Manager flushes the data to disk, the NTFS driver calls the EFS Callback function, EfsWrite, to encrypt the data.

Q: Can I use compression and encryption at the same time on a file?

A: The Windows 2000 interface clearly shows that compression and encryption cannot both be enabled at the same time on a file. The Windows interface has check boxes for the compression and encryption attributes.

Q: Can I store an encrypted file in a nonencrypted directory?

A: A user who is trying to mark a file for encryption, in a directory that is not marked for encryption, receives this message in a window: "You have chosen to encrypt a file that is not in an encrypted directory. The file can become decrypted when it is modified. Because files saved in encrypted directories are encrypted by default it is recommended that you encrypt the file and the parent folder." The user than chooses whether to encrypt the file and parent folder, or to encrypt the file only.

Chapter 7

IP Security for Microsoft Windows 2000 Server

Solutions in this chapter:

- Introduction
- Network Encroachment Methodologies
- IPSec Architecture
- Deploying Windows IP Security

Introduction

Security issues are of paramount importance to the network administrator. In the past, networks were lone entities. These lone networks typically ran NetBEUI in small workgroups of fewer than 200 computers and were not connected to any other networks. The major security concerns in an isolated environment typically revolved around employees located at the site. You could focus your security efforts on local access controls, such as locking down floppy drives on employee workstations, and checking briefcases and handbags for printed materials.

Today's network is very different from the isolated NetBEUI network. It is likely that your network is connected to other networks via dedicated leased lines, the Internet, or your organizational remote access server.

Each of these points of access represents an ever-increasing security risk. Previously, electronic documents had to be copied to a floppy disk or printed in order to leave your premises; now, it is as easy as sending an e-mail attachment over the Internet. The organization's prized database can just as easily be posted to electronic newsgroups. Hackers can snoop the network and gain usernames and passwords that allow them to bypass normal access controls. Innocent experimenting by fledging systems engineers and power users can corrupt or destroy data just as effectively as the most malignant of hackers.

Effective network security standards are the sum total of a well-planned and -implemented security infrastructure. These measures include hardware security, file and folder access controls, strong passwords, smart cards, social security, physical sequestration of servers, file encryption, and protection of data as it moves across the wire within the organizational intranet and outside the organization.

This chapter focuses on protecting the integrity and confidentiality of information as it moves through the network. First, it looks at some of the common security risks incurred as data moves across the wires. The next section discusses the basics of cryptography and how they function within the framework Microsoft's new IPSec capabilities. The last and most comprehensive section covers the specifics of implementing IP security in your network.

Network Encroachment Methodologies

Hackers can use a number of methods to circumvent your network security and gain access to information, including:

- Snooping
- Spoofing
- Password compromise
- Denial of service attacks
- Man-in-the-middle attacks
- Application-level attacks
- Key compromise

Snooping

Most data sent over the network is in clear text. Individuals with a network sniffer such as the Network Monitor program that comes with Systems Management Server, or third-party programs such as Sniffer Pro, can easily read the clear text messages as they traverse the network.

Some server applications that maintain their own username and password lists allow for the logon information to cross the network in free-text format. The network snooper, using easily accessible sniffing programs, can plug into an available port in a hub or switch and access this information. The use of clear text makes it easy for the snooper to access information. Such information might include: credit card numbers, Social Security numbers, contents of personal e-mail messages, and proprietary organizational secrets.

Spoofing

The source and destination IP address are prerequisite for establishing sessions between computers on a TCP/IP-based network. The act of IP spoofing involves falsely assuming the identity of a legitimate host computer on the network in order to gain access to computers on the internal network. Another term for spoofing is *impersonation*. The intruder is impersonating a computer with a legitimate IP address. A common spoofing-based attack is the TCP/IP Sequence number attack.

TCP/IP Sequence Number Attack

The Transmission Control Protocol (TCP) is responsible for reliability of communications on a TCP/IP-based network. This includes acknowledgment of information sent to the destination host. In order to track bytes sent over the network, each segment is given a sequence number. A sophisticated attacker can establish the sequencing pattern between two computers because the sequence pattern is not random.

First, the attacker must gain access to the network, and then the attacker must connect to a server and analyze the sequence pattern between the server and a legitimate host it is communicating with at the time. The TCP/IP Sequence Number attacker then will attempt a connection to the server by spoofing (falsely assuming) a legitimate host's IP address. In order to prevent the legitimate host from responding, the spoofer will start a denial of service attack on the legitimate host.

Since the legitimate host cannot respond, the spoofer will wait for the server to send its reply and then will respond with the correct sequence number. The server now believes that the spoofing computer is the legitimate host, and the spoofer now can begin data transfer.

Password Compromise

Users who have illegitimate access to network passwords can access resources they are not otherwise able to use. There are a number of ways an attacker can gain knowledge of passwords:

- **Social Engineering.** The attacker contacts an individual using an assumed identity, and then makes a request for a password from an individual who has access rights to the information of interest.

- **Sniffing.** Many network applications allow the username and password to cross the network in clear text. The attacker can use a network sniffer application to intercept this information.

- **Cracking.** The cracker uses a number of different techniques to gain illegal access to passwords. Examples of cracking techniques include dictionary attacks and brute force attacks.

If an administrator password is compromised, the attacker will then have access to all resources on the network that are protected with access controls. The intruder now has access to the entire user account database and can use this information to access all files and folders, change routing information, and alter information unbeknownst to users who are dependent on that information.

Denial of Service Attacks

There are a number of different denial of service attacks. All these techniques have in common the ability to disrupt normal computer or operating system functioning on the targeted machine. These attacks can flood the network with useless packets, corrupt or exhaust memory resources, or exploit a weakness in a network application. Denial of service attacks include:

- TCP SYN attack
- SMURF attack
- Teardrop attack
- Ping of Death

TCP SYN Attack

When computers on a TCP/IP-based network establish a session, they go through the three-way handshake process:

1.   The originating client sends a packet with the SYN flag set to ON. This host includes a sequence number in the packet. The server will use this sequence number in the next step.

2.   The server will return a packet to the originating host with its SYN flag set to ON. This packet will have a sequence number that is incremented by 1 over the number that was sent by the requesting computer.

3.   The client will respond to this request with a packet that will acknowledge the server's sequence number by incrementing the sequence number by 1.

Whenever a host requests a session with a server, the pair will go through the three-way handshake process. The attacker can take advantage of this process by initiating multiple session requests that originate from bogus-source IP addresses. The server keeps each open request in a queue as it is waiting for step 3 to occur. Entries into the queue are typically emptied every 60 seconds.

If the attacker is able to keep the queue filled, then legitimate connection requests will be denied, so service is denied to legitimate users of e-mail, Web, ftp, and other IP-related services.

SMURF Attack

The SMURF attack attempts to disable the network by flooding the network with ICMP Echo Requests and Echo replies. The attacker will spoof a source IP address and then issue an Internet Control Message Protocol (ICMP) to a broadcast address. This will cause all the machines on a segment to reply to the bogus request. If the attacker can maintain this attack for an extended period of time, no useful information can be passed though the network because of the flood of ICMP Echo Request and Reply messages traversing the wire.

Teardrop Attack

The teardrop attack is executed using a program, such as teardrop.c, which causes fragmentation similar to that seen in the

Ping of Death attack. It takes advantage of a weakness in the reassembly process and can cause a system to hang or crash.

Ping of Death

The Ping of Death exploits features of ICMP and the Maximum Transfer Unit (MTU) sizes of various network architectures. The Ping command issues an ICMP Echo Request and is returned an ICMP Echo reply by the destination host. The ICMP Echo request message is encapsulated in an IP packet that is limited by 65,535 octets. The MTU defines the maximum size of a unit for a defined network architecture, which varies with the media type.

If the size of a packet is larger than the MTU, the packet will be fragmented and then reassembled at the destination. It is possible to send a packet with more than the legal number of octets. When packets are fragmented, an offset value is included with the packet. This offset value is used to reassemble fragments at their destination. The attacker could include with the last fragment a legal offset and a larger packet size. This will exceed the legal number of octets in the data portion of the ICMP Echo request. When reassembly is attempted, the destination computer may respond by rebooting or crashing.

Man-in-the-Middle Attacks

A man-in-the-middle attack occurs when two parties believe that they are communicating only with each other, but in fact there is an intermediary silently listening in to the conversation. The man in the middle can intercede in the conversation by impersonating the identity of either the sender or receiver. During the attacker's intercession, he can alter or destroy messages during transit.

By using a network sniffer, the attacker can record and save messages for later use. This can allow the intruder to issue a subsequent replay attack. The man in the middle, having recorded aspects of a conversation, can replay this information in order to get around network authentication mechanisms in the future. This is known as a replay attack.

Application-Directed Attacks

Application-oriented attacks seek to take advantage of weaknesses inherent in certain network applications. By exploiting weaknesses in these network applications, an intruder can:

- Corrupt or alter important operating system files
- Change the content of data files
- Cause the network application or the entire operating system to operate abnormally, or even crash
- Disrupt normal security and access controls maintained by the application or operating system
- Plant a program or programs that can return information back to the attacker. Back Orifice is an example of such an application.

There are numerous examples of such application-directed attacks. Web servers are often the target of such attacks. On July 17, 1998, there was a report of vulnerability in the Microsoft Data Access Components (MDAC) that could allow Web site visitors to take unauthorized actions on Web sites hosted by Internet Information Server 3.0 and 4.0. This weakness allowed unauthorized users to execute shell commands as privileged users, and access nonpublished files and directories on the IIS system itself. A patch quickly followed after discovery of the vulnerability.

These application-level attacks provide the most fertile ground for the would-be intruder. Many network applications have not completed the degree of security assessment and testing that is required to optimize their immunity to attacks aimed against them.

Compromised Key Attacks

A key is a number, or cipher, that can be used to either verify the integrity of a communication or encrypt the contents of a communication. There are different types of keys. One type of key is known as a secret key. A sending computer encrypts the contents of a message using the secret key, and the receiving computer decrypts the message with the same secret key. Using this shared secret, two computers can communicate in private.

Another type of secret key is the private key. The secret private key can be used to confirm the identity of the sender. This is known as signing a message. A recipient who receives a message signed by someone's private key can be confident that the person who claims to have sent the message is indeed that person.

An attacker who somehow gains access to these keys can then communicate with an assumed identity by using someone else's private key. An attacker who gains access to a shared secret key can then decrypt messages that had been encrypted by that key.

When secret keys no longer remain secret, they are said to be compromised. After they are compromised they can no longer be used to secure identities and information. Discovering that a key has been compromised is often a difficult endeavor. Often the only way a compromised key is discovered is after some vital piece of information is found to be no longer secret, as in cases of corporate espionage.

IPSec Architecture

IPSec defines a network security architecture that allows secure networking for the enterprise while introducing a minimum of overhead. IPSec allows you to secure packets at the network layer. By performing its services at the network layer, IPSec secures information in a manner that is transparent to the user and also to the protocols that lie above the transport layer. IPSec provides layer-3 protection.

The IPSec security architecture exercises an end-to-end security model. Only the endpoints of a communication need to be IPSec-aware. Computers and devices that serve as intermediaries of message transfer do not need to be IPSec-enabled. This allows the administrator of a Windows 2000 network to implement IPSec for end-to-end security over diverse network infrastructures, including the Internet. Transit network devices such as bridges, switches, and routers can be oblivious to IPSec without compromising its efficacy.

This end-to-end capability can be extended to different communication scenarios, including:

- Client-to-client
- Gateway-to-gateway

When IPSec is used to protect communications between two clients—for example, on the same LAN—the machines can utilize IPSec in what is known as transport mode. In transport mode, both clients must use TCP/IP as their network protocol. In this example, the endpoints of the secure communication are the source machine and the destination host.

By contrast, with a gateway-to-gateway solution, information traversing a transit network (such as the Internet) is protected by IPSec. Packets are protected as they leave the exit gateway and then decrypted or authenticated at the destination network's gateway. In this scenario, the host and destination computers do not employ IPSec, and can use any LAN protocol supported by IPSec (IPX/SPX, AppleTalk, NetBEUI, TCP/IP).

When gateways represent the endpoints of secure communication, IPSec works in tunnel mode. A tunnel is created between the gateways, and client-to-client communications are encapsulated in the tunnel protocol headers. Tunnels can be created using IPSec as the tunneling protocol, or you can combine IPSec with L2TP, which stands for Layer 2 Tunneling Protocol and allows for data encryption via IPSec. In this case L2TP, rather than IPSec, creates the tunnel.

Overview of IPSec Cryptographic Services

IPSec is able to ensure security of communication by employing a variety of cryptographic techniques. Cryptography is the making and deciphering of hidden or scrambled messages in such a manner that if the message or communication is intercepted, the thief cannot ascertain the contents of the message.

There are several component features of a good security system. The IPSec security architecture is designed to provide these features:

- Integrity
- Confidentiality
- Authentication

Message Integrity

The term *integrity* refers to the assurance that the message received was indeed the message sent. Integrity is violated if the communication is somehow altered between the sending and receiving computer. Message integrity can be assured via the creation of digital signatures. A digital signature is a fingerprint. This fingerprint can be a representation of the contents of the document. If someone were to capture the message in transit and change its contents, the intruder would leave a fingerprint on the message that is different from the original fingerprint. The destination machine would detect that other hands had touched the document, and therefore would consider its content invalid. We can use hash functions to create the original fingerprint.

Hashing Messages

You can hash a message by running it through a hashing algorithm. A key is used together with the hashing algorithm to create a hash so that only computers that know the key can create the same hash output of a message. The hashed output is always the same length. This hashed output is often referred to as a message digest, or hash signature. You cannot reverse-engineer the digest to get the original message. Each packet must have a different hashed result.

For example, if I send you a message that says "Hi Mom," I will hash the message using a secret key that only you and I know about. After sending "Hi Mom" through the hash algorithm using the secret key, we get a message digest of "12345."

Now I will send you the message, together with the message digest. In order to make sure that the original message was "Hi Mom," you will send the contents of the message through the same hash algorithm and check the result. If you get "12345," then it matches the digest sent to you. You know that indeed "Hi Mom" was the original content of the message.

If a man in the middle had intercepted the message, he might have changed the content of the message to say "Hi Dad." When you received the message, it would read "Hi Dad." You would then run "Hi Dad" though the hash algorithm, and the result would be "12389." This does not match the message digest included with the message. This message has had its integrity violated and should not be considered valid.

These message digests are also known as Hash Message Authentication Codes (HMAC). To derive an HMAC, Microsoft's implementation of IPSec uses one of two algorithms:

- **Message Digest 5 (MD5).** This algorithm was developed by Ron Rivest of MIT and is defined in RFC 1321. MD5 processes each message in blocks of 512 bits. The message digest ends up being 128 bits.

- **Secure Hash Algorithm (SHA-1).** This algorithm also processes messages in blocks of 512 bits. However, the resulting message digest is 160 bits long. This confers a greater degree of confidence, but is a bit more processor-intensive, and therefore slower than MD5.

A shared secret key is required to make this hash method work. In order to ensure the validity of the secret key, you must utilize other technologies, such as a public key infrastructure.

Message Authentication

Authentication is concerned with establishing the identity of the sender or the recipient. Integrity concerns itself with making sure the message has not changed during transit. Authentication focuses on confirming the identities of the participants of the conversation. It would be of little value to receive a message of uncompromised integrity from an imposter.

IPSec uses three methods to carry out message authentication:

- Preshared key authentication
- Kerberos authentication
- Public key certificate–based digital signatures

Preshared Key Authentication

Preshared key authentication schemes depend on both members of the communication having pre-selected a secret key that will be used to identify them to each other. Data leaving the sending computer is encrypted with this agreed-to key, and is decrypted on the other end with the same key.

Both members of the communication assume that if the other side has access to this preselected key, then both are who they claim they are. This is accomplished in this way:

1. The sending computer can hash a piece of data (a challenge) using the shared key and forward this to the destination computer.

2. The destination computer will receive the challenge and perform a hash using the same secret key and send this back.

3. If the hashed results are identical, both computers share the same secret and are thus authenticated.

While preshared keys are effective in authenticating that each member has access to the same shared secret, this solution is not easily scalable. This is because the shared secret must be manually keyed into the IPSec policy. This is not an issue if the same policy applies to the entire domain tree, but it can become cumbersome when subdomains, organizational units, and individual machines require different IPSec policies.

Kerberos Authentication

The Kerberos authentication method is also based on the shared secret principle. In this case, the shared secret is a hash of the user's password. For details on the Kerberos Authentication proto-col, see Chapter 3, "Kerberos Server Authentication."

Public Key Certificate-Based Digital Signatures

A message digest is a hash of the contents of the message. The com-bination of a key and a hash algorithm is used to create the mes-sage digest. A digital signature is an encrypted message digest. A message is authenticated when the digest can first be decrypted, and then the decrypted hash must match the hash derived at the destination host.

The sending computer uses its private key to complete this process. Public key–based authentication is based on the principle that each computer has a public and private key pair created for it in advance. The public key is freely available to anyone who wants it; the private key is only available to the computer that owns it. In order for a public key infrastructure to work, the private key must be kept private. If a private key is compromised, all messages from that computer should be consider suspect and possibly originating from an imposter.

A viable public key infrastructure includes these elements:

- Secret private keys
- Freely available public keys
- A trusted third party to confirm the authenticity of the public key

The trusted third party is required to digitally sign each party's public key in order to prevent attackers from providing a public key that they claim is theirs, but is in fact not the public key of the per-son they are impersonating.

This central authority will digitally sign each user's public key. In this way, if I send you my public key, you can be sure that it is truly mine, since a trusted third party has already confirmed my identity and signed my public key. This third party is known as a certificate authority (CA).

Here are two scenarios that illustrate the need for digital certificates and digital signatures: In the first scenario, I want to authenticate you by using your public key. One way I can do this is by sending you a challenge message, which you encrypt with your private key. You then send it back to me after you have encrypted it. I then use your public key to decrypt the message. If the message that I decrypt is the same as the message that I sent to you, then I can confirm that indeed it was you that I was communicating with.

The problem is that I received your public key from you, yourself. How do I know that you, and not someone impersonating you, sent me your public key?

We solve this problem by having a mutually trusted third party digitally sign your public key. We both trust that this third party has verified the identity of anyone for whom the third party signs its public key.

You want to be sure that I am who I say I am. You do not have my public key at this point, so you ask me to send it to you. I will send you my signed certificate (the certificate is essentially my public key signed by the trusted third party). You already have the public key of the trusted third party. You use the third party's public key to verify the signature on my certificate. You know this verified key was my public key, which I sent to you. You can now send a challenge to confirm that you are indeed communicating with me.

Public key authentication is used when non-Kerberos-enabled clients need to be authenticated and no preshared key has been established. You must also use public key authentication when you use L2TP tunneling and IPSec.

Confidentiality

Neither integrity nor authentication is concerned with protecting the privacy of our information. Confidentiality is a matter of keeping your private information private. In order to ensure confidentiality, you must encrypt your information using an encryption algorithm.

Data Encryption Standard (DES)

The most commonly used encryption algorithm used with IPSec is the Data Encryption Standard (DES) algorithm. DES is the current U.S. government standard for encryption. The DES algorithm is an example of a symmetric encryption algorithm. A symmetric encryption algorithm has each side of the communication employ the same secret key for encryption and decryption. This is in contrast to a public key infrastructure, in which the two different keys are used. The public key approach is referred to as asymmetric encryption.

DES works on 64-bit blocks of data. The DES algorithm converts 64 input bits from the original data into 64 encrypted output bits. While DES starts with 64-bit keys, only 56 bits are actually used in the encryption process. The remaining 8 bits are used for parity.

A stronger version of DES is also available for use in Windows 2000 IPSec. This is called 3DES, or triple DES. Triple DES processes each block three times, which increases the degree of complexity over that found in DES.

Cipher Block Chaining (CBC)

Because the blocks of data are encrypted in 64-bit chunks, there must be a way to chain these blocks together. The chaining algorithm will define how the combination of the unencrypted text, the secret key, and the encrypted text (also known as ciphertext) will be combined to send to the destination host. These chaining algorithms also solve another problem.

Imagine someone is sniffing electronic transactions. The sniffed person is transferring a personal paycheck into an online account. This is a transaction the person performs every week. These transactions are always encrypted with DES. The sniffer would see the same ciphertext each week. However, what if the person got a raise or a new job? The sniffer would have information about a change in the person's current financial situation. This information can be integrated with other facts during an investigation.

In order to prevent each block from looking the same, DES can be combined with cipher block chaining (CBC). This DES-CBC algorithm will make each ciphertext message appear differently by using a different initialization vector (IV), which is a random block of encrypted data that begins each chain. In this fashion, you can make each message's ciphertext appear differently, even if you send the exact same message a hundred times.

IPSec Security Services

IPSec engages two protocols to implement security on an IP network:

- Authentication header (AH)
- Encapsulating security protocol (ESP)

Authentication Header (AH)

The authentication header ensures data integrity and authentication. The AH does not encrypt data, and therefore provides no confidentiality. When the AH protocol is applied in transport mode, the authentication header is inserted between the original IP header and the TCP header, as shown in Figure 7.1. The entire datagram is authenticated using AH.

Figure 7.1 The datagram as it appears after the authentication header is applied in transport mode.

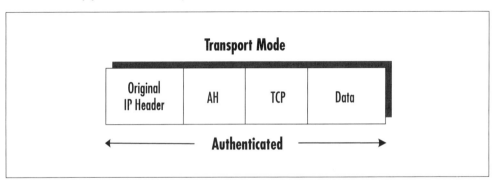

Encapsulating Security Payload (ESP)

The encapsulating security payload protocol can provide authentication, integrity, and confidentiality to an IP datagram. Authentication services are available with ESP, but the original IP header prior to application of the ESP header is not authenticated. The ESP header, in transport mode, is placed between the original header and the TCP header, as shown in Figure 7.2. Only the TCP header, data, and ESP trailer are encrypted. If authentication of the original IP header is required, you can combine and use AH and ESP together.

Figure 7.2 The datagram after the encapsulating security payload header is applied in transport mode.

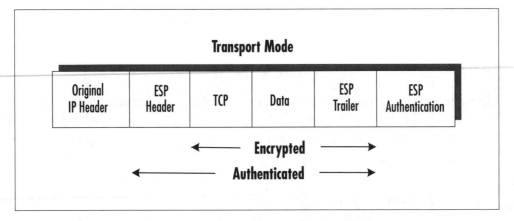

Figures 7.1 and 7.2 demonstrate packet configurations when AH or ESP is used in transport mode. Transport mode is used when point-to-point communications are taking place between source and destination computers. AH and ESP can be applied at a gateway machine connecting the LAN to a remote network. In this case, tunnel mode would be utilized.

In tunnel mode, an additional IP header is added that denotes the destination tunnel endpoint. This tunnel header encapsulates the original IP header, which contains the IP address of the destination computer. Figure 7.3 shows a packet constructed for tunnel mode.

Figure 7.3 A datagram with ESP header in tunnel mode.

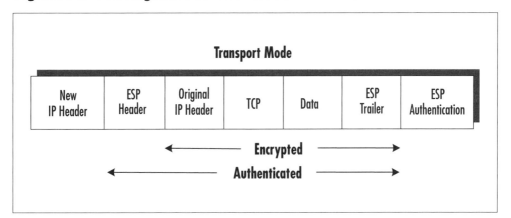

Security Associations and IPSec Key Management Procedures

When two computers establish a connection using IPSec, they must come to an agreement regarding which algorithms and protocols they will use. A single security association (SA) is established for each link a computer maintains with another computer via IPSec. If a file server has several simultaneous sessions with multiple clients, a number of different SAs will be defined, one for each connection via IPSec.

Each security association has associated with it these parameters:

- An encryption algorithm (DES or 3DES)
- A session key (via Internet Key Exchange or IKE)
- An authentication algorithm (SHA1 or MD5)

A Security Parameters Index (SPI) tracks each SA. The SPI uniquely identifies each SA as separate and distinct from any other IPSec connections current on a particular machine. The index itself is derived from the destination host's IP address and a randomly assigned number. When a computer communicates with another computer via IPSec, it checks its database for an applicable SA. It then applies the appropriate algorithms, protocols, and keys and inserts the SPI into the IPSec header.

An SA is established for outgoing and incoming messages, necessitating at least two security associations for each IPSec connection. In addition, a single SA can be applied to either AH or ESP, but not both. If both are used, then two more security associations are created. One SA for inbound and one SA for outbound communications will be created.

IPSec Key Management

Keys must be exchanged between computers in order to ensure authenticity, integrity, and confidentiality. Key management defines the determining procedure in how the keys are formed, the strength of the keys, how often they are changed, and when they expire. The establishment of a shared secret key is critical to secure communications. You can manually establish the shared secret using the prearranged key method, but this technique does not scale very well because of its inherent lack of flexibility.

Automated key management is the preferred method of key exchange. Automated key management uses a combination of the Internet Security Association Key Management Protocol and the Oakley Protocol (ISAKMP/Oakley). This combination of protocols is often referred to collectively as the Internet Key Exchange (IKE). The IKE is responsible for exchange of key material (groups of numbers that will form the basis of new key) session keys, SA negotiation, and authentication of peers participating in an IPSec interaction.

The Internet Key Exchange takes place across two phases: Phase 1, in which the two computers agree upon mechanisms to establish a secure, authenticated channel, and Phase 2, where Security Associations are negotiated for security protocols, either AH, ESP, or both.

The first phase establishes what is called the ISAKMP security association (ISAKMP SA), and the second phase establishes the IPSec SA.

Phase 1: Establishing the ISAKMP SA

This is what takes place during the ISAKMP SA:

- The computers establish a common encryption algorithm, either DES or 3DES.

- A common hash algorithm is agreed upon, either MD5 or SHA1.

- An authentication method is established. Depending on policy, this can be Kerberos, public key encryption, or prearranged shared secret.

- A Diffie-Hellman group is agreed upon in order to allow the Oakley protocol to manage the key exchange process. Diffie-Hellman provides a mechanism for two parties to agree on a shared master key, which is used immediately or can provide keying material for subsequent session key generation. Oakley will determine key refresh and regeneration parameters.

Phase 2: Establishing the IPSec SA

After a secure channel has been established by the creation of the ISAKMP SA, the IPSec SAs will be established. The process is similar, except that a separate IPSec SA is created for each protocol (AH or ESP) and for each direction (inbound and outbound). Each IPSec SA must establish its own encryption algorithm, hash algorithm, and authentication method.

One important difference is that each IPSec SA uses a different shared key than that negotiated during the ISAKMP SA. Depending on how policy is configured, the IPSec SA repeats the Diffie-Hellman exchange, or reuses key material derived from the original ISAKMP SA. All data transferred between the two computers will take place in the context of the IPSec SA.

Deploying Windows IP Security

In the implementation of IPSec in an organization, planning takes on special importance in the design of a security infrastructure.

After the planning phase comes the implementation phase. Windows 2000's graphical interface makes it easy to develop an IPSec policy for any organization. IPSec policy, filters, and filter actions and interoperability with downlevel clients and other operating systems are a vital part of implementation.

Evaluating Information

Identify your technology assets. You can break down your investment in IT resources by enumerating your software, hardware, intellectual (data), and human assets. What would it cost the organization if those assets were lost or destroyed? What expenditures in time and money would you incur if these assets were to fall in to the hands of unscrupulous individuals?

Developing a security plan starts with the awareness that security represents a balance. Total security means no one has access to

Table 7.1 Categorizing Corporate Assets

Type of asset	Examples
Software	Word processor, spreadsheet, database, operating systems, accounting, inventory, human resource, utilities, diagnostic programs, drivers, communication programs, enterprise integration systems
Hardware	Workstations, servers, RAM, hard disks, monitors, network interface cards, hubs, switches, bridges, routers, SANs, tape devices, modems, ISDN terminal adapters
Intellectual property (data)	Customer databases, human resource databases, payroll records, research and development databases and files, project development files, sales information, marketing information, backup tapes, offline storage facilities, floppy disks, removable hard disks, audit logs, information crossing the wire, documentation and help databases
Human	Executives, administrators, developers, marketing, sales, clerical, help desk, hardware technicians

anything. All assets would be protected at the cost of no one being able to use them. On the other end is total openness; no security controls are placed on assets or resources. No one will have difficulty obtaining the information or resources they need. The cost is that your assets have essentially become public domain.

In order to implement an effective security policy, you must balance accessibility with security. The more secure the resource, the more difficult it will be to access, even for those who are allowed access. Keep this in the forefront when you develop a security plan.

Use Table 7.1 to categorize your assets.

Evaluating the "Enemy"

The "enemies" of your security plan are all those who access a resource to which they have no explicit right. Most administrators envision the black-hat hacker as the foremost enemy of their information store. This is not entirely true. More likely dangers are:

- The power user who is interested in what can be done over the network

- The casual user who stumbles upon information that was not secured properly

- The authorized user who accesses a document or file that has poorly designed access control, leading to a misinformation situation that can create havoc in the organization

- The disgruntled employee seeking revenge on a former employer

- The greed-driven individual who sells legitimate access controls to others for a profit

- The competition that hires agents to carry out corporate espionage in order to access proprietary secrets

A common thread is that most risk emanates from within the organization. While it is important to shore up portals to the

Internet and other external networks, the security analyst's major concerns is often breaches from within.

It is easy for someone within the organization to plug a notebook computer into an available port at a hub or switch and run sniffing software. These insiders listening on the wire are those you must be most concerned about.

Determining Required Security Levels

A mainstay approach to assessing security levels is to consider what the cost would be if resources are lost, altered, or stolen. Consider how important the various resources are to the organization in the short, intermediate, and long term. How much time and money will it cost to return to normal operations?

Security level assessment can be accomplished by assigning an impact level to each item in your list of secure objects. Objects that do not appear to be the focus of security concerns should not be considered to have no impact on your security plan, because unsecured objects can create a backdoor access route to secured objects.

Rate your assets as high, medium or low in terms of their impact on the organization should they be compromised. Table 7.2 provides some examples of how you would categorize security requirements for different types of information.

Table 7.2 Categorizing Impact Level for Different Data Types

Type of information	Impact level
Corporate accounting data	High
Research data	High
Proprietary or patented information	High
Marketing information	Medium
Human resource information	Medium
Prospects database	Low
Parking permit database	Low

The security level assessment is not the sole province of the security analyst. You will need to meet with all department managers to assess their views and level of understanding of security issues. Polling nonmanagerial employees is important in making the security assessment, since they are often the first ones to be encumbered when they try to access needed information that has been secured.

Building Security Policies with Customized IPSec Consoles

IPSec configuration and deployment is intimately intertwined with Active Directory and group policy. You must create a policy in order to deploy IPSec in your organization. A policy can be applied to a forest, a tree, a domain, an organizational unit, or a single computer.

It is within the group policy that we can choose from built-in policies or create custom policies to meet our specialized needs. We configure these policies by creating an MMC and then using the appropriate MMC plug-in.

It is possible to configure a custom IPSec console that is used to configure IPSec policy and monitor significant IPSec-related events.

Building an IPSec MMC

1. Create a new console by starting the Run command and typing "mmc." Click OK to open an empty console.

2. Click the Console menu, and then click Add/Remove Snap-in. Click Add, select Computer Management, and click Add. A dialog box will appear that will want to know which computer the snap-in will manage. Select Local Computer (the computer this console is running on). Then click Finish.

3. Scroll through the list of available snap-ins and select Group Policy and click Add. At this point a wizard will appear that will query you on what group policy object you want to manage. In this case, confirm that it says Local Computer in the text box and click Finish. If you want to

define a policy for another group policy object, click Browser and select from the list.

4. Scroll through the list of group policy objects again, this time looking for Certificates. Select Certificates and click Add. A dialog box will appear asking you what you want the snap-in to always manage certificates for (see Figure 7.4). Select Computer Account, click Next, and then select Local Computer for the computer that you want the snap-in to manage. Then click Finish.

Figure 7.4 The way to confirm a certificate management plug-in for the local computer.

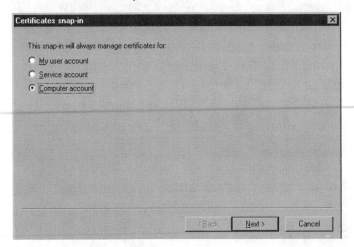

5. Click Close on the Add Standalone Snap-in dialog box and then click OK in the Add/Remove Snap-in dialog box. Expand the first level of each of the snap-ins (see Figure 7.5).

It will be from this custom IPSec Management Console that you will configure and monitor IPSec policies. In this example, IPSec policy is managed for this single machine. This might be appropriate if you were configuring IPSec policy for a file or application server. If you wanted to manage policy for an entire domain or organizational unit, you would select the appropriate policy when selecting the Group Policy snap-in configuration.

Figure 7.5 The Custom IPSec Security Management Console.

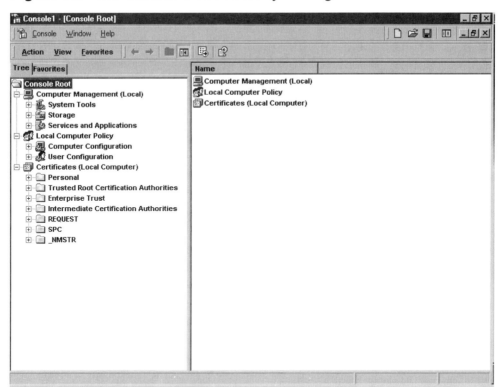

Flexible Security Policies

Now that we have our console, we can get to the business of building IPSec security policy. Because IPSec policies are implemented via group policy, there is a great deal of flexibility in the places where they are implemented. You can choose from three built-in IPSec policies, or create your own custom policies..

To begin, you need to find where the IP security policies are located. Expand the Local Computer policy; expand the Computer Configuration object; expand the Windows Settings object; then click IP Security Policies on Local Machine. In the right pane you will see listed the three built-in IPSec Policies: Client (Respond Only), Secure

Server (Require Security), and Server (Request Security). Your screen should look like that seen in Figure 7.6.

Figure 7.6 The IPSec Security Console demonstrates the three built-in IPSec policies.

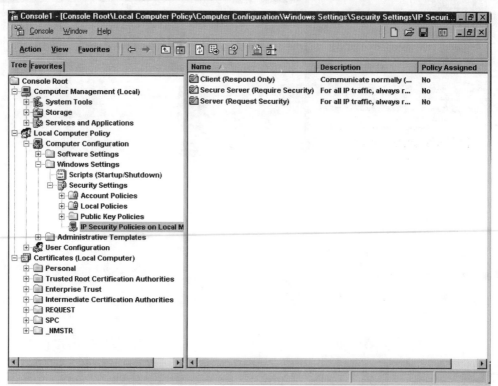

The Client (Respond Only) policy is used when you require secure IPSec connections when another computer requests them. For example, you are using a machine as a workstation that wants to connect to a file server that requires IPSec security. The workstation with the built-in Client policy enabled will negotiate an IPSec security association. However, never does this client require IPSec security; it will only use IPSec to secure communications when requested to do so by another computer.

The Server (Request Security) policy is used when you want to request IPSec security for all connections. This might be used for a file server that must serve both IPSec aware (Windows 2000) clients and non-IPSec-aware clients (such as Windows 9.x and NT). If a connection is established with an IPSec-aware computer, the session will be secure. Unsecured sessions will be established with non-IPSec-aware computers. This allows greater flexibility during the transition from mixed Windows networks to Native Windows 2000 networks.

The Secure Server (Require Security) policy is used when all communications with a particular server need to be secured. Examples include file servers with high impact information and security

For IT Professionals

IPSec Security and Network Services

Implementing IPSec security will afford you a large measure of comfort in knowing that traffic as it traverses the wire is safe from interception and manipulation. However, IPSec can have some significant influences on network service interoperability.

Network servers that run the DHCP, WINS, or DNS services are a point of concern. This is particularly problematic when you run the Secure Server policy on a machine providing one of these services. Should you need to do so, be aware that negotiation will fail on non-IPSec-enabled computers. The result of the failed negotiation is that those clients will not be able to use that network service.

A special case is when you use DNS names in the IP filter list, and the DNS server you are using is not IPSec aware. The unaware DNS server will not be able to successfully negotiate secure communication, and therefore name resolution attempts will fail, with cascading results. In order to solve this problem, create a new filter list and rule to exempt traffic from the DNS from IPSec negotiation.

When you set the rule, use the Permit option to allow traffic to flow unimpeded. The filter should be for computer-to-computer IP addresses (not network IDs), and for the Port number.

gateways at either end of an L2TP/IPSec tunnel. The server with the Secure Server policy will always request a secure channel. Connections will be denied to computers not able to respond to the request.

Security policies are bi-directional. If our Secure Server attempts to connect to non-IPSec-aware network servers such as DNS, WINS, or DHCP servers, the connection will fail. It is imperative that you test all scenarios in a lab that simulates your live network before you implement IPSec policies on your live network. During the testing phase you must assiduously check the event logs to ascertain what services fail because of IPSec policies.

Rules

An IPSec policy has three main components: IP security rules, IP filter lists, and IP filter actions. Double-click the Server Policy to see the Server (Request Security) Properties sheet, as shown in Figure 7.7.

Figure 7.7 The Server (Request Security) Properties sheet.

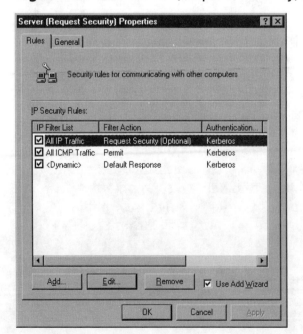

Rules are applied to computers that match criteria specified in a filter list. An IP filter list contains source and destination IP addresses. These can be individual host IP addresses or network IDs. When a communication is identified as a participant included in an IP filter list, a particular filter action will be applied that is specific for that connection.

The All IP Traffic filter list includes all computers that communicate with the server via TCP/IP. Any instructions in the filter action associated with All IP Traffic will be applied.

First, double-click All IP Traffic filter list. This opens up the Edit Rule Properties dialog box for the All IP Traffic filter. You should see a tabbed dialog box consisting of five tabs, as shown in Figure 7.8.

The option button for the IP filter list is selected and a description is included which explains the purpose of the list. Double-click All IP Traffic filter list to see the details of the All IP traffic filter. The

Figure 7.8 The All IP Traffic Edit Rule Properties dialog box.

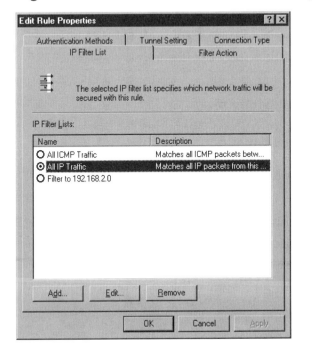

Figure 7.9 The IP Filter List Details dialog box.

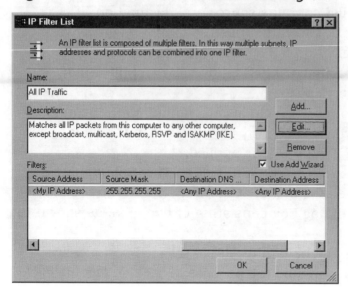

Name, Description, and the details of the filter are displayed in the details (see Figure 7.9).

If you want to see more details regarding the Addressing, Protocol, and Description of the filter, you can click Edit. Click Cancel twice to return to the Edit Rules Properties dialog box.

Filter Actions

Filter Actions define the type of security and the methods by which security is established. The primary methods are: Permit, Block, and Negotiate security. The Permit option blocks negotiation for IP security. This is appropriate if you never want to secure traffic to which this rule applies. The Block action blocks all traffic from computers specified in the IP filter list. The Negotiate security action allows the computer to use a list of security methods to determine security levels for the communication. The list is in descending order of preference. If the Negotiate security action is selected, both computers must be able to come to an agreement

Figure 7.10 The Request Security (Optional) Properties dialog box.

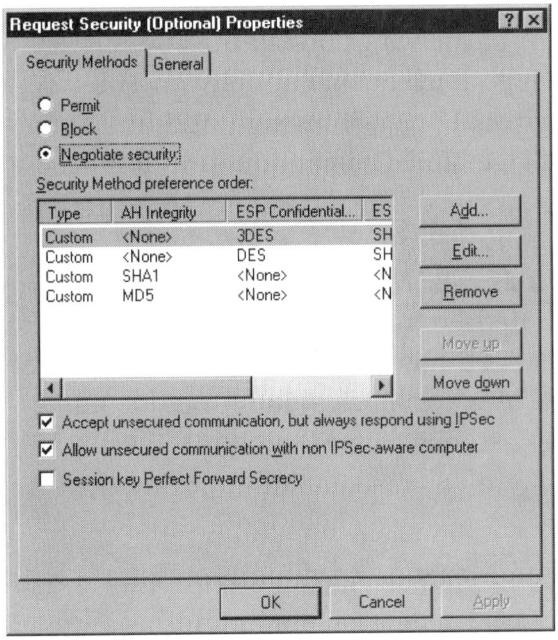

regarding the security parameters included in the list. The entries are processed sequentially in order of preference. The first common security method is enacted.

Click the Filter Action tab, and click Request Security (Optional) to view these options, as shown in Figure 7.10.

Note the check boxes on the bottom of the dialog box. "Accept unsecured communication, but always respond using IPSec" allows unsecured communication initiated by another computer, but requires the computers to which this policy applies to always use secure communication when replying or initiating. This is essentially the definition of the Secure policy. The Allow unsecured communication with non IPSec-aware computer option allows unsecured communications to or from another computer. This is appropriate if the computers listed in the IP filter lists are not IPSec-enabled. However, if negotiations for security fail, this will disable IPSec for all communications to which this rule applies.

Perhaps the most important of these options is the session key Perfect Forward Secrecy. When you select this option you ensure that session keys or keying material are not reused, and new Diffie-Hellman exchanges will take place after the session key lifetimes have expired.

Click cancel to return to the Edit Rule Properties dialog box. Click the Authentication Methods tab. Here you can select your preferred authentication method. Kerberos is the default authentication method. You can include other methods in the list, and each will be processed in descending order. You can click Add to include additional authentication methods, as shown in Figure 7.11.

Figure 7.11 The Authentication Methods configuration tab.

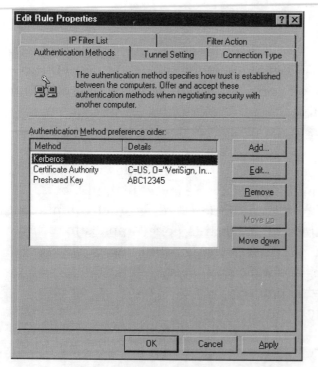

Click the Tunnel Setting tab if the endpoint for the filter is a tunnel endpoint. Click the Connection Type tab to apply the rule to All network connections, Local area network (LAN), or Remote access, as shown in Figure 7.12.

Figure 7.12 The Connection Type setting dialog box.

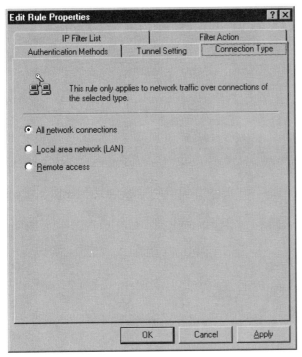

You cannot delete the built-in policies, but you can edit them. However, it is recommended that you leave the built-in policies as they are, and create new policies for custom requirements.

Flexible Negotiation Policies

Security method negotiation is required to establish an IPSec connection. You can use the default security policies, or you can create your own custom policies. You can do so by using a wizard-based approach. To add a new filter action, which will be used to create a new security policy, click Add after selecting the Filter Action tab. When the wizard has completed, you can edit the security negotiation method.

When you double-click on the Request Security (Optional) filter action, you will see the Request Security (Optional) Properties dialog box. If you select the Negotiate security option, and then click Add, you can add a new security method, as shown in Figure 7.13.

Figure 7.13 The New Security Method dialog box for security negotiation.

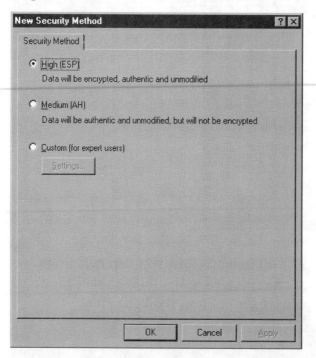

You may fine-tune your security negotiation method by selecting the Custom option, and then clicking Settings. After doing so, you will see the Custom Security Method Settings dialog box, as shown in Figure 7.14.

Figure 7.14 The Custom Security Method Settings dialog box.

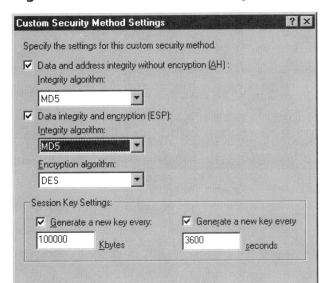

Here you can configure whether you want to use AH, ESP, or both. For each option, you can select either the integrity algorithm, encryption algorithm, or both. All algorithms supported in Windows 2000 are included. Session key lifetimes can be customized by entering new key generation intervals by amount of data transferred or time span.

Filters

Rules are applied to source and destination computers or networks, based on their IP addresses. To create a new filter, you can avail yourself of the New Filter Wizard. To do this, return to the Edit Rule Properties dialog box, click on the IP Filter List tab, and then click Add. This brings up the IP Filter List dialog box, where you enter in the Name of the new filter and a description of the filter. Click Add to start the wizard.

When the wizard starts, you see the Welcome dialog box. Click the Next button. As shown in Figure 7.15, you choose the source address of the wizard. Your options appear after you click the down arrow on the list box. Note that you can identify the source by individual IP address, all IP addresses, DNS name, or subnet. Click Next to continue.

Figure 7.15 The way to specify a source IP address for a new filter.

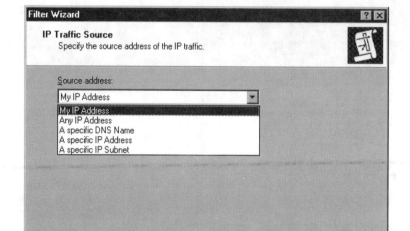

The next dialog box asks for the destination IP address. You are afforded the same options as when you designated the source. Click Next to continue through the wizard. At this point, you can select which protocols will be included in the filter. All protocols are included by default, but you can select from a list of protocols or define your own by selecting Other and entering a protocol number. The IP protocol selection dialog box is shown in Figure 7.16.

Click Next, and then click Finish. Your new filter will appear in the IP filter lists included in the IP Filter List tab of the Edit Rule Properties dialog box.

Figure 7.16 Select the protocol included in the new filter.

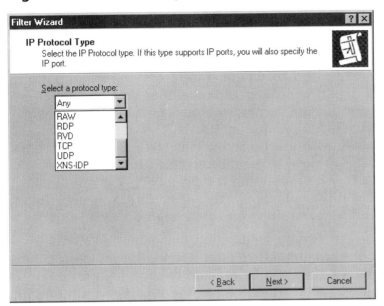

Creating a Security Policy

You are the administrator of the network for a large hospital. The network is subdivided into multiple subnets. The medical records department contains a large amount of data that must be kept secure. The hospital would suffer a large amount of liability if security were breached. Computers within the medical records department are closely monitored, and therefore the overhead of confidentiality is not required, but authentication and integrity should be applied to intradepartmental communications.

The medical records department must regularly send information to the hospital floor. The network infrastructure is more open to attack between the well-guarded medical records department and the less secure, open hospital environment. All computers within the medical records department are located in network ID 192.168.1.0, and all floor computers that access medical records database information are located on network ID 192.168.2.0. The default Class C subnet mask is used.

In order to implement your new security policy, you need to:

1. Create a security policy for the hospital's domain. In this way, all computers in the domain will inherit the IPSec policy.

2. Computers in the medical records department need to communicate with two sets of computers: machines within their own department, and the machines on the hospital floor. Characterizing these machines by subnet, you could say that machines on subnet 192.168.2.0 need to communicate with machines on 192.168.1.0, and machines on 192.168.1.0 need to communicate with machines on 192.168.2.0. When selecting the protocols, you would select All so that all IP traffic is filtered. Therefore, you need to create two filters, so that you can assign different filter actions to each filter.

3. Now you need to create two filter actions (negotiation policy); the first filter action will be applied to intradepartmental communications, in which just authentication and integrity are important, and the second filter action will be applied to extradepartmental communication, where authenticity, integrity, and confidentiality are required. The first filter action might use AH, which provides for authenticity and integrity. The second filter action might use a combination of AH and ESP, to provide the highest level of authentication and integrity, while also providing confidentiality.

By implementing these combinations of filters and filter rules, you can effectively secure traffic in a customized fashion. You can easily implement this solution by invoking the Security Rule Wizard after you create the new security policy.

Making the Rule

The rule will create a filter for all communications emanating from 192.168.1.0 that are directed to 192.168.2.0. After the filter is created, you will create a filter action. In this case, you need to ensure secure communications, because you are communicating with the unsecured hospital floor. You need to ensure integrity, authentication, and confidentiality.

1. Click Start | Programs | Administrative Tools | Active Directory Users and Computers. After the Active Directory Users and Computers console is open, right-click on a domain name, then click Properties. In the Domain Properties dialog box, click on the Group Policy tab.

2. Select Default Domain Policy and click Edit.

3. This opens up the Group Policy Editor. Expand Computer Configuration, expand Windows Settings, expand Security Settings, and then right-click on IP Security Policies on Active Directory. Click Create IP Security Policy.

4. A wizard starts up, welcoming you. Click Next.

5. You now need to enter the name of the Policy. Name it "MedRecToFloor," then click Next. Remove the check mark in the Activate the default response rule check box. Click Next.

6. Now you are at the end of the wizard. Leave the check in the Edit Properties box, and click Finish. Figure 7.17 shows the results of The Wizard

Figure 7.17 The properties of the MedRecToFloor IPSec policy.

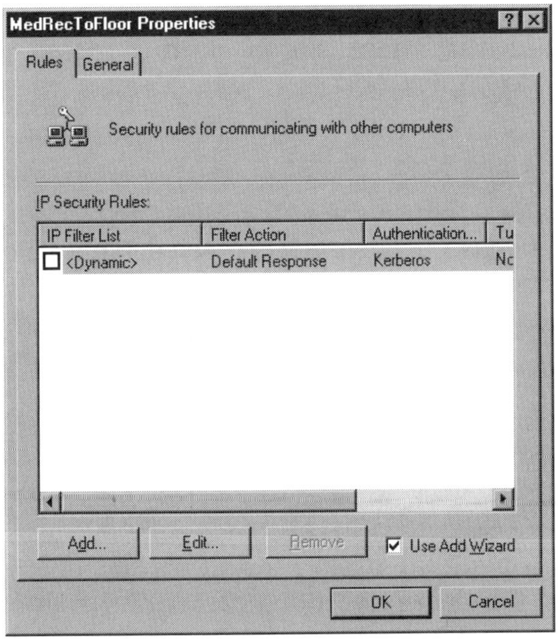

Figure 7.18 Select the Authentication Protocol.

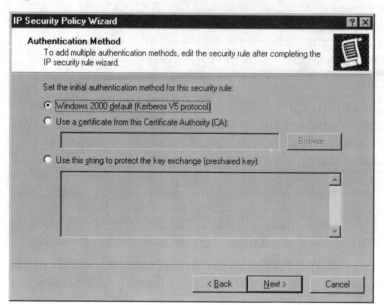

7. At this point, you have no IP filter lists. Use the Add Wizard to create a new filter list and filter action. Together they create a filter rule. Make sure there is a check in the Use Add Wizard check box and click Add.

8. This takes you to the Security Rule Wizard. The first dialog box is a welcome box. Click Next.

9. The next dialog box asks whether the rule applies to a tunnel endpoint. In this case, it does not, so select This rule does not specify a tunnel. Click Next.

10. The wizard now asks what network connections this rule should apply to. Select All network connections, then click Next.

11. Now decide which default authentication protocol should be used. Select Windows 2000 default (Kerberos V5 protocol), as shown in Figure 7.18. Then click Next.

12. Create the IP filter list by adding a filter for all traffic sent from 192.168.1.0 with the destination of 192.168.2.0. Click Add, as shown in Figure 7.19.

Figure 7.19 Add a new filter list.

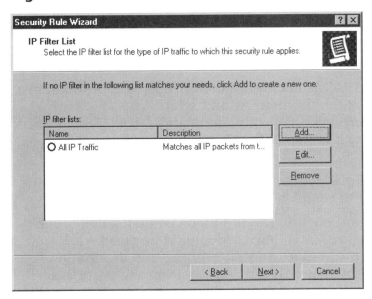

13. You now see the IP Filter List dialog box. Type "Secure from MedRec to Floor," and make sure the Use Add Wizard check box is filled, as shown in Figure 7.20. Now click Add.

Figure 7.20 The IP filter list.

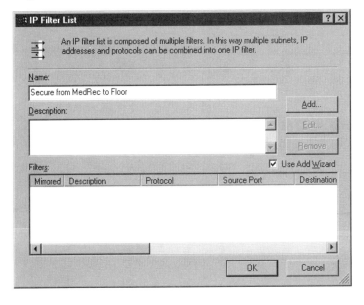

14. The IP Filter Wizard (yes, another wizard!) appears. Click Next to move past the Welcome dialog box. Now you are at the IP Traffic Source dialog box. Click the down arrow under Source address and select A specific IP Subnet. Type 192.168.1.0 and a subnet mask of 255.255.255.0. Then click Next.

15. Now enter the IP traffic destination. Under the Destination address click the down arrow and select A specific IP Subnet. Then type the destination subnet 192.168.2.0 with a subnet mask of 255.255.255.0. Click Next.

16. You want all the protocols to be included in the filter, so select Any for the protocol type and click Next, and then click Finish to complete the wizard.

17. This takes you back to the IP Filter List dialog box. Click Edit (see Figure 7.21). Mirrored should be checked. Match packets with the exact opposite source and destination addresses, to ensure that machines from the destination subnet are also included in the incoming filter. Click OK to

Figure 7.21 The Filter Properties dialog box.

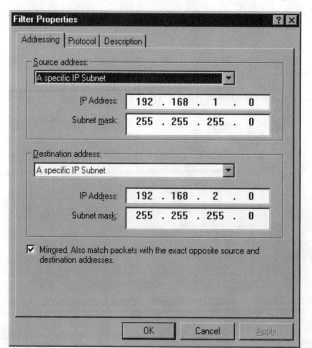

close the dialog box, and then click Close. You are now back to the IP Filter List dialog box in the Security Rule Wizard. Select the Secure from MedRec to Floor filter list and then click Next.

18.   At this point, configure a filter action. Select the Require Security option. Make sure there is a check mark in the Use Add Wizard check box, and then click Add, as shown in Figure 7.22.

Figure 7.22 The Filter Action dialog box of the Security Rule Wizard.

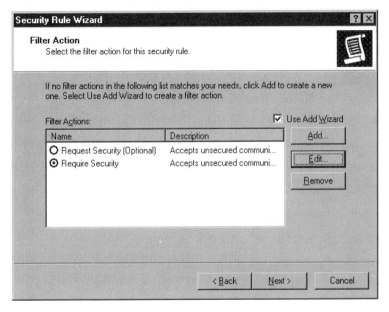

19.   The IP Security Filter Action Wizard starts. Click Next to move past the Welcome dialog box. Here you are asked for a name; enter SecureMedRec, and click Next.

20.   The Filter Action General Options dialog box asks for a filter action behavior. Select Negotiate security and click Next.

21.   This dialog box asks whether you want to support communications with computers that do not support IPSec. Select the Do not communicate with computers that do not support IPSec option, as shown in Figure 7.23. Click Next.

Figure 7.23 Prevent communication with non-IPSec computers.

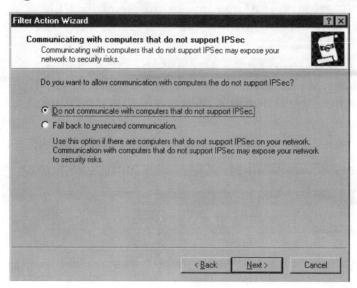

22. Now select the security method for IP traffic. To ensure confidentiality, authentication, and integrity, select Custom and then click Settings (see Figure 7.24). Select the Data and address integrity with encryption check box and then click the down arrow and select SHA1. Make sure there is a

Figure 7.24 The Custom Security Method Settings.

check mark in the Data integrity and encryption (ESP) check box, and select MD5 and DES. Do not set the session key settings; you will select Perfect Forward Secrecy later. Click OK, then click Next. The final dialog box appears. Ensure that a check is in the Edit box and then click Finish.

23. You are brought to the New Filter Action Properties dialog box. Check Session key Perfect Forward Secrecy, as shown in Figure 7.25. Click OK to return to the Security Rule Wizard, then click Next.

Figure 7.25 The way to enable Perfect Forward Secrecy.

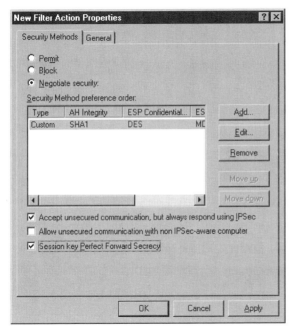

24. This is the last dialog box for the Security Rule Wizard. Click Finish. Click OK to close the New Rule Properties dialog box. You are returned to the MedRecToFloor properties box. Click the General tab (see Figure 7.26). You can configure how often the Policy Agent checks for policy changes here. Click Advanced to control the Internet Key Exchange Process.

25. Here you control the security of the Internet Key Exchange process, as shown in Figure 7.27. Click Methods to

Figure 7.26 The General tab for the IPSec Policy properties box.

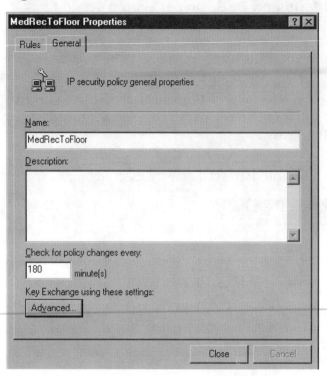

Figure 7.27 The Key Exchange Setting dialog box.

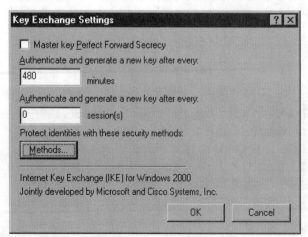

Figure 7.28 The Key Exchange Methods dialog box.

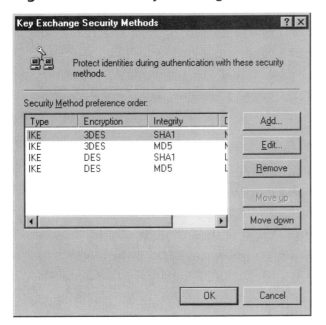

configure the security methods that are used to protect identities during the Key Exchange process, as shown in Figure 7.28.

26. Click OK, click OK, and then click Close. Your new security policy appears in the console.

As you can see, what looks easy on paper can be somewhat daunting when you actually apply the principles! With the rule you created, all traffic leaving 192.168.1.0 to 192.168.2.0 will be secured according to the filter rule you set up. Because it is mirrored, the same rule applies in the other direction.

Compatibility Notes

In order to fully engage the capabilities of the IPSec security architecture, your entire enterprise must use IPSec-aware devices. The only Microsoft Operating System that is IPSec aware at this point in time is Windows 2000. All communications to or from any other version of Windows cannot be secured via IPSec. Microsoft source materials indicate possible client functionality for Windows 9.x computers in the future, but there is no strong indication of commitment. Research is ongoing regarding Windows CE and IPSec compatibility.

Summary

Windows 2000 provides the administrator with a new tool to defend against security violations. IPSec allows the administrator to secure information as it crosses the network. IPSec secures data at the Network Layer and carries out its activity transparently in the background. Users and applications do not need to be aware of IPSec. IPSec's implementation at the network layer gives it an advantage over security protocols, such as SSL, that applications must be specifically written for to support.

Hallmarks of secure communications ensure authentication, integrity, and confidentiality. Authentication assures the receiver that a message was indeed sent by the individual who claimed to have sent it. Data integrity ensures that content of messages have not been altered during transit. Confidentiality ensures that others cannot read data during transit. Combining all three provides solid end-to-end security between any two communicating hosts.

To meet the goals of authentication, integrity, and confidentiality, algorithms are used to represent the original data in a different fashion. Authentication methods available include Kerberos, public key certificates, and preshared keys. Integrity algorithms used by Windows 2000 IPSec include MD5 and SHA1. Confidentiality is ensured by scrambling messages using either DES or 3DES (triple DES).

Algorithms must work with keys in order to carry out their functions. Computers must have access to the same shared secret key when they perform forward and reverse operations using these algorithms. IPSec implements Internet Key Exchange, which is a combination of ISAKMP and the Oakley protocols. Key management techniques ensure that intruders cannot compromise security by accessing a single key.

IPSec utilizes two protocols that add their own headers to IP datagrams. The authentication header (AH) provides for authentication and integrity, but not confidentiality. The encapsulating security payload (ESP) provides for authentication, integrity, and confidentiality. The two protocols can be combined to provide for a higher degree of security.

Each IPSec connection a computer establishes has its own Security Association (SA). There are two types of SAs: the ISAKMP SA and the IPSec SA. The ISAKMP SA provides a secure channel for the exchange of keying information to provide for a master key, and the IPSec SA defines parameters for each secure IPSec channel between computers. A separate IPSec SA is created for both inbound and outbound connections. Each IPSec SA is individualized by assigning it a Security Parameters Index (SPI).

Planning security requirements involves taking an inventory of your hardware, software, intellectual (data), and human resources. After the inventory, you should assess the cost to the organization if any of these assets are lost or compromised. Assign each asset an impact value, and focus security concerns on the basis of the value you assign. Your enemy is most likely to be inside your organization.

Network security enabled by IPSec is policy-driven. Policies are integrated into Active Directory on domain machines, or they can be implemented as local machine policies. Each IPSec-aware computer uses a policy agent, which checks for IPSec policy during startup, and periodically afterward.

IPSec policies are implemented as a series of rules. These rules include IPSec filter lists and IPSec filter actions. If a computer seeks to establish a session with a computer whose IP addressing information matches a number in one of the filter lists, then a filter action affiliated with that list will be triggered. The creations of IPSec policies, filter lists, and filter rules can be easily accomplished via wizard-driven interfaces. You can create your own policies, or use one of the three built-in policies. The built-in policies are the Client, Server, and Secure Server IPSec policies.

It is vital to take compatibility issues into account when you enable IPSec in your organization. The only Microsoft operating system that is IPSec aware is Windows 2000. Connection failures will result if a computer configured with the Secure Server policy interacts with non-IPSec-aware machines.

FAQs

Q: What happens if a computer attempts to connect to a computer with the Secure Server IPSec policy and it fails to authenticate?

A: The server will not accept connections from that host for at least one minute, and as long as five minutes. This is something to be aware of when you troubleshoot connectivity problems with IPSec-enabled machines.

Q: Can I use Kerberos authentication for my users who are using an L2TP/IPSec tunnel to dial in to intranet servers?

A: No. VPN connections must use certificate-based public key authentication.

Q: Our internal network uses NAT (Network Address Translation) rather than public IP addresses. Can I use L2TP/IPSec tunnels to allow remote access VPN clients to access my internal resources?

A: No. Because of incompatibilities between NAT and IPSec, you cannot use both at the same time. L2TP over IPSec traffic is not translatable by a NAT because the UDP port number is encrypted.

Q: What is Perfect Forward Secrecy?

A: Perfect Forward Secrecy ensures that a key used to protect a transmission, in whichever phase, cannot be used to generate any additional keys. If the key used was derived from specific keying material, that material cannot be used to generate any other keys. This provides a high level of protection. If an intruder is able to access data and obtain a key, that key will not be valid on other packets, making the cracking process very difficult.

Q: I am using a firewall to protect my intranet from Internet traffic; are there any special considerations I need to be aware of when I implement IPSec in this environment?

A: Yes. You will need to open up inbound and outbound IP ports 50 and 51 to support AH and ESP traffic. You will also need to open UDP port 500 for the Internet Key Exchange (IKE) to take place.

Q: Is there a tool that I can use to monitor IP traffic for troubleshooting purposes?

A: Yes. From the Run command, type "ipsecmon" and click OK. You will be offered a graphical interface to monitor IPSec traffic.

Chapter 8

Smart Cards

Solutions in this chapter:

- **Introduction**
- **Interoperability**
- **Smart Card Base Components**
- **Enhanced Solutions**

Introduction

With the modern world being computerized more and more every day, such things as face-to-face conversations and paper mail are becoming a thing of the past. Why walk to the other end of the building to ask a question when you can send an instant message or e-mail? Why pay a long-distance fee to talk around the world when you can use the Internet or even the company's local Intranet? With each new emerging technology, our lives are made easier as we put greater trust in computers.

Unfortunately, a problem has arisen in many organizational environments that is different from problems encountered in the home. The problem is security. Would you send a piece of mail with no envelope? Would you conduct financial transactions on a post-card? Of course not. So why would you send an insecure piece of electronic mail? When an electronic message (which could be e-mail or any other application's data that flows over a network) is sent unsecured, it is available for the entire world to see. As part of the effort to solve these problems, many products and technologies have been developed that enhance the security of messages by digitally signing and encrypting them. One of the most popular of these tech-nologies is public/private key technology, which requires that each user has a private key that only that user possesses and for which only that user knows the password. A smart card offers a secure place to physically store and access that key.

Realized advantages of smart cards include electronic entry to restricted areas, secure logons, user authentication, secure e-mail, and, in the future, even consolidation of personal information, bank accounts, medical history, and more on a single portable interface. Before storing your most personal information on a little plastic card, you should know more about the reliability and confidentiality of a smart card. One of the goals of the smart card is to protect your information from misuse by third parties. To make this possible, the data is stored on a card that is always in your possession—not stored on your home computer, your office computer, or some computer located on a network. By being in your pocket, it is already more secure than it ordinarily would be. Now consider the process of using your card. The reason you have data on the card, after all, is so that you can use it somehow. Usually, when you interact with data, it is manipulated on the host PC. This may be fine for some applications, but would you really want your bank information, medical records, private keys, and other secret information to reside on an insecure machine for even a second? I wouldn't. The smart card allows you to store and process information on the card without ever placing it in danger of being compromised. And what happens if you lose your card? As long as you didn't write your secret PIN on it, you'll be fine. No one can access that card without a valid PIN. Some cards even support a "three strikes and you're out" protection scheme. If too many bad PIN numbers are entered, the card becomes disabled. And since a security certificate usually identifies the card, canceling your card is as easy as revoking your certificates. Still worried? Recent advancements in technology have brought us even closer to biometrics security, an example of which would be an integrated scanner that reads your thumbprint instead of making you enter a PIN. With biometrics security you can be assured that no one but you will be able to access your data.

Smart card technology has roots dating back to 1974, when Roland Moreno was issued the first patents for his "chip cards." At the time, the cards were highly advanced and expensive and therefore were not taken seriously by the general public for the first few years. By 1978, chip miniaturization made mass production possible, and it has led to the current popularity of smart cards. France, which seems to have realized the most benefit from this technology, continues to deploy more and more every year. Since 1985, over 600 million smart cards have been produced in France, with 110 million of those in 1994 alone. The technology has been around for quite a few years, but its main problem in reaching widespread use has concerned compatibility issues. Because the cards, readers, and software have been mostly proprietary until recently, companies have been reluctant to deploy systems for fear of being at the mercy of a single vendor.

Interoperability

A common plague in new computer technologies has been the absence of standards and common models of operation. The International Standards Organization sought to solve this problem with smart cards. Companies such as Europay, Visa, MasterCard, the European telecommunications industry, and major international software and hardware companies later built on their solution.

ISO 7816, EMV, and GSM

In order to promote the smart card movement, the Industry Standards Organization (ISO) took steps to ensure future interoperability among smart cards and readers by establishing the ISO 7816 standard. This standard contains detailed specifications for the operations of the devices on a physical, electrical, and data-link level. In 1996, Europay, MasterCard, and Visa (EMV) defined a standard based on the ISO 7816 recommendations that incorporated new data types and encoding rules developed specifically for the financial industry. The Global System for Mobile communications (GSM) was developed by the European telecommunications industry, also based on the ISO 7816 specifications. This system allows mobile phone users to be identified and authenticated by using a smart card in conjunction with a cellular phone.

While the ISO 7816, EMV and GSM specifications were definitely a vast improvement over the previously nonstandard proprietary device models, there were still no industry standards for interfacing the readers and cards with computer programs. Because of this, there was little interindustry support for the cards until the PC/SC Workgroup was established.

PC/SC Workgroup

In May 1996, major PC and smart card companies formed the Personal Computer/Smart Card Workgroup. Participants included Microsoft, Hewlett-Packard, Groupe Bull, Schlumburger, and

Siemens Nixdorf. The group's sole purpose has been to resolve the remaining software-hardware interoperability problems that existed with ISO 7816. In December 1997, the group released its version 1.0 of the specifications.

NOTE

As of this writing, the PC/SC Version 1.0 specifications can be found at http://www.pcscworkgroup.com. All specifications regarding smart cards created by the PC/SC Workgroup are for the ICC Smart Cards.

The Microsoft Approach

This is Microsoft's approach:

- A standard model enabling smart card readers and smart cards to communicate with PCs
- Application Programming Interfaces (APIs) that are device-independent and are used for enabling smart-card-aware applications
- Use of familiar tools for the development of software
- Integration with Microsoft platforms.

A Standard Model for Interfacing Smart Card Readers and Cards with PCs

A standard model is a set of specifications that allows software to communicate with any compliant hardware device using a common language. A hardware manufacturer has only to develop drivers that allow the device's language to be translated into the PC's language. This process is used by many different devices with many software components in Windows. Figure 8.1 shows how the model works logically: First, the application makes a request to the operating system (that is, "Have the modem dial 555-1234"). Next, the operating

Figure 8.1 A logical look at how an application communicates with a hardware device.

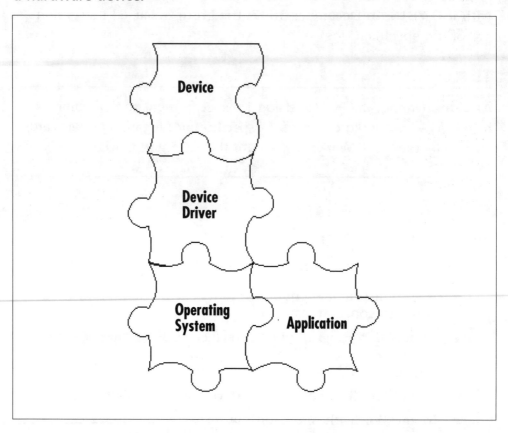

system makes a call to the device driver. Lastly, the device driver performs a translation and passes the call to the device for completion. This model makes it easy to see that adherence will permit almost unlimited flexibility in device design while still allowing for complete interoperability.

Device-Independent APIs for Enabling Smart-Card-Aware Applications

The Smart Card SDK is now included with the Microsoft Platform Software Development Kit (SDK). This now provides Windows programmers an easy solution for supporting these devices. Since there is now a common model, a developer can create smart card solutions as easy as any other common device found on a PC. The Platform SDK can be obtained from Microsoft's MSDN site at http://www.microsoft.com/msdn/sdk. For an application developer, three choices exist for accessing the services supported by the smart card: CryptoAPI, Win32 API, and SCard COM. The three access mechanisms vary in ease of use and capabilities.

CryptoAPI

CryptoAPI is a set of tools that allows developers to integrate cryptography into their Windows 2000 program without having to actually know about its inner workings. Without any knowledge of the cryptographic algorithms involved, a developer can create cryptographic-enabled programs that carry out the public key routines on the PC while performing private key operations on the smart card itself. This helps by reducing the security risk of rogue programs' examining any computations and isolating private information from system components that do not need to know about them. CryptoAPI is also supported on Windows 95, 98, and NT.

NOTE

If you are interested in developing with CryptoAPI, you can receive information on obtaining a kit by visiting http://www.microsoft.com/security and selecting "Technologies" followed by "CryptoAPI." Because CryptoAPI is capable of strong encryption, it is regulated under U.S. export laws and requires that you answer some questions so that it can determine whether you can legally obtain the kit.

Win32 API

While the Win32 APIs are the most complicated noncryptographic interfaces to use, they also allow you to have the maximum control available over a card or reader's services. To use the APIs effectively, you need to have a broad and deep understanding of how Windows operates and how cards and readers function. If a developer needs maximum flexibility and control over how a smart card system works, then the Win32 API extensions will fill the order best.

SCard COM

SCard COM is a generic noncryptographic interface implementation for accessing smart card services. The COM components are basic interface elements used to build richer and more functional services for an application. These functions can be implemented in various languages such as C, C++, Java, and the Microsoft Visual Basic development system. In general, the developer does not need to know the specifics of how a card's functions operate in order to make use of COM components. This helps speed development of Windows-based applications, saving time and money and allowing the developer to operate in an already familiar environment. Due to the nature of COM and the isolation of system components (as illustrated in Fig. 8.1), this also prevents products from becoming obsolete as soon as the technology suffers a minor change.

Integration with Various Microsoft Platforms

Microsoft is one of the participants in the PC/SC Workgroup and has accordingly implemented the solutions into its own software. Windows 2000 contains native support for smart card access and Smart Card Interactive Login by certified cards and readers. These certified cards and readers can be identified by the Windows 2000 Compatibility Logo. This allows a user to walk up to a computer and log in by inserting a card into a card reader and entering a personal identification number (PIN). Support for smart cards for Windows 95, 98, and NT 4.0 is also available without the secure login feature. Internet Explorer 4.0 and later, as well as Outlook 98 and later, all support Secure MIME (S/MIME) communications by utilizing smart cards.

A new platform by Microsoft, called Smart Card for Windows, which will be to smart cards what PalmOS is to a PalmPilot, is a low-cost, easy-to-program OS with 8K of ROM. It can run Visual Basic applications and is designed to extend the PC environment into smart card use. In addition to supporting major Visual Studio development tools, Smart Card for Windows is part of the PC/SC program. This means that any card that uses the OS will be able to be read by any certified Windows card reader. A drawback to Smart Card for Windows is that currently there are no native cryptographic functions. This means that all smart card manufacturers will have to implement their own security algorithms. If you are a developer interested in developing smart-card-aware applications, you can still program the software that is resident on the host computer by using CryptoAPI, Win32 APIs, or SCard COM.

Smart Card Base Components

The smart card base components are the drivers and utilities that are required for smart card services to function through Windows. As of this writing, version 1.0 of these components has been released for Microsoft Windows 95 and NT 4.0. They are available on Microsoft's Web site at http://www.microsoft.com/security/tech/smartcards.

Service Providers

Every card must have at least one service provider installed in order for Windows-based applications to access the card and make use of its services. Depending on the type of card and the issuer, some may have multiple service providers available. In general there are two different types of service providers: cryptographic and standard. This distinction is necessary due to export control regulations on cryptography components in the United States.

Cryptographic Service Providers

Cryptographic Service Providers (CSP) can be either software-based, like the Windows CSP that ships standard with all Windows platforms today, or it can be a hardware solution, in which the actual crypto-engine resides on the smart card or other piece of hardware attached to the computer. A CSP associated with a smart card is referred to as a Smart Card Cryptographic Provider (SCCP), in order to distinguish it from a software-based CSP. Both CSP and SCCP expose cryptographic services through CryptoAPI, such as random number generation, key generation, key exchange, bulk encryption, and digital signatures.

Smart Card Service Providers

Smart Card Service Providers (SCSP) expose the services that are not cryptographic in nature. To do this, they expose interfaces similar to COM components while providing the protocols necessary to invoke the services and making assumptions regarding the context of the services.

A smart card can register support for an interface by binding an association to the interface's globally-unique identifier (GUID). This binding between card and interface is done at the time the card is first introduced to the system, typically when the SCSP is installed. A card service provider registers its interfaces at the time the card is introduced to the system in order to allow applications to locate smart cards based on a specific interface or GUID. For example, a cash card could make itself available to Windows applications by registering its purse scheme.

As part of the Smart Card Base Components 1.0 release, Microsoft shipped several base-level service providers for performing generic operations on a card. They were implemented as COM objects to allow developers to use them as building blocks to develop higher-level services and applications.

Cards

The term "smart card" has been used to describe a class of credit-card-sized devices with varying degrees of capabilities. The three types of smart cards are stored-value cards, contactless cards, and integrated circuit cards (ICC). All these cards differ substantially from each other and their visually similar ancestor, the magnetic-stripe card. The magnetic stripe card is currently being used in applications such as credit, debit, and ATM cards.

Stored-Value Smart Cards

Stored-value smart cards are simply cards that hold information on them. These are good for providing access to buildings and computer systems that don't require that the key be hidden from the host PC. Since the card can't perform any complex operations, it can't do such things as key exchange and digital signing. This means that any operations necessary for authentication or encryption will have to be done by the host PC connected to the reader. This may or may not present a problem. A stored-value card's storage capacity varies by manufacturer but generally contains only enough room to store a few digital keys. Before purchasing any smart card, be sure to contact the manufacturer and verify that the card has enough storage capacity to fit your organizational needs. The card may require the user to enter a secret PIN before access to the card is granted. This requirement is also manufacturer-specific and should be considered before a purchase is made.

Contactless Smart Cards

Contactless smart cards perform the same function as do stored-value cards but differ in that you do not have to insert them into a reader. Figure 8.2 shows a contactless smart card. An example application would be a secure building's entry. On the door frame there would be a sensor slightly larger than the card itself. You would hold up your card next to the sensor, and within a half

Figure 8.2 An example of a contactless smart card.

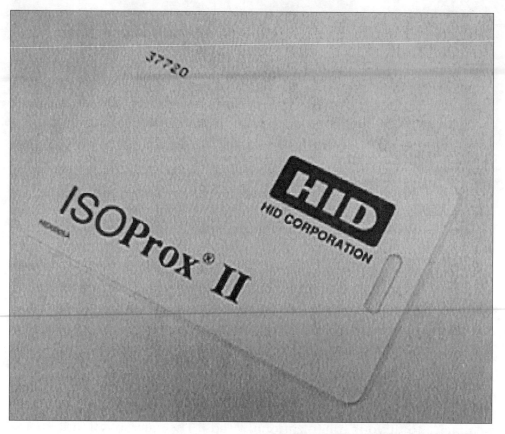

second it would beep and unlock the door. Sure does beat trying to find your keys in the dark! The problem with contactless cards is that if you lose the card, the result is the same as if you lose your door key. Since there's not always a keypad to enter a PIN, anyone can use your card to gain access. Bear in mind that the solution to this problem (canceling a user's smart card access) is much easier than changing your locks.

ICC Smart Cards

ICC smart cards are the smartest of all smart cards. They can be contact or contactless and can have all the functionality of stored-value cards, with the addition of being able to perform more complex operations involved in key exchanging and digital signing. This enables you to send secure e-mail and perform encryption operations without having to temporarily store your private key on a computer. Since the key is retained on the smart card, and all the operations performed on your private key are also done on the card, there is no reason to have the key stored on the local PC. This prevents hackers from obtaining it and attempting to compromise it and also protects against rogue applications or other processes monitoring the secure transaction. Your key information is on a need-to-know basis with regard to which system components have access to it. The ICC smart card is the type of card used to devise specifications by the PC/SC Workgroup. Figure 8.3 shows a contact smart card for a digital cellular phone. Figure 8.4 shows the function of each area of the contact pad based on ISO 7816-2.

Figure 8.3 An example of a contact ICC smart card.

Figure 8.4 A description of each section of the contact pad for a contact smart card based on the ISO 7816-2 standard.

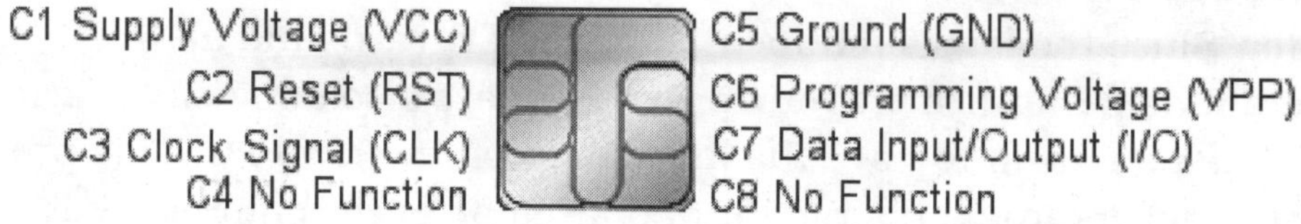

C1 Supply Voltage (VCC)   C5 Ground (GND)
C2 Reset (RST)   C6 Programming Voltage (VPP)
C3 Clock Signal (CLK)   C7 Data Input/Output (I/O)
C4 No Function   C8 No Function

For Managers

Smart Card Costs

We have discussed various features of smart cards and seen the strengths of using them, but we have not discussed how much it will cost to implement in your organization. Prices do vary based on the quantity purchased, so the size of your organization is important, especially if you plan to roll out smart cards and smart card readers to the entire organization.

The GemSAFE smart card presents an example of smart card costs. Gemplus sells the cards in a four pack for $70. The GemSAFE card supports 128-bit encryption, which is used by the domestic versions of Netscape Navigator and Internet Explorer. If you needed to purchase in quantity, you could arrange better pricing from Gemplus or any other smart card vendor.

Smart card readers vary significantly in price, depending on whether you require internal readers, external readers, or mobile readers. One vendor sells internal smart card readers for $97 each when they are purchased one at a time. The price goes to $54 each for a quantity of 500 and $35 each for a quantity of 10,000. Plan wisely when you decide to roll out a smart card strategy for your organization.

For IT Professionals

Transactions

Transaction-based processing is a key component to the success of messaging between the resource manager and the smart card device. If the application makes a request that consists of three different commands that would normally be performed simultaneously, the request is forwarded to the resource manager for processing. When the resource manager receives the request, the request is split into three separate transactions that are completed individually. If any of the transactions does not fully complete, the request is returned as a failure. If the third transaction fails, the resource manager will undo whatever the first two transactions did. By returning the system to the original state, the resource manager ensures that the affected components are not corrupted. The request from the application is then returned as failed, and the application can determine whether or not to try again. If it elects to retry, it can do so without worrying about having certain items being corrupt because of the previous failure. With transactions, either the whole request completes or the whole request fails.

Resource Manager

The resource manager is responsible for delegating between an application using services provided by the smart card or reader and the device itself. It runs as a trusted service in a single process. When an application needs to make use of a smart card or reader, it sends a request to the resource manager, which then makes the request of the device, enabling a virtual connection between the application and the device. This solves three basic problems in managing multiple readers and cards: First, it enables the devices to be identified and tracked. Second, it manages the multiple readers and

Figure 8.5 The interaction between smart card application and smart card reader.

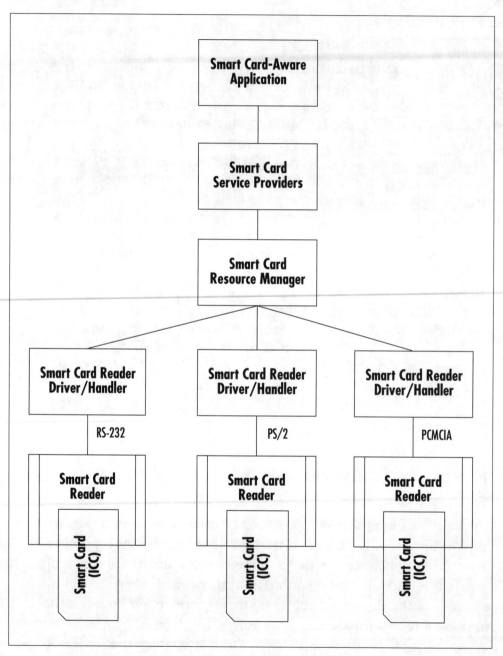

keeps track of their respective resources. Third, it supports a transaction-based method of accessing available services on a given card. This is important because current smart card devices are only single threaded, but some requests may take multiple commands to complete. Figure 8.5 shows how the interaction process works between the application and the card.

Enhanced Solutions

Now that you have a good idea of how smart cards came to be and how they work, you should understand how they can positively affect your environment. Smart cards offer solutions to security concerns, such as authenticating that users on the network are who they claim to be, allowing for secure automated logins, and making it possible to send securely-encrypted and digitally-signed e-mail. In some states, an e-mail message signed with a digital signature is just as legally binding as a signed paper message.

Client Authentication

Client authentication is the process of verifying an alleged user's identity. After verification, a secure communications channel such as Secure Sockets Layer (SSL) or Transport Layer Security (TLS) can be opened. These secure transport protocols are generally used in conjunction with a public key certificate. The client could be running Microsoft Internet Explorer 4.0 or later, and the server could be running Microsoft Internet Information Server 4.0 or later. This is just an example, as there are many solutions available for a secure connection to be established.

The secure session is established using public key authentication with a key exchange to derive a unique session key that can be used to validate any messages sent over the connection as complete, intact, and confidential. Mapping individual users or groups to certificates with preconfigured access permissions and restrictions can further enhance security. The smart card enhances the security process in two ways. First, it allows the user's private key to be stored securely on the card and to be accessible only to the holder of a custom PIN. Second, if the card is an ICC card, it allows the actual key exchange to take place on the card, which further isolates the secure components from the insecure components.

Public-Key Interactive Logon

In the past, interactive logon has been the process of inputting credentials into a logon screen in the form of a user name and password that is then shared with other resources that require validation for access. With public key interactive logon, the process has changed significantly. Windows 2000 supports the use of an X.509v3 Certificate stored on the smart card alongside the user's private key. Instead of a user name and password, the user inserts his or her smart card and inputs the PIN into the graphical identification and authentication (GINA). If the PIN is correct, the user is authenticated to the card (see Figure 8.6).

Figure 8.6 Windows 2000 Professional is ready for smart card authentication.

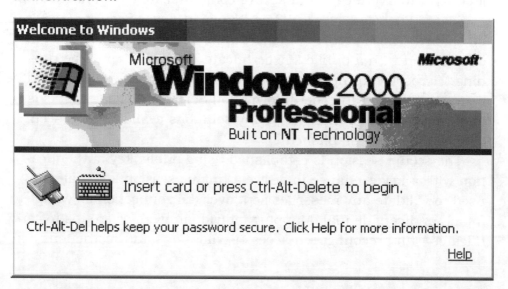

The user's public key certificate is retrieved from the card through a secure process and is verified to be a valid certificate issued from a trusted provider. During the authentication process, a challenge is issued to the card based on the public key contained within the certificate. If the card can verify that it is indeed in possession of and can use the private key, the user identity contained within the certificate is used to reference the user object stored in Active Directory and to build an access token for it. The client is then issued a ticket-granting ticket (TGT). Public key logon has been integrated with the Microsoft implementation of Kerberos v5.

In order to enable the public key interactive logon feature of Windows 2000, you need to first install a smart card reader and enable the card to store certificates.

Smart Card Reader Installation

Smart card readers generally install via an RS-232 or PC Card interface. In the future there will be support for Universal Serial Bus (USB) and maybe even FireWire (IEEE 1394). When you purchase a reader, you should look for the Windows 2000-Compatible logo. Microsoft has compiled detailed specifications on how to make a reader work optimally with its operating systems and grants the logo to compliant products (similar to the "Works with Windows 95" logo). Please refer to the Windows Hardware Compatibility List (HCL) for a list of currently supported readers at http://www.microsoft.com/hcl. Smart card readers should come with manufacturer instructions on how to install any necessary cables. To install software support in Windows for the devices, follow these steps:

1. Ensure your computer is powered down.
2. Connect the smart card reader to the computer according to the manufacturer's instructions.
3. Power up your computer and log on.
4. The Hardware Wizard will automatically detect the smart card reader if it is Plug and Play compliant. Follow the instructions presented by the wizard. If prompted, insert

the manufacturer's driver disk(s) and/or the Windows 2000 CD.

5. Set the Smart Card service to start automatically. To do this, select the Start button, choose Settings, and click Control Panel. Double-click Administrative Tools, double-click Computer Management, double-click Services and Applications, and select Services. Right-click Smart Card, select Properties, and then choose Automatic from the Startup option. Figure 8.7 shows the service set to run automatically.

6. Click OK and reboot if prompted.

If the device is not automatically detected upon startup, then it is either not Plug and Play compatible or not installed correctly. Consult the manufacturer's documentation for further assistance.

Figure 8.7 Smart Card service is set for automatic startup.

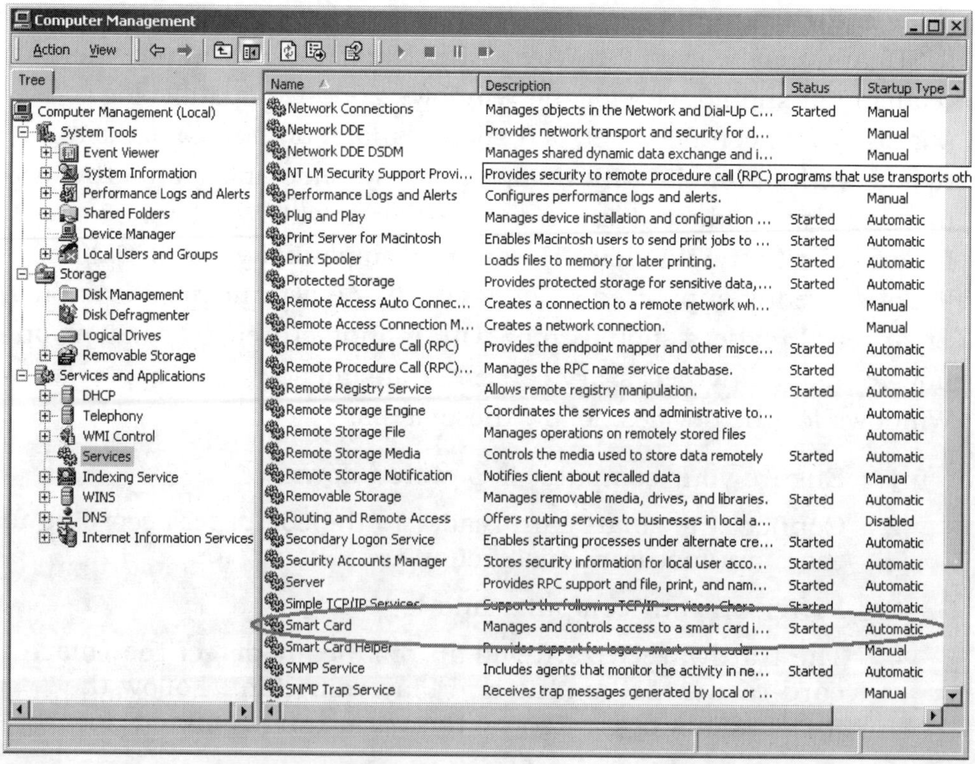

Now that your reader is installed correctly, you can proceed to configuring the certificate parameters.

Smart Card Certificate Enrollment

In order for a user to enroll for either type of smart card certificate (authentication or authentication plus e-mail), the user must have access to the certificate template stored in Microsoft's Active Directory. This is done because enrollment for smart card access needs to be a controlled procedure similar to the procedure used for obtaining a ID badge for work. Microsoft's recommends configuring badges through the "Enroll on-Behalf-of Station" that is integrated with Certificate Services.

When an enterprise certificate authority (CA) is installed, the installation includes the Enroll On-Behalf-Of Station. This station allows an administrator to act on behalf of a specific user and request that a certificate be installed on the user's smart card. Since the cards themselves are partially proprietary, the station cannot offer card customization features such as building a file directory or changing the PIN. To perform these operations, consult the manufacturer's documentation and software.

Before proceeding, make sure you have set up Active Directory and added to it a CA that supports public/private key certificates. An administrator should perform these procedures:

1. To connect to a CA, open Internet Explorer and type http://<machine-name>/certsrv into the address bar. Be sure to replace <machine-name> with the computer name of the issuing CA.

2. The Microsoft Certificate Service Welcome page appears as shown in Figure 8.8. Select Request a certificate, and then click Next to continue.

3. Select Advanced request from the Choose Request Type page and click Next.

4. Select Request a certificate for a smart card on behalf of another use, using the Smart Card Enrollment Station from the Advanced Certificate Requests page, and click Next.

Figure 8.8 The Welcome screen from the Microsoft Certificate Services.

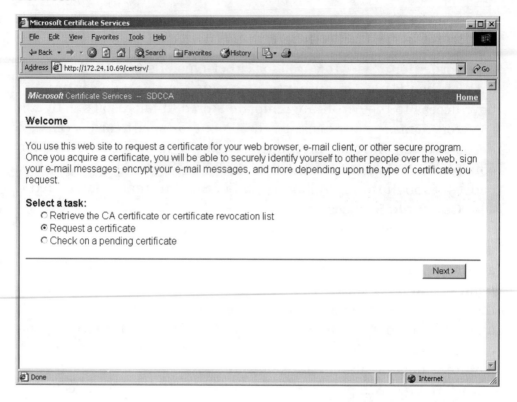

5. The first time you use the enrollment station, a digitally-signed ActiveX control is downloaded from the CA to the station computer. To use the station, select Yes from the Security Warning dialog box to install the control.

6. Five items need to be completed on the Smart Card Enrollment Station page before you submit the request.

    ■   There are several certification templates to choose from. For smart card usage, you are only concerned with two: Smart Card Logon and Smart Card User. Remember that the Smart Card Logon template is for access to public key interactive logon, and the Smart Card User template is for both logon and user authentication through e-mail. Select either Smart Card Logon or Smart Card User.

- Select a Certification Authority.

- Select a Cryptographic Service Provider.

- Select an Administrator Signing Certificate if one is not already selected.

- Select the user by clicking Select User.

7. You are now ready to submit the certificate request as shown in Figure 8.9. Click Enroll on the Smart Card Enrollment Station page.

Figure 8.9 Select criteria to enroll a new Smartcard User.

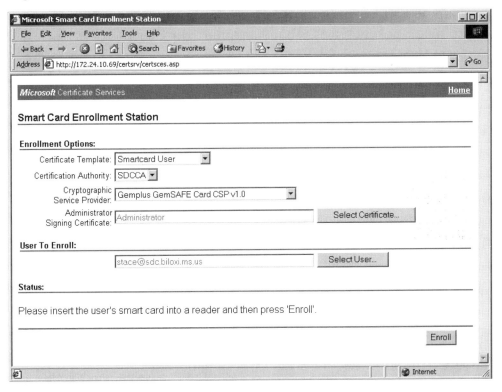

8. If the card is not already inserted into the reader, you will be requested to insert it. Insert the card and click OK.

9. The request must be digitally signed by the private key that corresponds to the public key included in the certificate

request. Because the key is stored on the card, the signature requires that the card owner verify the PIN and prove ownership of both the card and the key. Type the PIN for the card and click OK.

10. If the CA successfully processes the certificate request, the station will inform you that the smart card is ready. You can now either view the certificate by clicking View Certificate or you can specify a new user by clicking New User.

Smart Card Logon

Logging on with a smart card is a relatively simple and straightforward task. Approach a PC that has smart card logon enabled and perform these steps:

1. You will see a logon screen that reads "Insert card or press Ctrl-Alt-Delete to begin," as was shown in Figure 8.6. Insert your card into the smart card reader.

2. The Log On to Windows dialog box will prompt you to enter your PIN. Enter it.

3. You are now logged on. To lock a workstation without logging off, press Ctrl-Alt-Delete and select Lock Workstation. To unlock it with a smart card, simply insert your card and enter your PIN.

Secure E-Mail

Secure e-mail is one of the most exciting aspects of public key technology. It allows you to finally put that envelope over your letter and superglue it shut. Secure e-mail works like this:

1. The sender composes a message in a public-key-aware messaging application, such as Microsoft Outlook Express or Microsoft Outlook 98.

2. The sender retrieves the recipient's public key certificates from a trusted security provider and uses them with his or

her own private key to digitally sign and encrypt the message.

3. The message is sent to the recipients over the network.

4. Upon receipt of the message, the recipient uses a private key to verify and decrypt the message. This is the only way an encrypted message can be opened other than by forcibly hacking your way into it.

5. The recipient's private key analyzes the data stored in the message to determine whether it has been tampered with in transit. It also compares the data with the sender's public key. This allows the recipient to verify the authenticity of the message and to be sure that it was not forged.

In a process similar to the one used in the public key interactive logon, the smart card adds the same amount of security to the e-mail process. The key is the sole possessor of the private key and, depending on the card type, the sole processor of any data destined to it, thereby reducing the private key's exposure to insecure systems.

Summary

This chapter introduced the basics of smart card theory and examined the interoperability issues involving smart cards in the present, past, and future with the ISO 7816, EMV, GSA, and PC/SC specifications. Microsoft's vision of the future of smart cards is evident in its products and services and the methods of implementing card services through CryptoAPI, Win32 API, and SCard COM. Finally, Enhanced Solutions shows what makes smart cards so practical and realistic for today's use by examining public key interactive logon, client authentication, and secure e-mail.

We are at the dawn of an information-based age. To protect ourselves from the side effects of all this information being transmitted over public networks, we need to secure our data. The smart card will play an important role in further enhancing this security, both now and in the future.

For IT Professionals

How Secure Is Secure E-Mail?

With all this talk of secure e-mail and messaging and encryption, you may be wondering how secure an e-mail message has to be to be secure. That all depends on your definition of the term. Not too long ago 56-bit encryption was thought to be very secure. This security has recently been broken by an organization that enables users worldwide to lend some of the users' computer processor time to the organization over the Internet. For more information, visit http://www.distributed.net. If you're brute-force hacking, you have a possibility of 2^{56} combinations. Now everyone considers 128-bit to be secure. When you determine an optimal level of security, you have to consider the technology factor of today and what it will be 10 years from now. If I encode a 128-bit message that is intercepted, chances are that by the time it is decoded, it will no longer matter. In the case of something more long-term, like financial records, if you work for an organization that archives its records each year and you encrypt the records with 128-bit protection, it is difficult to plan for a future in which a hacker may get hold of your file with a multigigahertz quadruple processor computer with a terabyte of RAM. We don't know where technology is going, so we need to remain constantly alert and plan ahead. I personally use 3000-bit encryption on any files that I deem personal and long-lasting. To put things in perspective, consider this: Your chances of being killed by lightning each day are 1 in 9,000,000,000 (nine billion) or 2^{33}. The chance of breaking my encrypted file is currently 1 in 2^{3000}.

FAQs

Q: What is Microsoft's smart card strategy?

A: Microsoft will ensure that the Microsoft Windows platform is ready for use by smart cards and readers, thereby allowing developers to create products based on standard APIs and tools.

Q: Will Microsoft support smart card logon on other platforms?

A: Microsoft will support smart card logon only in Windows 2000.

Q: What are the main differences between CryptoAPI, Win32 API, and SCard COM?

A: CryptoAPI is an interface for utilizing cryptographic functions such as digital signing and encryption. Because of this, it is a regulated export item. The other two interfaces are noncryptographic in nature. Win32 APIs allow the developer rigid control over the operation of smart cards and readers but require a broad understanding of Windows and smart card operations. SCard COM allows a developer to perform basic generic functions without a thorough knowledge of Windows or smart cards.

Q: How does smart card logon work in Windows 2000?

A: Windows 2000 uses the PKINIT protocol for public key, which is an extension to Kerberos v5. This allows an authorized user to insert a card in a reader, authenticate to the card, and use a certificate/private key to authenticate to the Microsoft Windows Active Directory. An authenticated user is then provided with a Kerberos ticket and can use that ticket to access resources in the domain.

Q: Does Microsoft plan to support smart card for Internet authentication and secure e-mail?

A: Yes. Microsoft currently has support for Internet Explorer 4.0 and 5.0 and Outlook 98 and 2000. These applications support user authentication and S/MIME e-mail today. This works with any card that supports RSA crypto-operations and has a CSP.

Q: How secure is secure e-mail?

A: That depends on the encryption level used. See the "For IT Professionals" sidebar earlier in this chapter.

Chapter 9

Microsoft Windows 2000 Public Key Infrastructure

Solutions in this chapter:

- **Introduction**

- **Concepts**

- **Windows 2000 PKI Components**

- **Certificate Authorities**

- **Enabling Domain Clients**

- **PK Security Policy in Windows 2000**

- **Applications Overview**

- **Preparing for Windows 2000 PKI**

Introduction

All organizations today rely on networks for access to information. These can range from internal networks to the Internet. Access to information is needed, and this access must be configured to provide information to other organizations that may request it. When we need to make a purchase, we can quickly check out vendors' prices through their Web pages. In order not to allow the competition to get ahead of our organization, we must establish our own Web page for the advertising and ordering of our products.

Within any organization, there may be many sites across the country or around the globe. If corporate data is available immediately to employees, much time is saved. In the corporate world, any time saved is also money saved.

In the past, Windows NT provided user security through account names and passwords. At logon, every user had to submit credentials, which were compared against a server's database for authentication. The matching of the username and password identified the user but failed to identify the corporate server. This environment allowed many man-in-the-middle attacks. A server could be configured by a hacker to impersonate the corporate server, thus intercepting the data from the user as well as from the corporate server. With the man-in-the-middle in place, when users sent information to the corporate server, sensitive data could be grabbed. The man-in-the-middle could have access to sensitive information when the server sent the information to the requesting user. The way to prevent any impersonation from occurring on the network is to have both the user and the server verify themselves to each other.

Windows 2000 includes new security features that will prevent man-in-the-middle attacks on corporate secrets. The new security features include the components that create the Public Key Infrastructure. As the name implies, the security is based on the use of public key pairs. Your environment will decide which components need to be implemented.

Concepts

The rapid growth of Internet use has given rise to new security concerns. Any company that does not configure a strong security infrastructure is literally putting the company at risk. An unscrupulous person could, if security were lax, steal information or modify business information in a way that could result in major financial disaster. To protect the organization's information, the man-in-the-middle must be eliminated. Cryptographic technologies provide a way to identify both users and servers during network use.

Public Key Cryptography

Encryption is the process of changing a cleartext message into an unreadable form to protect sensitive data. The transformation from the scrambled form, known as ciphertext, back to cleartext is called decryption.

Cryptography can be dated back to around 2000 B.C. in ancient Egypt. Through time and civilizations, ciphering text played an important role in wars and politics. As modern times provided new communication methods, it became increasingly more important to scramble information. World War II brought about the first use of the computer in the cracking of Germany's Enigma code.

In 1952, President Truman created the National Security Agency at Fort Meade, Maryland. This agency, which is the center of U.S. cryptographic activity, fulfills two important national functions: It protects all military and executive communication from being intercepted, and it intercepts and unscrambles messages sent by other countries.

There are three types of cryptographic functions. The hash function does not involve the use of a key at all, but it uses a mathematical algorithm on the data in order to scramble it. The secret key method of encryption, which involves the use of a single key, is used to encrypt and decrypt the information and is sometimes referred to as symmetric key cryptography. An excellent example of secret key encryption is the decoder ring you may have had as a child. Any person who obtained your decoder ring could read your "secret" information.

There are basically two types of symmetric algorithms. Block symmetric algorithms work by taking a given length of bits known as blocks. Stream symmetric algorithms operate on a single bit at a time. One well-known block algorithm is Data Encryption Standard (DES). Windows 2000 uses a modified DES and performs that operation on 64-bit blocks using every eighth bit for parity. The resulting ciphertext is the same length as the original cleartext. For export purposes, the DES is also available with a 40-bit key.

One advantage of secret key encryption is the efficiency with which it takes a large amount of data and encrypts it quite rapidly. Symmetric algorithms can also be easily implemented at the hardware level. The major disadvantage of secret key encryption is that a single key is used for both encryption and decryption. There must be a secure way for the two parties to exchange the one secret key.

In the 1970s, this disadvantage of secret key encryption was eliminated through the mathematical implementation of public key encryption. Public key encryption, also referred to as asymmetric cryptography, replaced the one shared key with each user's own pair of keys. One key is a public key, which is made available to everyone and is used for the encryption process only. The other key in the pair, the private key, is available only to the owner. The private key cannot be created as a result of the public key's being available. Any data that is encrypted by a public key can be decrypted only by using the private key of the pair. It is also possible for the owner to use a private key to encrypt sensitive information. If the data is encrypted by using the private key, then the public key in the pair of keys is needed to decrypt the data.

The public key is available to everyone, so there is no need for a secure key exchange channel. Users who wish to communicate just retrieve each other's public keys. Figure 9.1 shows the encryption process using the receiver's public key.

Figure 9.1 Public Key Encryption

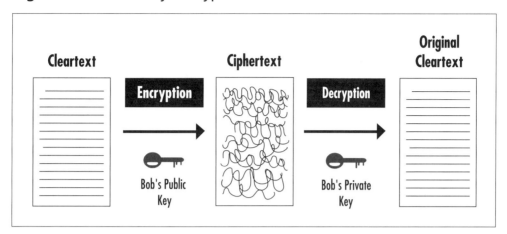

Public key cryptography can do everything that secret key cryptography can do, but at a much slower pace. To work around the speed problem of public key encryption, designers often incorporate the two encryption methods together. The designers of Windows 2000 did just that. Any data that requires a fast encryption method is handled by secret key encryption, while the encryption of the secret key itself is handled by public key cryptography. Public key encryption is slow, but because the secret key is small, this method of encryption does not have an impact on the overall process.

Public Key Functionality

Public key cryptography brings major security technologies to the desktop in the Windows 2000 environment. The network now is provided with the ability to allow users to safely:

- Transmit over insecure channels
- Store sensitive information on any commonly-used media
- Verify a person's identity for authentication
- Prove that a message was generated by a particular person
- Prove that the received message was not tampered with in transit

Algorithms based on public keys can be used for all these purposes. The most popular public key algorithm is the standard RSA, which is named after its three inventors: Rivest, Shamir, and Adleman. The RSA algorithm is based on two prime numbers with more than 200 digits each. A hacker would have to take the ciphertext and the public key and factor the product of the two primes. As computer processing time increases, the RSA remains secure by increasing the key length, unlike the DES algorithm, which has a fixed key length.

Public key algorithms provide privacy, authentication, and easy key management, but they encrypt and decrypt data slowly because of the intensive computation required. RSA has been evaluated to be from 10 to 10,000 times slower than DES in some environments, which is a good reason not to use public key algorithms for bulk encryption.

Digital Signatures

Document letterhead can be easily created on a computer, so forgery is a security issue. When information is sent electronically, no human contact is involved. The receiver wants to know that the person listed as the sender is really the sender and that the information received has not been modified in any way during transit. A hash algorithm is implemented to guarantee the Windows 2000 user that the data is authentic. A hash value encrypted with a private key is called a digital signature. Anyone with access to the corresponding public key can verify the authenticity of a digital signature. Only a person having a private key can generate digital signatures. Any modification makes a digital signature invalid.

The purpose of a digital signature is to prevent changes within a document from going unnoticed and also to claim the person to be the original author. The document itself is not encrypted. The digital signature is just data sent along with the data guaranteed to be untampered with. A change of any size invalidates the digital signature.

When King Henry II had to send a message to his troops in a remote location, the letter would be sealed with wax, and while the wax was still soft the king would use his ring to make an impression in it. No modification occurred to the original message if the seal was never broken during transit. There was no doubt that King Henry II had initiated the message, because he was the only person possessing a ring that matched the waxed imprint. Digital signatures work in a similar fashion, in that only the sender's public key can authenticate both the original sender and the content of the document.

The digital signature is generated by a message digest, which is a number generated by taking the message and using a hash algorithm. A message digest is regarded as a fingerprint and can range from a 128-bit number to a 256-bit number. A hash function takes variable-length input and produces a fixed-length output. The message is first processed with a hash function to produce a message digest. This value is then signed by the sender's private key, which produces the actual digital signature. The digital signature is then added to the end of the document and sent to the receiver along with the document.

Since the mere presence of a digital signature proves nothing, verification must be mathematically proven. In the verification process, the first step is to use the corresponding public key to decrypt the digital signature. The result will produce a 128-bit number. The original message will be processed with the same hash function used earlier and will result in a message digest. The two resulting 128-bit numbers will then be compared, and if they are equal, you will receive notification of a good signature. If a single character has been altered, the two 128-bit numbers will be different, indicating that a change has been made to the document, which was never scrambled.

Figure 9.2 illustrates the generation of a digital signature. The original message is processed with a mathematical function to generate a message digest. The sender's private key is used to encrypt the message digest, and the final result is a digital signature.

Figure 9.2 How a digital signature is generated.

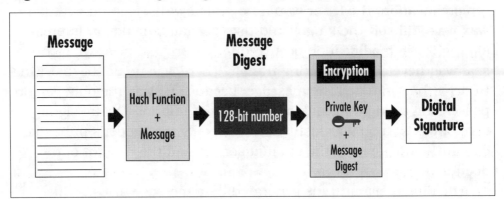

Authentication

Public key cryptography can provide authentication instead of privacy. In Windows 2000, a challenge is sent by the receiver of the information. The challenge can be implemented in one of two ways. The information is authenticated because only the corresponding private key could have encrypted the information that the public key is successfully decrypting.

In the first authentication method, a challenge to authenticate involves sending an encrypted challenge to the sender. The challenge is encrypted by the receiver, using the sender's public key. Only the corresponding private key can successfully decode the challenge. When the challenge is decoded, the sender sends the plaintext back to the receiver. This is the proof for the receiver that the sender is truly the sender.

For example, when Alice receives a document from Bob, she wants to authenticate that the sender is really Bob. She sends an encrypted challenge to Bob, using his public key. When he receives the challenge, Bob uses his private key to decrypt the information. The decrypted challenge is then sent back to Alice. When Alice receives the decrypted challenge, she is convinced that the document she received is truly from Bob.

The second authentication method uses a challenge that is sent in plaintext. The receiver, after receiving the document, sends a challenge in plaintext to the sender. The sender receives the plaintext challenge and adds some information before adding a digital signature.

The challenge and digital signature now head back to the sender. The digital signature is generated by using a hash function and then encrypting the result with a private key, so the receiver must use the sender's public key to verify the digital signature. If the signature is good, the original document and sender have at this point been verified mathematically.

Figure 9.3 uses Alice and Bob to demonstrate the plaintext challenge.

This type of authentication is referred to as proof of possession. The sender must prove he is who he says he is by having the correct corresponding private key. The process is always started by the receiver of the document. The document is never encrypted in this authentication process.

Figure 9.3 A plaintext authentication challenge.

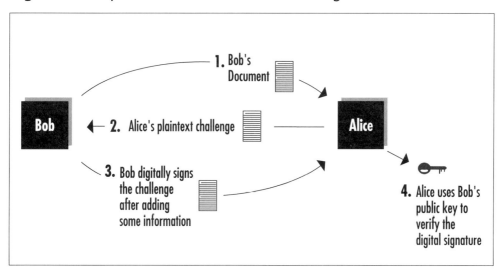

Secret Key Agreement via Public Key

The Public Key Infrastructure of Windows 2000 permits two parties to agree on a secret key while they use nonsecure communication channels. Each party generates half the shared secret key by generating a random number, which is sent to the other party after being encrypted with the other party's public key. Each receiving side then decrypts the ciphertext using a private key, which will result in the missing half of the secret key.

By adding both random numbers together, each party will have an agreed-upon shared secret key, which can then be used for secure communication even though the secret key was first obtained through a nonsecure communication channel.

Bulk Data Encryption without Prior Shared Secrets

The final major feature of public key technology is that it can encrypt bulk data without generating a shared secret key first. The biggest disadvantage of using asymmetric algorithms for encryption is the slowness of the overall process, which results from the necessary intense computations; the largest disadvantage of using symmetric algorithms for encryption of bulk data is the need for a secure communication channel for exchanging the secret key. The Windows 2000 operating system combines symmetric and asymmetric algorithms to get the best of both worlds at just the right moment.

For a large document that must be kept secret, secret key encryption is the quickest method to use for the bulk data. A session key is used to scramble the document. To protect the session key, which is the secret key needed to decrypt the protected data, the sender encrypts this small item quickly by using the receiver's public key. This encryption of the session key is handled by asymmetric algorithms, which use intense computation but do not require much time, due to the small size of the session key. The document, along with the encrypted session key, is then sent to the receiver. Only the intended receiver will possess the correct private key to decode the session key, which is needed to decode the actual document. When the session key is in plaintext, it can be applied to the ciphertext of the bulk data and then transform the bulk data back to plaintext.

Protecting and Trusting Cryptographic Keys

When secret key cryptography is implemented, both the sender and the receiver share a key, which they protect and keep private. In some secure fashion, both parties have agreed and exchanged this single key, which is used to encrypt and decrypt the data the two parties wish to keep secure.

In contrast to secret key cryptography, public key cryptography does not protect all the involved keys. In public key cryptography, only the private keys are protected, but the public keys are shared by the act of publishing them. Since the public key is not protected, in any Public Key Infrastructure the sender must be provided with a means to trust the relationship of the public key and its entity.

Unlike the case of secret key cryptography, in which the single key is exchanged by some secure contrived plan, the public key is available without passing any security checkpoints. The fact that the public key is available for public use limits security implementation in protecting it. Because public keys are not surrounded by any security measures, there is a need for some mechanism that ensures that the public key being used is really the entity's public key.

Certificates

Certificates are used to provide the assurance that the public key being used does in fact belong to the entity that owns the corresponding private key. A certificate is a digitally signed statement by its issuer that affirms the validity of both the public key and the subject's identity information. The certificate is the user's guarantee between the public key and the entity holding the corresponding private key.

The certificate contains the public key and a complete set of attributes. These attributes may include information about the holder's identity, what the holder is allowed to do, and under what circumstances the certificate is valid. The digital signature ties the attributes and the public key together on the certificate itself. The issuer's signature on the certificate is, in effect, the guarantee of authenticity.

A real-world example of a certificate is a passport. All passports contain a unique key, the registered passport number from the issuing government. Also included on every passport are the passport holder's full name, date of birth, place of birth, the date of issue, and the expiration date. U.S. passports are issued by the federal government and require a photo identification on the laminated information page. Any country that has agreed to accept these passports trusts that the information on the document is true as long as the passport does not seem to have been tampered with. This means that foreign countries are relying on the passport's authenticity, just as the user of a public key relies on the issuer's certificate.

The Public Key Infrastructure of Windows 2000 supports the International Telecommunication Union (ITU)-T X.509 version 3 standard for certificate creation. This X.509v3 standard defines the format and content of digital certificates. The use of a standard for certification creation allows the exchange of certificates between vendors and ensures true interoperability.

Certificate Authorities

Digital certificates provide a way to validate public keys. By definition, the issuer of a Public Key Certificate is known as a certificate authority. Certificate authorities are responsible for validating the identity of a person or organization and for joining that entity with a key pair. The certificate authority stores the public key and maintains the list of certificates that have been issued.

Certificate authorities vary greatly in size. At one end of the spectrum are commercial certificate authorities like Verisign and

GTE Cybertrust, which issue millions of certificates, while at the opposite end there are departmental certificate authorities that issue a small number of certificates. Many smaller certificate authorities are known to issue certificate authorities whose certificates are signed by a higher-level certificate authority, which can be inside or outside the organization.

Each certificate authority can decide what attributes will be included in the certificates it creates and also what method of verification it will implement at the time of creation. Every certificate authority has the responsibility to issue a certificate revocation list containing any certificate that has to be revoked. The certificate revocation list (CRL) is published, so clients can check the list before any authentication request is approved.

Figure 9.4 shows the Windows 2000 interface for identifying information that is used by the certificate authority in every certificate it creates and also in identifying all certificates that belong to it.

Figure 9.4 An example of certficate identification information.

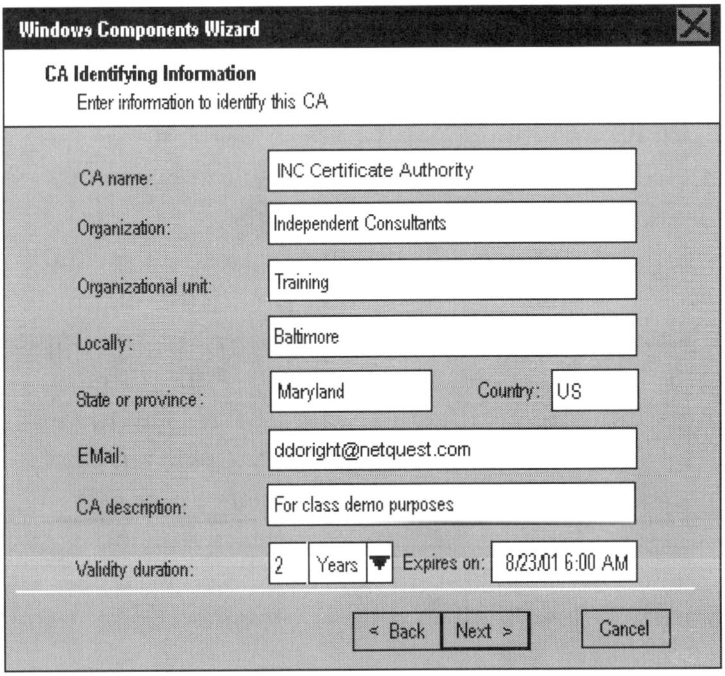

Certificate Types

The certificate authority provides the validation of the entity belonging to the public key, so the administrator must understand the four types of certificate authorities that are included with the Microsoft Certificate Services. The Enterprise Root certificate authority is at the top of the Public Key Infrastructure. Active Directory is used to verify a certificate requester's identity. Because it is at the top of the Public Key Infrastructure, the Enterprise Root certificate authority will sign its own CA certificate and then publish that certificate to every Trusted Root certificate authority on the network.

An Enterprise Root certificate authority uses predefined certificate templates for issuing and requesting certificates. When it uses certificate templates, the Enterprise Root certificate can verify user credentials during the certificate enrollment. Each template has an access control list that is evaluated at the time the user makes a certificate request in order to determine if the requester is in fact authorized to receive the template. An example of a template is one created for a smart card logon.

The Enterprise Root certificate authority can be used to issue certificates directly to the user, but it is generally used to authenticate the Enterprise Subordinate certificate authorities. The Enterprise Root certificate authority is integrated with Active Directory, so it helps simplify the issuing and revoking of certificates.

The Enterprise Subordinate certificate authorities are available in two different types: intermediate or issuing certificate authorities. All certificate authorities can issue certificates, but the implementation practice is to use the issuing certificate subordinate certificate authorities to issue certificates. The issuing certificate authorities issue, directly to users, certificates that will support client services such as smart card logons, the Encryption File System, and IP security. The intermediate certificate authority's job is not to issue user certificates, but to generate a certificate for issuing certificate authority validation and to provide a link in the chain back to the root certificate authority. If the Enterprise Root certificate authority itself signed its own certificate, the subordinate certificate authority gets its certificate from another certificate authority.

Not all Windows 2000 environments use Active Directory, which generates the need for the other two types of certificate authorities. When the environment does not have Active Directory services or is not a member in a Windows 2000 domain, the certificate authorities are referred to as stand-alone certificate authorities. The Standalone Root is at the very top of the certificate structure, but the stand-alone subordinate certificate authorities can be an intermediate or issuing certificate, much as in the Enterprise environment.

When the root certificate authority is determined, you must decide on the type of certificate authority to use as a subordinate. The common practice is to make the subordinate certificate authority of the same type as its root certificate authority. After you determine the use of Enterprise or stand-alone certificate authority, you must define each certificate authority's function and role. The administrator defines the primary role of the certificate authority and the type of certificate it can issue, and the administrator also indicates the users who can receive each certificate type.

Trust and Validation

When a receiver receives a signed message, the signature can be validated through the use of the sender's public key and a mathematical process. The receiver must be sure that the public key truly belongs to the sender; if Bob was the sender, Alice needs proof that this is Bob's public key.

This is where the certificate authority enters the validation process, providing the proof the receiver is looking for in the public key that was used. Receivers will look for a certificate for the sender's public key in a certificate authority they implicitly trust. They need to know that a certificate:

- Was issued by a trusted issuer
- Assures a binding between the sender and the sender's public key
- Has a valid signature from its issuer

The receiver uses the public key of the issuing certificate authority to verify the certificate.

The receiver needs to be sure that the public key of the certificate authority used to verify the sender's public key is not an impersonator. This chain reaction of verifying the verifier will continue up the certificate authority hierarchical structure. In the final step, a certificate issued to some certificate authority that the receiver implicitly trusts is used. This certificate, which does not require authentication, is known as a Trusted Root certificate, because it is at the very top of a hierarchy of keys and identities bindings accepted as truthful. When the certificate authority hierarchy is created, the parent-child relationship is established. A user who trusts a particular root certificate implicitly trusts all the certificates issued by the root and its subordinate certificate authorities.

Figure 9.5 shows the Certificate snap-in of the Microsoft Management Console. The left pane breaks the user certificate authorities down into five different groupings. The Trusted Root certificate authorities object has been expanded, and the list of Trusted Root certificate authorities is displayed in the right pane. From this interface, a user can add or remove a Trusted Root certificate authority.

Certificate authorities form a hierarchy that can be called the trust chain. Each member in the chain has a signed certificate held by a superior authority. The root certificate authority is trusted by everyone, and its private key is unknown to anyone. A receiver of a document will go up the chain until a trusted certificate authority is located. As a result, each subordinate certificate authority's public key is identified by its issuing superior certificate authority.

Figure 9.5 The Certificates snap-in of the MMC.

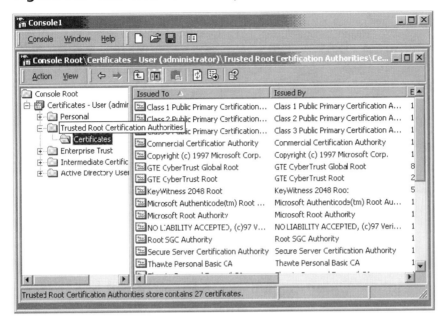

Windows 2000 PKI Components

In order to protect your organization on the Internet, you must use cryptographic technologies to create a secure infrastructure. Microsoft has built a comprehensive Public Key Infrastructure into the Windows 2000 operating system. The Public Key Infrastructure is designed to take full advantage of the Windows 2000 security architecture, and through public key cryptography, digital certificates, and certificate authority, it provides a flexible, secure infrastructure that is easy to use.

Any Public Key Infrastructure is a defined set of operating system and application services that makes the use of public key cryptography a seamless process. The PKI does not in any way replace or override the domain trust and authorization process based on the domain controller and Kerberos Key Distribution Center, but in fact enhances scalability. Because security is based on key use, a Public Key Infrastructure must give the administrator the ability to create and issue new keys as well as the ability to revoke any existing key. The Public Key Infrastructure must provide the client with a way to locate and retrieve a needed public key without any additional effort. When these two capabilities are in place, the application programmers can build even more secure applications.

It is commonly thought that Public Key Infrastructure is a single item, but PKI is really a collection of various components that work together to allow public cryptography to occur and at the same time are transparent to clients. Since operating systems provide numerous infrastructures, it should be no surprise in finding that Public Key Infrastructure is implemented in the Windows 2000 operating system.

Figure 9.6 shows the components of the Windows 2000 Public Key Infrastructure. The client machine is the focal point for all other components. In this view the components are identified but are not reflected on any physical piece of hardware.

Figure 9.6 The components of the Windows 2000 Public Key Infrastructure.

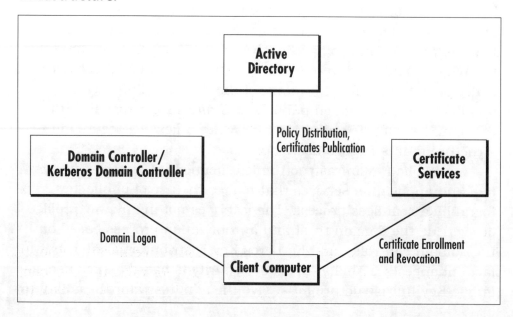

At the base of Windows 2000 Public Key Infrastructure is the Microsoft Cryptographic API, which provides the two major services for public key security: a cryptographic service and a certificate management service. The certificate management service is responsible for X.509 version 3 digital certificates. The cryptographic service is responsible for key generation, message hashing, digital signatures, and encryption. The Microsoft Cryptographic API makes available any installable cryptographic service providers. As Figure 9.7 shows, other services can benefit from using the Microsoft Cryptographic API to provide even more functionality for developers.

Figure 9.7 Services that benefit from the Cryptographic API.

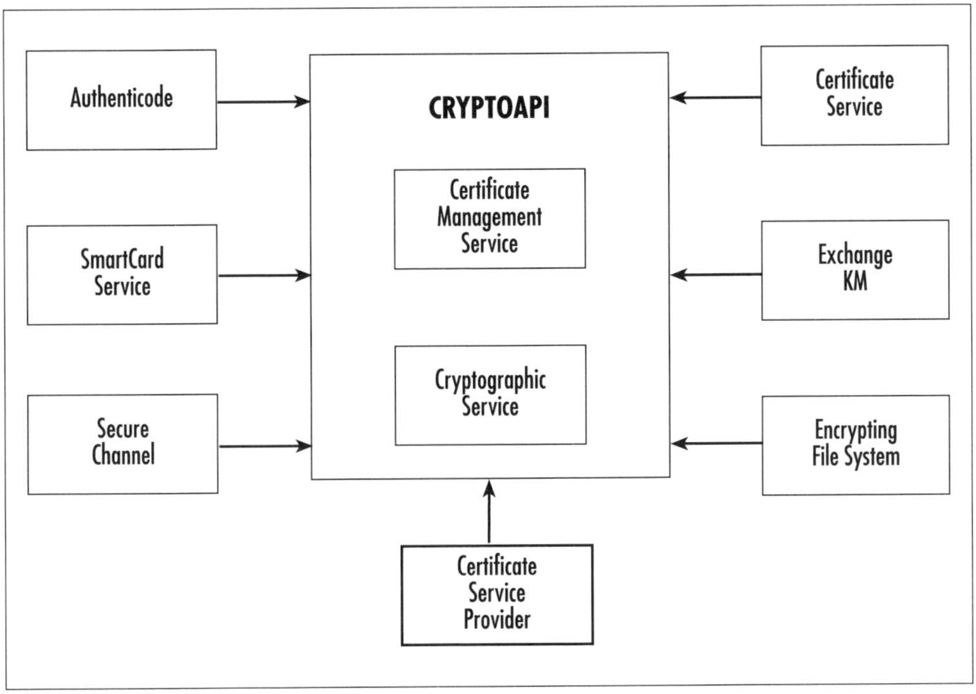

Certificate Authorities

The issuer of a Public Key Certificate is called the certificate authority. Any certificate authority has the responsibility for validating the identity of a person or organization and for associating that entity with the key pair it issued. The user places trust in the certificate authority's ability to distinguish between authorized and unauthorized certificate requests. The certificate authority stores and maintains the list of the certificates it has issued.

Windows 2000 contains a new version of the Microsoft Certificate Server Service. The original Certificate Server Service appeared in the IIS 4.0 for Windows NT 4.0 operating system. It was through this server that keys and X.509v3 certificates were issued and managed. The Certificate Server 1.0 allowed the user to use an Internet browser to retrieve or request the identification of certificate authority certificates.

The Certificate Service for Windows 2000 includes the ability to:

- Issue certificates to users, computers, or services
- Identify the requesting entity
- Validate certificate requests, as allowed under the Public Key security policy
- Support the local enterprises CAs as well as external CAs

Certificate Hierarchies

As with most hierarchical structures, the Public Key Infrastructure hierarchy makes administration easier and improves scalability. The hierarchy can contain one or more well-defined parent-child relationships. Multiple unconnected hierarchies may be implemented in environments that do not require that all certificate authorities share one top-level certificate authority parent.

The certificate authority at the very top of a certificate hierarchy is referred to as a root certificate authority. There is no one above the root CA, so nobody can vouch for its authenticity, and the root CA will simply sign its own certificate. Since the signing of its own identity is not really secure for the root certificate authority, a third party is often used to verify a root CA's certificate; thus verification of the entire certificate chain is possible. Children are issued certificates from the parent certificate authority.

Figure 9.8 Trusted Root certificate authorities.

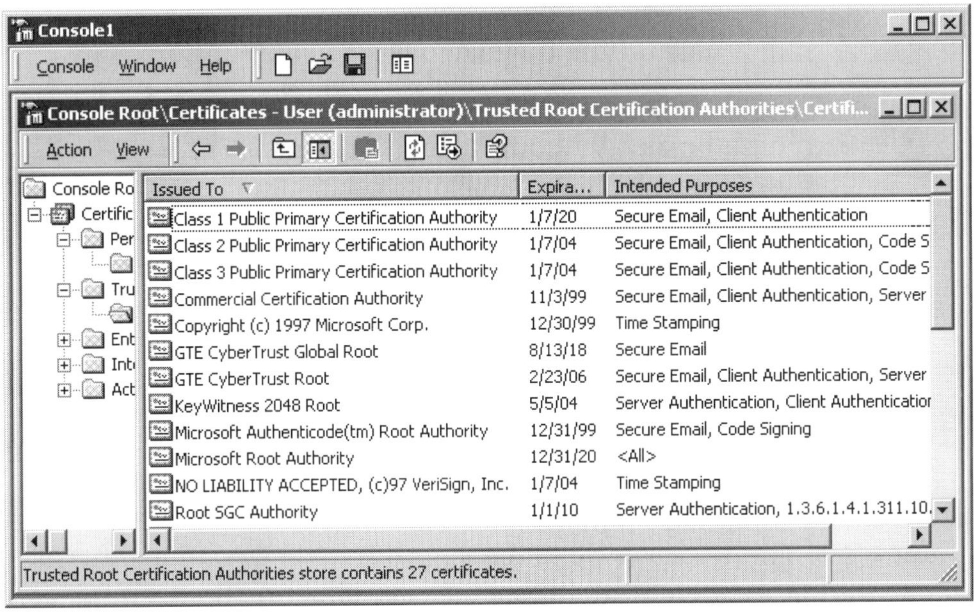

Any environment can have more than one Trusted Root certificate authority. Figure 9.8 shows one environment that contains 27 Trusted Root certificate authorities. The Windows 2000 dialog box not only displays the CAs but can also include the expiration date and the intended purpose for each listed CA.

When you set up your Public Key Infrastructure, you must choose a certificate authority hierarchical structure to implement. Each model comes with its own advantages and disadvantages. It is necessary to understand each hierarchy in order to plan Public Key Infrastructure deployment.

The practical reasons for supporting a model containing multiple certificate authorities may include:

- **Use.** Certificate may be issued for defined purposes such as smart card logons, and separation will provide a basis for administering different policies.

- **Geographic.** A large organization may have entities at multiple remote sites. The network connections between the multiple sites may require separate issuing certificate authorities.

- **Flexible configuration.** The most important certificate authority is the root, so you may decide to physically secure the computer and also install some special cryptographic hardware.

- **Shutdown.** Multiple certificate authorities enable you to turn off a branch without having an impact on the certificate authority hierarchy.

- **Organizational divisions.** A large organization may have entities at multiple remote sites. The network connectivity between the multiple sites may require separate issuing certificate authorities.

Deploying an Enterprise CA

The administrator does not have to configure a one-to-one relationship between the established Windows domains and the certificate authorities. The Windows domains may have trust relationships configured in a different way than the relationships between the certificate authorities. The bottom line is that the trust between domains and the trusts between the certificate authorities do not need to be mapped into a one-to-one relationship. A single certificate authority can be used by numerous Windows domains. A single domain can use multiple certificate authorities.

Microsoft recommends that the domains be created before the needed certificate authorities are set up on the network. Due to the hierarchical structure, the first certificate authority should be the root CA. The very top of the hierarchical structure is the root certificate authority, which automatically generates a self-signed CA certificate using its own key pair. The root certificate authority will also generate CA certificates for any of its subordinate certificate authorities.

A subordinate is a child to a parent and can take on one of two roles. A subordinate may be an intermediate certificate authority that is not a root but whose only purpose is to create certificates for other certificate authorities. The subordinate's other role is as an issuing certificate authority, and it has the responsibility of issuing end-entity certificates.

When child certificate authorities are installed, a certificate request is generated and is submitted to the parent certificate authority, which would be either an intermediate CA or the root CA. The certificate request can be sent automatically to the parent certificate authority defined in Active Directory; otherwise, the installer will have to get the certificate request to the parent certificate authority manually. When the certificate request is processed and a certificate is returned to the child, it must be installed before the certificate authority can become operational.

As with many services, Windows 2000 has a wizard to ease the installation of the certificate service. The wizard walks the installer through the entire process, periodically requesting input. Preplanning will, as always, make the installation run more smoothly. Before installing the Certificate Service, the administrator needs to identify what computer should run the service, considering such factors as current workload, physical security, connectivity, load balancing, and available hardware. The determination of the certificate name should involve some thought, because all issued certificates are tied to the certificate authority name of the issuer. After the certificate authority is created, there is no rename capability available. It is easiest to use the organizational naming convention probably already established for your organization.

During the Certificate Service installation, a public key pair will be generated for the certificate authority that is being created. This key pair is unique to the certificate authority. The installation process involves Active Directory, in that a certificate authority object and information about the CA configuration are added to Active Directory. If the environment does not include Active Directory service, the administrator has to add the certificate object and its information manually.

Trust in Multiple CA Hierarchies

The word "hierarchy" implies more than one level, and for most environments the Public Key Infrastructure will have more than one certificate authority. The Public Key Infrastructure of Windows 2000 must deal with the trust relationships across the multiple certificate authorities. The multiple CA hierarchies could be within the organization, or they could be other organizations that can include commercial certificate authorities as well as private CAs.

The system administrator has to create and enforce the certificate-authority-based trust relationships. For each individual Trusted Root certificate authority, the administrator has the ability to restrict the use of certificates that are created by the CA. An example would be a Trusted Root certificate authority that has been configured to validate only certificates issued by a CA for digital signatures; the same CA has to be set up to issue certificates for any purpose.

The user with the Public Key Infrastructure has the ability to add certificate authority trust relationships. Any trust relationship added by users has an effect only on themselves.

Multiple certificate authorities outside Windows 2000 sometimes are configured to use cross certificates, which provide a way to create a chain of trust from a single Trusted Root certificate authority to numerous other certificate authorities. The Windows 2000 environment can process such cross certificates and involve them in making trust decisions, but they are not a necessity in the Microsoft Public Key Infrastructure model. Microsoft's model excludes the use of cross certificates for these sound reasons:

- They are not really a necessity with Microsoft's model.

- Additional administrative work is needed to generate the cross certificates and to maintain them.

- Cross certificates were processed when current business agreements did not cover their use.

- Final evaluation within an organization, when certificate authorities implement distinct policies, is uncertain.

Enabling Domain Clients

One of the necessary components for any Public Key Infrastructure is the ability to generate and manage keys while making any activity being performed transparent to the user. To meet this requirement, Microsoft has written into the Windows 2000 operating system a set of core services that support development and use of public-key-based applications. Through the use of Active Directory, application management within any enterprise is integrated with the domain administration and policy. The core application services of Windows 2000 are designed for interoperability of the public key algorithms across the enterprise.

Generating Keys

To use a Public Key Infrastructure, the software must be able to generate and manage keys. The design of Windows 2000 allows installable Cryptographic Service Providers that will handle these two major tasks. The CryptoAPI defines standard interfaces that are the same for all Cryptographic Service Providers.

The way public key pair information is stored is dependent on the Cryptographic Service Provider being used. The Microsoft-provided CSP stores key information for a user or computer in any encrypted form. Microsoft's Cryptographic Service Provider allows full control over the use and export of the public key information. There is a CRYPT_EXPORTABLE flag that must be set before the key is generated in order to allow private key export from the CSP. Microsoft has also included a CRYPT_USER_PROTECT flag that can be used to notify the user when an application tries to use the user's private key. Other Cryptographic Service Providers may implement similar or different control mechanisms.

Key Recovery

Key recovery is compatible with the CryptoAPI architecture of Windows 2000, but it is not a necessary requirement. For key recovery, an entity's private key must be stored permanently. The storage of private keys guarantees that critical information will always be accessible, even if the information should get corrupted or deleted. On the other hand, there is a security issue in the backup of the private keys. The archived private key should be used to impersonate the private key owner only if corruption occurs on your system.

Windows 2000 does provide the ability to back up and restore the key pairs and their certificates through the Certificate Manager snap-in for the MMC. The exporting of a certificate can involve just the certificate, or the certificate and the associated key pair. If the associated key pair is exported, the information is encrypted as a PKCS-12 (Public Key Cryptography Standards) message. In the restoring of certificates and key pairs onto any system, the administrator uses the import function of the Certificate Manager.

Before doing an export operation of the certificate and public key pairs, the administrator should look at the cryptographic service provider being used. When the Microsoft cryptographic service provider is used, the exporting of key pairs will occur only if the exportable flag CRYPT_EXPORTABLE was set at the time the key was created. Some third-party Cryptographic Service Providers may not support the backup and the restoration of key pairs and their certificates. When this is the case, only a complete system image backup is possible.

Certificate Enrollment

The guarantee that the public key is truly owned by the entity lies in the public-key-based certificates. The Windows 2000 Public Key Infrastructure includes certificate enrollment to the Microsoft Enterprise certificate authority or to other third-party CAs.

The certificate enrollment used by Microsoft in Windows 2000 is based on the industry-standard PKCS-10 and PKCS-7. PKCS-10 is the standard for a certificate request message, and PKCS-7 contains the issued certificate or certificate chain. The Windows 2000 operating system currently supports certificates based on RSA key and signatures, Diffie-Hellman keys, and Digital Signature Algorithm (DSA) keys and signatures.

The Microsoft-supplied enrollment control XENROLL.DLL provides support for both PKCS-10 and PKCS-7. The dynamic link library allows enrollment to be Web based by use of scripts or through Interprocess Communication mechanisms such as RPCs and DCOM. Enrollment can be completed through e-mails, an enrollment wizard, and a policy-driven enrollment that occurs as part of the logon process. The enrollment allows the calling application to supply the needed attributes in the PKCS-10 message request. The certificate enrollment provides for the creation of an internal binding between the certificate, the key pair container, and the Cryptographic Service Provider. In the future, the certificate enrollment will be implemented under Certificate Request Syntax, which is an Internet Architecture Board (IAB) protocol that is currently in the draft stage.

Renewal

Much like a credit card's expiration date, a certificate, for security reasons, should be valid only for a period of time. The certificate renewal is processed more efficiently than the certificate enrollment, because the renewal certificate will contain the same attributes as the existing certificate, so verification is not needed. Currently in Windows 2000, only automatic enrolled certificates support renewal and may use the existing public key or a new public key. All other generated certificates are handled through a complete certificate enrollment process, including verification.

As with the certificate enrollment, the Internet community is working on a mechanism for defining the message protocol for a renewal certificate. We should expect to see this standard in Windows 2000 as soon as the protocol gets to the official standard stage.

Using Keys and Certificates

In the Windows 2000 operating system, the Local Security Authority Subsystem is in the user mode. This security subsystem in

Windows 2000 must take on additional functions to support the new security features. The Microsoft CryptoAPI subsystem manages both the cryptographic service provider and the certificate stores. Within the Windows 2000 Public Key Infrastructure, the keys are managed by the Cryptographic Service Providers (CSP), while the certificates are managed by the certificate stores.

Certificates and their properties are stored in the certificate stores. These stores are logical stores in that they present a systemwide view of available certificates that may exist on numerous physical stores. The applications can locate and decode the certificates by these services of the CryptoAPI subsystem.

Any Public Key Infrastructure defines five standard certificate stores:

- **CA.** Stores issuing and intermediate certificate authority certificates to use in the certificate hierarchical structure.

- **MY.** Stores a user's or computer's certificates for which the related private key is available.

- **ROOT.** Stores only the self-signed certificate authority certificates for trusted root CAs.

- **TRUST.** Stores the Certificate Trust Lists (CTLs). This is an alternate way to specify a certificate hierarchy.

- **UserDS.** Stores a logical view of a certificate repository that is located in the Active Directory and is used to simplify access to the certificate stores.

Roaming

The logon process of the Windows 2000 operating system allows the user to use any available computer in the domain. Microsoft had to make sure that a user's cryptographic keys and certificates are available wherever logon occurs. The user must be guaranteed to use the same public-key-based application no matter what computer is available for their use.

The Public Key Infrastructure of Windows 2000 supports the roaming user in two ways. The Microsoft-provided Cryptographic

Service Provider allows the roaming profiles to support the roaming use of keys and certificates. As with the Windows NT roaming profile, the process is transparent to the end user when roaming profiles are enabled. The second way to support the use of roaming keys and certificates is through the implementation of hardware devices such as smart cards, which contain the user's certificates and private keys. Because it is the size of a credit card, the smart card can be easily carried by the user.

Revocation

Certificates tend to be issued with an average lifetime of two or three years. Until the expiration date, there could be many reasons to cease trusting the credentials. From a security point of view, any of these circumstances would certainly warrant the revoking of a certificate:

- An entity's private key has been compromised.
- A project with another organization is completed.
- The employee has changed status within the company.
- A department is to cease having access to certain information.
- The certificate was obtained through forgery.

The Windows 2000 public key functions are based on distributed verification, so any revocation of certificates also will be handled in a distributed fashion. There is no need to create a central location for revocation information.

Microsoft designed Windows 2000 revocation around the industry standard certificate revocation lists. The Microsoft Enterprise certificate authority publishes the CRLs to Active Directory. From here the domain clients can obtain the information, cache it to the local machine, and then read it from the cache when certificates are verified. The clients can verify certificates when they use a commercial certificate authority or any third-party CA, as long as the published certificate revocation list is available over the network.

Trust

The client, in any Public Key Infrastructure environment, wants to trust the certificate verification. The client must have confidence in the certificate authority that says that the public key does in fact belong to the entity.

Two conditions must be met before any certificate verification is assumed to be valid. First, the entity's certificate must be shown to be linked to a known Trusted Root certificate authority of the client. Second, the intended certificate's use must be in line with the application. If either of these two conditions are not satisfied, the certificate is assumed to be invalid.

Trust relationships that the client has initially available should be automatically propagated as part of the Enterprise policy. As an exception, Windows 2000 will allow users to install or remove the root certificate authority they want to trust. These trusts affect only the users themselves. Any trust established with a root certificate authority can thus be configured with use restrictions.

PK Security Policy in Windows 2000

Windows 2000 fully uses the Kerberos security standard, thus providing single point logons at the enterprise level. Any policy, which would therefore include the security policy, can be globally established for the entire enterprise, a site, a domain, or an organizational unit. The security policy, once set, would then affect the groups of users or computers defined on the network.

The Public Key security policy is just one element of the overall Windows 2000 security policy and is a component of the Public Key Infrastructure. The security policy will be enforced globally, but for ease of administration, it can be centrally defined and managed.

Trusted CA Roots

Any user with the necessary software can generate a key pair, so there must be some means for the organization to guarantee that a key is in fact valid for a particular user or company. It is the responsibility of the certificate authorities to provide this needed guarantee. The certificate authorities can handle this task easily by storing the public key and maintaining a list of issued certificates.

The structure of the certificate authorities' model has been designed as a hierarchy, which contains multiple certificate authorities with defined parent-child relationships. The certificate authority at the very top of the hierarchy is referred to as a root CA. The children are certified by certificates issued for them by their parent. One advantage of a hierarchical structure over a linear structure is that few trusts are needed with the root certificate authorities.

The Microsoft Management Console Certificate snap-in is the administrative tool used to specify which certificate authority to trust. It is through this application that trusted root certificate authorities are defined so that the proper certificate authority is used by the clients in verifying certificates. If you create a certificate authority, its certificate should be added so it is used as a trusted certificate authority. The trust created by default is for only one computer, but through the group policy editor the certificate authority can be set for global implementation. If there is a certificate authority that you do not want to trust, make sure that this certificate authority is removed.

The hierarchical model allows trust relationships with other organizations to be implemented easily. For example, if ABC Corporation is a subordinate certificate authority of the public root of which XYZ Corporation is also a subordinate, the two corporations automatically trust each other. Figure 9.9 shows the relationship between the two companies and the root certificate authority.

The certificate authority contains numerous properties that are tied to its use. The administrator can use the Microsoft Management Console Certificate snap-in to specify the certificate policy that will control the generation and use of certificates by the CA, as shown in Figure 9.10. When they are specified, the properties will restrict when certificates are valid. A user can use the certificate to validate secure mail but may not be allowed to use the certificate's private

Figure 9.9 A certificate authority's hierarchical structure.

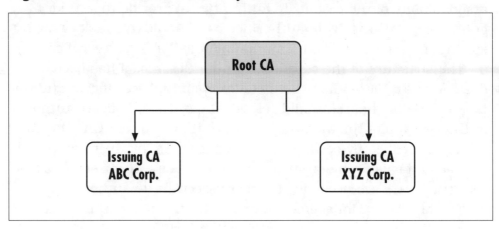

Figure 9.10 Certificate authority properties.

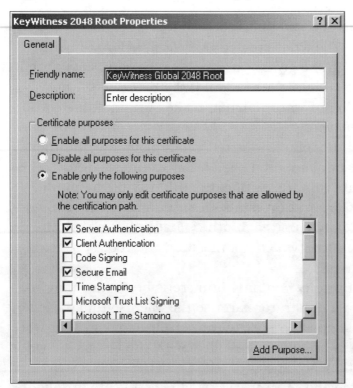

key for digital signatures. These objects may be restricted in any combination:

- Server authentication
- Client authentication
- Code signing
- E-mail
- IP Security end system
- IPSec tunnel
- IPSec user
- Time-stamping
- Microsoft Encrypted File System

To make the public key infrastructure transparent to the user, Windows 2000 had to make it possible to support automatic certificate enrollment, which is controlled by certificate types and auto-enrollment objects. Both of these elements are integrated with the group policy object, so they can be defined at the site, the domain, the organizational unit, the computer, or the user level.

Certificate Enrollment and Renewal

Certificate types are templates used to define policies that control the generation and use of a certificate. The template is identified by having a common name that usually associates with the group for which the template was designed, such as the template named Engineers.

The template defines components that will be incorporated into the certificate, such as:

- Name requirements
- Expiration date
- Cryptographic service provider
- Public Key generation algorithm

Templates are created for users and for computers through the use of the Template Creation Wizard.

Smart Card Logon

Smart card logon is controlled by the policy established with the user object. The policy can be set in one of two ways. The smart card logon policy can be set to enforce smart card logon, so password-based logon is not available. The disadvantage of setting the policy in this fashion is that users must have their smart card and a computer available with a smart card reader in order to log on. The second way to set the policy for smart card logons is to enable smart card logon, which will still allow password-based logons to occur on the network. Both smart card policies will add security to prevent unauthorized access.

Applications Overview

The Public Key Infrastructure gives the Windows 2000 operating system a way to integrate services and tools to manage the public-key-based applications. As application programmers implement the secret-key- or public-key-based security model into their code, organizations gain new security functionality. Some applications already have the public key mechanisms available, because the programmers have made use of the Public Key Infrastructure. When the Public Key Infrastructure has been configured, an application can use the public key cryptography. If it is correctly written, this will keep all the encryption process transparent to the user.

Web Security

Windows 2000 provides support for both Secure Sockets Layer /Transport Layer Security (SSL/TLS) and Server Gated Cryptography (SGC) to ensure secure Web communications. Server Gated

Cryptography is an extension to SSL3.0 that was defined to secure online banking sessions.

The Transport Layer Security can be used to access any kind of Web site. Due to export restrictions, the Transport Layer Security comes in a 128-bit and 40-bit encryption version. The secure channel is established by the use of certificates and public keys. The client will first send a hello message to the server and will then receive the server's certificate. The server is authenticated by the client, using the certificate authority's public key. After the server is guaranteed, the client generates a session key of the appropriate size. The client then secures the session key by encrypting it with the server's public key. When the server receives the encrypted session key, it uses its private key to decrypt this session key. Now both the client and the server will securely use the session key to exchange sensitive data.

The Server Gated Cryptographic process is similar to the Transport Layer Security process. The first major difference is that the server's certificate must come from an authorized certificate authority. Server Gated Cryptography will reset and then restart the handshake after the SGC Certificate is detected. The final major difference between Transport Layer Security and Server Gated Cryptographic is that a 128-bit session key is always generated, even if one party is outside the United States.

To take advantage of TLS and SGC, both the client and the server must have certificates issued by the same trusted certificate authority. Only when the two parties are using a common certificate authority can the parties authenticate each other. The certificates exchanged rely on the use of key pair encryption in order to end up with a secretive session key.

Web security involves the authentication of both the client and the server. It also involves the encryption of data between the two parties to prevent public readability. The client guarantees the server by comparing the certificate authority's public key to the certificate authority's signature on the server's certificate. The server guarantees the client by using its private key to get to the session key. The session key has been encrypted with the public key, so the only way to decrypt the session key is through the private key out of the key pair.

Secure E-mail

Secure e-mail has always been part of the Exchange Server product. Exchange Server's advanced security enables users to keep data private during message transfer through encryption and digital signatures. The Key Management server component stores and manages the security database, and it creates and maintains backups of public and private encryption keys and the Certification Revocation List. Exchange Server supports S/MIME mail, which is part of a PKI.

In order to send an encrypted mail message, first the message is composed that contains the sensitive data. The sender obtains the public key of the receiver. A bulk encryption key is generated, and then the sensitive data is encrypted with this key. After the document is in ciphertext, the bulk encryption key is encrypted, using the receiver's public key. The message is now ready to be delivered. The receiver uses the private key in order to gain access to the bulk encryption key. The receiver then uses the bulk encryption key to return the document to plaintext.

The process of using a digital signature with e-mail will assure both the sender and the receiver that the message has not been tampered with in transit. When the user indicates through the e-mail interface that the message should have a digital signature, the private key is used to hash the message and produce the message digest. The document and the message digest are then sent to the receiver. The e-mail interface will indicate to the receiver that the message contains a digital signature. In the verification of the digital signature, the sender's public key is used to decrypt the digital signature. The document is hashed by the receiver's generating a 128-bit number. If the decrypted digital signature matches the generated 128-bit number, the receiver knows that the sender is really the person who is indicated on the message and that the body of the message has not been tampered with before the receiver received it.

Digitally-Signed Content

Microsoft Public Key Infrastructure includes a code-signing technology, Authenticode, with the release of Windows 2000. As more people use the Internet to download information, the question of security comes to the surface quickly. Authenticode ensures the integrity and origin of software distribution by vendors over the Internet. This is, in effect, a digital signature; Authenticode is based on digital signature technology. Authenticode adds a digital signature, a code-signing certificate, and a timestamp in the downloadable software. The software that Authenticode can guarantee includes Java applets, Active X controls, cabinet files, dynamic link libraries, executable files, and catalog files.

Authenticode does not stop with the download process; it also verifies downloaded code before you use it on your local computer. Authenticode uses code signing and code verification to perform its tasks.

Before you can sign code, you need to obtain a code-signing certificate from a certificate authority. This is sometimes referred to as obtaining a software publishing certificate. With this code-signing certificate, you can then use from the Active X Software Developer's Kit the Authenticode signing functions. The digital signature will be created by a hashing algorithm used on the code you wish to secure, and the private key is then used to sign the hash. The software will then build a signature block that contains the digital signature and the code-signing certificate. The timestamped signature block is then bound to the original software code. At this point you are ready to publish the signed software on your Web site for downloading purposes.

Built into the Internet Explorer is the second technique of Authenticode, code verification. Before any signed code can run, it calls up the code verification function to check three important items: the signature, the publisher's certificate, and the timestamp. A security warning window will display the name of the code, the name of the organization, when the publisher authenticated the code, and the name of the certificate authority that issued the code-signing certificate. The user has the ability at this time to decide to accept or reject the published software. Figure 9.11 shows a security warning window received while the Internet Explorer application is used.

Figure 9.11 A Windows Security Warning dialog box.

Internet Explorer allows the user to set up a security policy for Authenticode with four security levels: high, medium, low, and custom. Table 9.1 identifies each security level.

Table 9.1 Security Levels

Level	Function
High	Does not execute damaged code.
Medium	Warns you before running potentially damaged code.
Low	Always runs the code.
Custom	Can choose the security level setting for software codes and security zones.

Encrypting File System

Windows 2000 enables users to encrypt files that contain sensitive information as long as they are stored on a NTFS partition. The Encrypting File System can be set at both the directory and the file level and is transparent to users when they have indicated that they want encryption to be implemented. Applications will have access to encrypted objects in the same fashion as nonencrypted objects.

Windows 2000 uses both symmetric and asymmetric algorithms to encrypt a file. The file is encrypted using the secret File Encryption Key, along with the DESX algorithm. To protect the File Encryption Key from hackers, it is then encrypted by the owner's public key. This means that the owner's private key is needed in order to decrypt the file.

No additional configuration steps are needed for the user who works with sensitive data. When the file or directory is marked for encryption, all the encrypting and decrypting activity is transparent to the user. The user can identify for the operating system what files are to be encrypted through either Windows Explorer or the Cipher command line utility.

The Encrypting File System also supports a recovery policy in the Windows 2000 operating system. The administrator has to designate trusted Recovery Agents, which generate a recovery key pair and will be issued a certificate by the certificate authority. The certificates of the Recovery Agents are published to domain clients with the group policy object.

Smart Card Logon

Smart card service can be implemented as a component of the Public Key Infrastructure in Windows 2000. A smart card is about the size of a credit card and can store the owner's certificates and private keys on an erasable programmable ROM, so changes can be made if necessary. The smart card is protected by a password and runs a card operating system that resides in ROM. The smart card requires that a smart card reader be attached to the user's computer.

The portability of the smart card allows the user to store an issued certificate and use the certificate whenever needed. The International Organization for Standards (ISO) developed the ISO 7816 standard for smart card hardware. The Personal Computer/Smart Card group specified standards for smart card, smart card readers on the PCs. Microsoft also has a device-independent smart card Software Development Kit for programmers.

One major important use of the smart card is for public key logon. In this process, the private certificate is used to log on a Windows 2000 domain. You must supply your secret PIN after inserting the smart card into the smart card reader. Windows 2000 authenticates you as the true owner of the smart card, because the PIN you entered matched the PIN on record. The Local Security Authority will send the certificate, found on the smart card, to its Kerberos Key Distribution Center. The certificate's issuer and validation are checked by the KDC. After the KDC completes the verification, Active Directory is referenced for your user object. After the object is founded, the ticket-granting ticket is built. For security purposes, the ticket-granting ticket is encrypted with a session key by the Windows 2000 domain controller. You can then use your public key to encrypt the session key. After the encrypted ticket-granting ticket is received by the smart card, you decrypt the session keyby using the private key on your smart card. Finally, the Local Security Authority logs you on the Windows 2000 domain.

Smart card logon can be either enabled or enforced. When a smart card use is just enabled, the password-based logon can still be used by the user. If the Smart Card policy is changed to enforced, users will not be able to log on if they forgot their smart card or if the only available computer does not contain a smart card reader.

IP Security (IPSec)

IPSec is a protocol that implements network encryption at the IP protocol layers. IPSec uses state-of-the-art cryptography techniques and does not require a public key algorithm. A public key algorithm provides the organization with a distributed trust environment that can be scaled to any size. The Internet Engineering Task Force has implemented IPSec devices so that through the use of public key algorithms they can mutually authenticate each other and agree on encrypting keys.

IPSec was designed for interoperability and is independent of the current cryptographic algorithms, so it will be able to support new changes as they become available. IPSec is a mandatory part of IPv6 and is also supported by IPv4.

Microsoft, as a member of the IPSec workgroup, is actively working on these standards to support interoperable certificates and the management and enrollment protocols. The Windows 2000 operating system is designed to support any new standard evolved from the IETF.

Preparing for Windows 2000 PKI

Microsoft Exchange Server is a useful tool for an organization preparing to use Windows 2000's Public Key Infrastructure. S/MIME is based on a Public Key Infrastructure, and it allows Exchange clients to encrypt mail and send digitally-signed messages. The Exchange Server product allows the Public Key Infrastructure to exist within the entire organization, and it also allows support to exchange keys to other organizations outside your own.

If you are just starting to use Exchange Server, Microsoft recommends that you install version 5.5 along with Service Pack 3. The client software to be used in your Public Key Infrastructure should be Microsoft Outlook 2000, which supports S/MIME e-mail. The Public Key Infrastructure is built around these components:

- A Key Management Server with recovery features
- S/MIME clients using CryptoAPI
- LDAP-based Exchange directory services
- Certificate Authority X.509 version 3

Public Key Infrastructure Standards

Public Key Infrastructure standards that are written into the Windows 2000 operating system are listed in the Table 9.2.

Table 9.2 Public Key Infrastructure Standards

Standard	Defines	Why included
Secure Sockets Layer—V3	Encryption for Web Sessions	Security Procotol used on the Internet. Export Restrictions exists.
Server Gateway Cryptography	Secure session between U.S. and other countries for online banking sessions	Used by financial organizations. Always uses 128-bit session key
X.509 Version 3	Digital certificates format and content	Allows certificate exchange between vendors
Certificate Revocation List v2	Format and content of certification lists	Provides revocation information
PKCS family	Format and behavior for public key exchange and distribution	Requests and certificate movement understood by all vendors
PKIX Public Key Exchange	Format and behavior for public key exchange and distribution	New technology that is replacing PKCS family
PC/SC Personal Computer Smart Card	Interface for smart card on PCs	Group-defined standards for smart cards and smart card reader on PCs

Continued

Standard	Defines	Why included
IPSec	Encryption for an IP session	Encrypts the network connection
PKINIT	Log on where Kerberos is used by public key	Allows certificate on smart card to be used as logon credentials

These major components are included in Exchange Server 5.5 and Microsoft Outlook 2000 to protect e-mail messages that contain sensitive information. Microsoft has stated that they will provide a migration path for Exchange users to move to the generalized Public Key Infrastructure that Windows 2000 will implement when the product is released.

Any new product involves the learning process, so include training time in your plans. System administrators need to understand how keys and certificates are used so they can take care of the management side of these new items. It would also be to the system administrators' advantage to do some research on Public Key Infrastructure case studies, which are helpful to anyone setting up a Public Key Infrastructure for the first time. The latest information, which can be obtained on the Microsoft Web site or from TechNet, should be used in preparation for the Windows 2000 Public Key Infrastructure.

Summary

There are three types of cryptographic functions. The hash function uses a mathematical algorithm on the data in order to scramble it. The secret key method of encryption uses a single key to encrypt and decrypt the information. Secret key encryption encrypts a large amount of data quickly and is sometimes referred to as symmetric key cryptography. The disadvantage of secret key encryption is that a secure method must be in place for the parties to exchange the one secret key. The disadvantage of secret key encryption was removed in the 1970s with public key encryption, which is based on the use of key pairs. The public key is made available to everyone, but the private key of the key pair is available only to the owner. Public key encryption is also referred to as asymmetric cryptography. The public key is usually used to encrypt the sensitive data, which means that only the matching private key can decrypt the ciphertext. If a user wants to make information available to everyone with the guarantee that readers are getting information that has not been tampered with, the owner can use the private key to encrypt the data. Under these circumstances the matching public key is needed for the decryption process, and it is available for everyone's use. The disadvantage of public key encryption is that it is slow and therefore cannot protect a large amount of data.

Windows 2000 uses cryptography extensively. A digital signature is a hash value encrypted with a private key. By using the corresponding public key, receivers can be guaranteed that the document contains no modifications and that senders are really who they claim to be. With a digital signature, the document itself is not encrypted. Digital signatures involve the creation of a message digest, which is signed by the sender's private key. A message digest is a 128-bit number generated by hashing the original message.

Public key cryptography can provide authentication instead of privacy. Authentication involves the use of a challenge initiated by the receiver of the data. The challenge can be sent encrypted or in plaintext. Either way, the result is proof for the receiver that the sender is authentic. This type of authentication is referred to as proof of possession. Windows 2000 also uses public key cryptography for bulk data encryption and exchanging a secret key through a nonsecure communication channel.

Certificates are used to provide assurance that the public key used does in fact belong to the entity that owns the corresponding private key. The issuer of a public key certificate is known as a certificate authority. The job of the certificate authority is to validate the identity of a person or organization to the public key.

The certificate hierarchy consists of multiple certificate authorities that have trust relationships established between them. The certificate authority at the very top of the certificate hierarchy is referred to as a root. Nothing is above the root CA, so it simply signs its own certificate. A subordinate is a child to a parent and can take on the role of an intermediate certificate authority or an issuer CA.

The subordinate's certificate is generated by its parent certificate authority. The intermediate certificate authority's purpose is to create certificates for other certificate authorities. The issuer certificate authority is responsible for issuing end entity certificates.

Four types of certificate authorities are available with the Microsoft Certificate. The four types can be broken down into two major categories: Enterprise and Standalone. The Enterprise certificate authorities rely on the Active Directory services of the Windows 2000 operating system. The Standalone certificate authority is implemented when Active Directory or membership in a Windows 2000 domain is not available. The four types of certificate authorities are: Enterprise Root, Enterprise Subordinate, Standalone Root, and Subordinate.

The Public Key Infrastructure is not a single item but rather a collection of various components working together to allow public cryptography to occur. The main components of the Public Key Infrastructure are:

- **Active Directory.** Policy distribution and certificate publication
- **Certificate Service.** Certificate creation and revocation
- **Domain Controller/Kerberos Domain Controller.** Domain logon
- **Client.** Where most of the activity is initiated

The Windows 2000 operating system makes many core application services available to domain clients. For the use of public key encryption, public keys must be generated, and they must be enrolled with a certificate authority. If for some reason a key pair gets lost or corrupted, there must be a way for a client to have key recovery. Keys have an expiration date, so the operating system must include a mechanism for necessary renewal.

Windows 2000 provides core services for domain clients through the Public Key Infrastructure. The generation and use of keys is transparent to the user. The Public Key Infrastructure is a mechanism for creating, renewing, and revoking keys on an as-needed basis. Generated keys can be automatically enrolled with a certificate authority, and in the event of key corruption, the Windows 2000 Public Key Infrastructure makes it possible to recover keys. Since it is possible to log on Windows 2000 with any computer, the Public Key Infrastructure enables clients to use their keys from any network location.

Public key security relies on Trusted Root certificate authority, certificate enrollment and renewal, and smart card logon. The responsibility of the certificate authority is to attest to the public key being used. The top of the hierarchical structure is the Trusted Root certificate authority. Through the Certificate snap-in the Trusted Root certificate authorities are defined. Administrators must add the appropriate Trusted Root certificate authorities and also remove any root certificate authority they do not want to trust. Certificate templates must be created to define policies that control how to create and then use a certificate. Smart card logon is controlled by the policy that has been established with the user. If the policy is set to enforce smart card logons, the user cannot log on without a smart card and a computer with a smart card reader. If the smart card policy is set to Enabled, password logons are still available.

Public Key Infrastructure includes the applications written to support public key encryption. Windows 2000 provides security support for both Transport Layer Security (TLS) and Server Gated Cryptography (SGC). TLS and SGC require both the client and the server to have certificates issued by a certificate authority. Certificate exchanges rely on the use of key pair encryption in order to end up with a secretive session key. E-mail can be secured by using the Exchange Server and Microsoft Outlook products. The process of digital signatures guarantees both the sender and the message for e-mail. Windows 2000 includes a code-signing technology known as Authenticode, which ensures the integrity and origin of software distribution from vendors over the Internet. The Encrypting File System allows any user to encrypt sensitive data by marking the directory or just the individual file for encryption. Windows 2000 also supports smart cards for public key logons.

FAQs

Q: What components are needed to build a complete Public Key Infrastructure?

A: Five major components are needed to build a Public Key Infrastructure. Certificate authorities are needed to issue certificates and for certificate revocation lists. The certification publication point, based on any kind of directory service, makes certificates and the certificate revocation lists available at any time. Any structure needs some kind of management tool, so a Public Key Infrastructure also provides a utility for key and certificate management. The fourth component is the set of well-written applications that make public cryptography transparent to the user when the user has indicated what must be completed. The final component in Public Key Infrastructure is hardware that supports cryptographic technologies. The hardware ranges from smart cards used to store secure keys to PCI cards that handle on-board encryption/decryption processing. The fifth component of a complete Public Key Infrastructure is completely optional.

Q: What are the primary components of the Windows 2000 Public Key Infrastructure?

A: The Microsoft Certificate Services make it possible for you to create your own certificate authorities and to issue and manage digital certificates. This means that the Microsoft Certificate Service is your certificate authority and Management tool. The Active Directory service is your Certificate Publication Point. The third component is the set of well-written applications that work seamlessly with the Windows 2000 Public Key Infrastructure, including Microsoft Internet Explorer and the Internet Information Server, as well as many third-party vendors. The final primary component of Windows 2000 Public Key Infrastructure is a component from the Exchange Server software, the Exchange Key Management Service. The optional hardware support in cryptography is available through the use of smart cards.

Q: Are the security features easy to use?

A: Microsoft has designed the Public Key Infrastructure to be easy to use for everyone, from the end user to the administrator. The Public Key Infrastructure components are included with the Windows 2000 operating system, so there is nothing extra to buy or install. Departments can be set up with their own certificate authorities, because the CA software is part of the operating system. The administrator and the end user can use already familiar tools such as the Microsoft Management Console and Internet Explorer to create certificates, view their certificates, view other certificates, validate their authenticity, and set what certficates are authorized to do. By using Internet Explorer, the user can access the Microsoft Certificate Service to request that a certificate be created. The Certificate Request Wizard will supply appropriate fields, and the request will automatically be forwarded to the appropriate certificate authority. When the certificate is generated, the public key information is automatically stored in Active Directory, and the private information is delivered to the requester.

Q: For the administrator, how easy is the Public Key Infrastructure to maintain?

A: The management of the Public Key Infrastructure is a regular daily task once the Public Key Infrastructure is installed. From the Certificate Service, a Microsoft Management Console snap-in, the administrator can perform the daily PKI maintenance tasks. Most the tasks can be completed by merely selecting the appropriate menu item. Normal maintenance includes:

- Revoking certificates when necessary
- Defining templates for certificate attributes that will automatically be inherited by newly created certificates
- Viewing the certificates and their properties
- Viewing the properties of a certificate revocation list
- Changing group policy settings for users, groups, and computers
- Seeing certificates pending requests
- Viewing failed certificate requests

Q: What does it really mean when people state that you can export DES?

A: In 1996, the U.S. export regulations on cryptography were put under the purview of the Department of Commerce. In the fall of 1998, export restrictions were relaxed. The regulations for exporting cryptographic material and key recovery requirements are:

- The key recovery requirements for export of 56-bit DES and equivalent products are eliminated.
- Export of unlimited strength encryption under license exceptions is now broadened to include others besides the financial industry for 45 countries.
- Export of recoverable products is granted to most commercial firms for a broad range of countries in the major commercial markets, excluding items on the U.S. defense list.
- Export license to end users may be granted on a case-by-case basis.

Q: How does the RSA algorithm really work?

A: The RAS algorithm works this way:

1. Take two large primes, and q. (These must be kept secret.)
2. Find their product (p * q = n).
3. N is called the modulus.
4. Choose a number, e, that is less than n and relatively prime to (p-1)(q-1).
5. Find its inverse ed=1 mod (p-1)(q-1).
6. The public key is the pair (n,e).
7. The private key is the pair (n,d).

Simple RSA encryption could use the equation $c = m\string^e \bmod n$ where e and n are the receiver's public key.

Simple RSA authentication could use the equations:

Sender: $S = m \string^ d \bmod n$, where S is the digital signature created by the sender's private key (d and n).

Receiver: $m = S \string^ e \bmod n$, where e and n are the sender's private key.

Windows 2000 Server Security Fast Track

Introduction

A basic security framework will be presented here. After this foundation is laid, we can move forward into more esoteric questions such as: "What is my organization's security like?" "Do we have a clear security policy?" "If so, what does it say? If not, what do I do?" These types of security issues must be addressed if we are going to have a proper context in which to evaluate any product in terms of its security features, strengths, and weaknesses.

In order to understand the good, bad, and indifferent issues surrounding Windows 2000 security, you must know what is important to you and your organization. If a certain component of the security model presented here is not supported, or supported well enough as defined by the user's security plan, then the network administrator, manager, or executive should go into a Windows 2000 deployment with this in mind. It may be necessary to augment Windows 2000 supplied security mechanisms with third-party or custom solutions. This is fine, but it should be understood beforehand.

What Is Windows 2000 Server Security, and Why Do You Need to Know About It?

Security is important to anyone using a computer. How can you trust what your data tells you? How can you trust other peoples data? Where does Windows 2000 fit into all this? First, let's look at one way to explain what security is.

How Do You Spell "Security"?

The terms "computer security," "information systems security," and "network security" all have different meanings to different people. Depending on your background, experience, and particular area of concern, you may be more focused on different security components than your counterpart in a different industry or environment.

To the chief information officer of a mortgage company, the term "security" might mean secure password protection. Thus, the CIO wants to ensure that only people who should have access to certain information are actually the ones who can get to it. A webmaster for an online shopping site may be concerned with accurately and reliably transmitting credit card information. A human resources manager might be concerned that salary or personal information about company employees remains confidential. All these individuals have security concerns, but in order to take an objective look at security features, we need a framework that addresses a vast array of definitions. In order to do this, we can view security as involving these components:

- Authentication
- Authorization
- Privacy
- Integrity
- Auditability

Each of these components creates a "Secure Environment" when it is implemented individually. When all the components are combined, a secure environment can be created that should be able to make even the most paranoid system administrator sleep at night.

Authentication

It is generally agreed among security circles that before we can do anything with you, we need to know who you are. Authentication, therefore, is the practice and technique involved in doing just that. A nontechnical means of authentication might be producing a driver's license or passport when requested by a law enforcement officer. There are huge parallels in this simple example to the computer systems world of authentication.

By seeing a document that has been issued by a trusted third party (a government agency, department of motor vehicles, and so on) an authenticator, our law enforcement official, in this case, can be assured that the person presenting the document is who he or she claims to be. In a sense, what has happened is that a department, organization, or certificate authority has gone to great lengths to ensure the validity of this person's claim to identity. The document is proof of that investigation and certification by the external entity that this person is who she or he claims to be.

This is the same type of activity that would be performed during the process of logging in to a computer system or secure domain. If the process is providing a password, scanning a bar code or magnetic stripe, giving a fingerprint, retina scan, or blood sample, the end result is the same. All we have done at this point is prove to the concerned parties that you are, in fact, who you claim to be. This is a separate and distinct process from the other components of the security model.

Authorization

Now that we know who you are, we can make decisions as to what you should be able to do. For example, I have a passport issued to me by the government. This is my authentication mechanism. Having one of these, and being able to prove who I am, has nothing to do with whether or not it is legal for me to drive a car, fly a plane, practice medicine, or any number of other things that I need special authorization to do.

Continuing this idea through our computer model, authorization becomes the act of allowing or disallowing operations on objects. Am I allowed to perform the delete operation on this file? Am I allowed to change the permissions associated with this printer? Am I allowed to edit the contents of this directory? These are all authorization decisions. It also follows that in order to make correct authorization decisions, I must already know who you are. This is what binds authentication and authorization together. If I know who you are, I can then enforce what you can and cannot do. There is no point to authorization without authentication; nor is there any sense in my authenticating you unless it matters to me (or my system) from an authorization standpoint.

For example, the FAT file system we had with DOS was perfectly adequate for years. We had no authentication process on DOS machines because we had no permissions on the file system. There was no need to authenticate users, because we had no authorization scheme anyway!

Privacy

In broad terms, privacy deals with making sure that a conversation I have with someone else is not subject to interception and interpretation by someone other than the individual I intend to communicate with. In the computer world, this includes conversations with myself, such as files I am working with. It also includes conversations with others, such as a credit card I am sending across the Internet.

Generally, when we are talking about privacy in information circles, we are talking about encryption. Encrypted messages, stored data, and the like allow me a certain guarantee that only the recipient for whom I intend the message is able to read it. This may have relative weighting issues as well. For example, it may take an unintended recipient a week to decrypt my message and read it. If the nature of the data is such that its privacy is irrelevant to me five minutes after I send it, then this is acceptable. If, on the other hand, it is important to me that this data be private for a month, then the encryption used to prevent unauthorized access for one week is insufficient.

Note that I used the term "unauthorized access." Those able to read my private message or data are determined by authorization, which in turn relies on authentication.

Integrity

If you present a $50 bill to a store clerk, the presumption is that the Treasury Department in fact issued the bill you are using, and therefore it will be honored. If you write a check at the store, you may be asked for one or more pieces of identification to prove that you are the one who can spend money from that account. Did you ever skip a day of school only to be asked to produce a signed note from a parent authorizing such activity? These are all examples of data integrity issues.

Integrity deals with the idea that if you get an e-mail from me, you can be sure it really came from me and that it has not been tampered with on the way to you. Integrity deals with the idea that if I put data down on a disk and pick it up later, it is in the same condition as it was when I wrote it out.

Auditability

Finally, we need to be able to audit events that occur. This means being able to track a series of events in time. We must trust that we can accurately reconstruct or observe these events in the order that they occurred. We may need to understand who was involved in the events occurring, what data was or was not changed, and so on. Auditability involves the logs, trails, messages, and histories kept by a system as it is being used. This differs from other system messages that might report errors.

When the auditability of a system is examined, we generally refer to being able to define what events are important to us without restriction from the system. We want to be like accountants, tracking the cash flow through a business. If petty cash accounts are not important to us, we should be able to ignore them. If accesses to certain data are unimportant to us, we should not be bothered with those details. However, if reading, writing, accessing, or changing something is important to us, we should be able to get that information quickly, accurately, and without concern for the integrity of the trail we are viewing.

The Component Security Model

Just as the network folks have their seven-layer OSI model, information security has its multilayered model. Table 10.1 summarizes these components and describes their responsibilities. It should become apparent that the broad term "security" refers to several possible concerns. The next time someone asks you about security, ask them what is meant by the term. Most computer professionals have little or no idea that several very specific pieces go into making a security model.

Table 10.1 Security Components

Component	Provides	Example
Authentication	Confirms identity	Username/Password, thumbprint, voice recognition
Authorization	Allows/disallows access	Read/Write privileges to a file, print to a printer, see the contents of a directory
Privacy	Confidentiality	IP Security Model (IPSec), Data Encryption Standard (DES), RSA Inc. Encryption
Integrity	Trust in the source	PKI, Secure RPC
Auditability	History	Log files

Bringing It All Together: A Security Policy

A security policy is the implementation of these components to achieve a desired result. If we combine these components and examine what needs to happen at each of the different layers, we can then discuss an organization's security policy and how a given set of products or technologies might support this policy. If we determine that a product correctly supports the privacy component of our policy, for example, we can then determine whether its other characteristics are acceptable. These characteristics might include things like price, usability, deployment, management tool set, total cost of ownership, and integration with our existing and future systems.

Now that we have all the pieces in place, we can see that the CIO who was concerned with his data only being viewed by those who need to view it actually had several security concerns. He or she was expressing a data privacy concern. Since privacy relies on authorization (who should and should not be able to do something), we first need to determine who a person is (authentication) before applying authorization.

The webmaster with the credit card problem needed to be sure that the data had integrity. He or she needs to make sure that the person performing the transaction is authorized to do so, and that the credit card number, order information, shipping information, and the like was what the customer intended. There is also a privacy issue, in that the customer probably does not want the conversation to be heard by unauthorized eavesdroppers.

The human resources manager also has security concerns that address many, if not all, of these individual components.

Armed with an understanding of what security is, and how it affects us, let's take a look at Windows 2000 and examine how these security components might be addressed by the Windows 2000 operating system.

The Historical Perspective: A Review of Windows NT Security

In the dawn of the information age, all computing was done in a central location, which was usually a well-protected "glass house" with many smart people being paid very well to keep the organization's computer running. With all the processing done here, the only way for users to interact with the processing of the computer was via terminals that provided windows into the tasks that the computer was performing. Breaching security here essentially amounted to breaching the authorization process by intercepting a user's name and password combination. While this was at times sufficient to create some havoc in the system, the most that could be done was limited to reading, printing, or altering data that the impersonator had access to via the stolen identity. Today, however, with the increasing dependence upon computing machines for so many common daily tasks, the role of security has increased dramatically. As the computing power available in "user space" increases, and more and more connectivity becomes available, this encourages remote access and manipulation of datasets. The security issues become more complex.

We don't want to make our security policies and tools discourage use of the system we are protecting. We do not want to be so prohibitive as to discourage use of the system. For example, if we made access to our electronic commerce site so difficult as to discourage unauthorized access, we might in fact turn shoppers away too! The use of several difficult passwords, with frequent changes as a requirement inside a network, might have the users making little yellow sticky notes as the password storage medium of choice, thereby defeating the whole password scheme! While the social aspects of security are still open to definition by managers and IT professionals, Windows 2000 can help quite a bit with the technical issues involved.

Since the beginning, Windows NT has provided outstanding support for each of the security model components. In small, medium, and large enterprise environments, Microsoft has addressed these security concerns in a fairly consistent manner. Let's take a quick look at how these security components were handled in Windows NT versions 3.x and 4.0.

Authentication

In a small workgroup model, NT has provided us with the Security Accounts Manager (SAM) database. Each Windows NT machine maintains this database of users and related information. As a result, each machine's administrator can decide whether this machine should authenticate a user; if so, what the parameters for authentication are; and how these parameters should be enforced. Examples of this include password length, password expiration parameters, and forced password changes. Giving this authentication authority to each system in the network allows the owners of each system the ability to decide who they will authenticate, and how. This is a great solution unless you have a small IT team responsible for hundreds or thousands of systems. For this, Windows NT provided us with the Domain Security model.

In the Domain Security model, authentication is centralized on domain controllers. These machines are responsible for storing, managing, and replicating user and machine account authentication information. Each machine in the network still maintains its own SAM database and can authenticate users on its own, but in a large environment, having each machine trust a central repository of authentication information is not only easier; it would be impractical to do it any other way. By allowing authentication to take place centrally, a user account need exist only in one place. This account may then be granted rights to any machine or object in the security domain.

If there are too many machines and users to manage in a single domain, trust relationships can be created between domains. These trust relationships essentially allow one domain's controllers to authenticate the legitimacy of a user who is requesting access to a resource in another domain. Before this happens, however, the administrator or administrators responsible for these domains must create the trusted relationship. Effectively, one or more domains "trust" one or more other domains to authenticate a user's identity.

Figure 10.1 The authentication models in Windows NT.

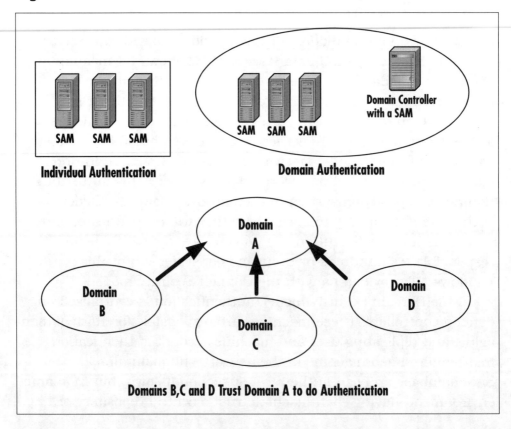

Authorization

Windows NT provides two basic file system authorization mechanisms. The NTFS file system and its associated Access Control Lists provide file system level authorization. This allows an administrator to create pairs of entries in an ACL that list a user (who was authenticated as above), and the things that they can do to the file system: Read, Write, Change, List, and so on. This authorization is located on the disk, close to the data, and will be enforced whether the user logs on locally or across the network.

Windows NT's network access permissions, sometimes called "share permissions," govern what a user may or may not do when accessing a file system across the a network. These work in the same way as NTFS permissions on the file system work: by using ACLs.

When all these permissions are used in conjunction with each other, the resulting permission set is a combination of both access permissions and NTFS permissions.

Privacy

Windows NT 3.x and 4.0 support some encrypted network protocols such as CHAP and PAP for allowing encrypted remote logons over nonsecure lines. Windows NT also provides support for Virtual Private Networks but provides no on-disk file system encryption to ensure privacy. This was actually considered a security hole, as data placed on tape backups would be considered vulnerable to attack and compromise.

Integrity

Much of the data integrity in Windows NT is based on the concept of the Remote Procedure Call (RPC). The RPC architecture has been in use in other operating systems such as various UNIX implementations, and has been defined in the Open Group's Distributed Computing Environment. Since Windows requires machine accounts in a secure domain, we can use the same type of authentication for machines as we used for our user accounts. Therefore, we can challenge a machine sending a RPC to prove its identity. By doing this, we can guarantee that all who send us data via an RPC call are who they claim to be, thus providing a level of integrity.

Auditability

Logging of security events has been with us since the beginnings of Windows NT. Using the Event Viewer, an administrator can audit security events, including successful/unsuccessful logons, permissions usage, object access, and the like. This is an important and often overlooked aspect of a security story. An administrator must have an audit trail that keeps track of such things in order to claim a complete understanding of who is doing what to a system.

Important Features or Design Changes

Since Windows NT's release and resulting adoption by industry as a standard computing platform, many issues have arisen around security issues in the enterprise environment. As a result, Microsoft has enhanced many security features in Windows 2000. These include, but are not limited to:

- Adoption of the Kerberos v5 authentication standard
- Implementation of Public Key Infrastructure (PKI) support
- Encryption of the NTFS file system
- IPSec—Cryptographic Services for IP
- Inclusion of Security Management Snap-ins for MMC

Industries and Companies Affected by Windows 2000 Security

Clearly, the prolific nature of the Windows family of operating systems is going to continue for the foreseeable future. The older, legacy Windows NT 3.x and 4.0 operating systems and Windows 2000 will not only continue to be used by industry, government, and small and large businesses, but will most likely be found in more and more environments as we move into the twenty-first century. The addition of these new security features and enhancement of existing security mechanisms will no doubt aid in the adoption of the Windows operating system into more mission-critical and security-sensitive areas.

Increased confidence in the secure nature of Windows 2000 should allow for its increased use in government and military applications. C2 Level security—the type required by many government organizations—was available in a previous version of Windows NT, which provided that the computer would not be attached to a network, that various service packs would be installed, and so on. Many industry observers expect that the introduction of Kerberos and IPSec will allow Windows 2000 Server to become C2 certified, even when it is attached to a network, much like competitor Novell and its NetWare product line, which have had C2 Level certification for many years.

This added security certification has connotations in the private sector as well. In addition to companies that perform contract services for government agencies, several specific industries would benefit from stronger Windows operating system security including:

- Medical
- Insurance
- Financial
- Education

This includes, essentially, any industry that deals with information considered sensitive and that needs authorization to access, privacy to store or transmit, and integrity to guarantee the originator or recipient.

One huge business sector is the booming e-commerce arena. This single area of the technological world has the potential to touch virtually all business activities and personal business transactions. A

1998 Forester Research report predicts the growth of electronic commerce activity to exceed $3 trillion by the year 2001. Transactions in retail, wholesale, business-to-business, services, merchandise, and information services are moving toward an electronic marketplace. The Internet certainly has a place here, but so do technologies that allow wholesalers, suppliers, purchasers, and the like to conduct transactions privately. Any additional security that can be implemented in these environments will be welcome, provided of course that the security processes do not impede business process.

Advantages and Disadvantages

All these security facilities come with pros and cons. There are some real strengths to the way security is implemented in Windows 2000, but there are drawbacks as well. While some of these are obvious and intuitive, some are a bit more obscure and might not be apparent right away. To determine whether Windows 2000's security features are going to meet your organization's security needs, it should be evaluated within the context of a predefined security plan.

Crafting a security plan is a serious undertaking for any organization and is beyond the scope of this book. Suffice it to say, if you do not have a clear understanding of the data your servers are storing and the implications involved if that data falls into the wrong hands, you need to start at that point prior to implementing security tools from any vendor. Here are some quick guidelines:

- Most organizations have different security needs for different data. This is where the terms "company confidential," "internal use only," "for public viewing," and the like come from.

- A good general rule for considering security policy is to have an understanding of the financial impact of a security violation. Ask these kinds of questions: "If this data were made available to our competitors, customers, and so on, would we suffer financially?" "Would we lose sales?" "Would we lose reputation?" "Would we lose competitive advantage?" or even "Would it put us out of business?"

- Once these issues are resolved at an organizational level, then the IT organization can define processes that meet the organization's needs. This is when the advantages and disadvantages of a particular tool or technology are discussed.

- Defining the security value of data is the responsibility of the creator/owner of the data. You don't want to have an IT department resource committed to understanding all the organization's data and determining its value. IT should be responsible only for understanding clearly defined "security buckets," then creating, managing, and protecting those buckets in accordance with the organization's definition of different security classifications.

Advantages of Windows 2000 Server Security

While any organization can benefit from increased security features, if they are difficult to use, they won't be used. It is a generally accepted idea that if a security scheme is obtrusive, the administrators or users of the system will devise ways to get around the system, thus defeating it. Perhaps the single greatest strength regarding the security features of Windows 2000 Server security is its integration with the operating system itself.

Many legacy operating systems utilize an add-on or external security provider. Windows 2000 integrates strong security features integral with the operating system. For example, the Kerberos authentication protocol, which is pervasive throughout Windows 2000, is totally integrated to the logon and authentication process.

The Encrypting File System (EFS) that is new in Windows 2000 is a key addition to the security of the operating system. For the first time, Microsoft has provided the tools integral to the operating system to support privacy files as they reside on disk. In addition, the implications of saving data off to tape and having it restored to another machine as a security issue is removed. If you weren't aware of it before, tape is not a private place for your data. With EFS, we protect the organization's data not only as it sits on the server, but also while it sits on tape in the backup vault.

The tools that are used to implement IPSec, PKI, and other security components are integral to the Windows 2000 operating system. This greatly reduces the time that an administrator needs to learn the "hand-waving" involved in setting up and managing security. Since all the tools have that familiar look and feel of the Windows 2000 operating system, an administrator can focus on implementing the security plan instead of learning management tools.

The Microsoft Management Console allows the placement of security management tools in the hands of the administrators that will use them. In addition, by assigning different authorization schemes to various sections of the Active Directory Tree, an organization could have someone responsible for managing user accounts in one logical area of the network, while that same administrator might not be able to do anything in another area. Similarly, several administrators might have networkwide responsibilities, while regional or site administrators could have complete administrative privileges, but be constrained to their site or region. This allows the distribution of administration responsibilities, as well as the partitioning of the areas for which administrators are responsible. This addresses classic issues not only with security management, but also with training, logistics, and ultimately the total cost of ownership as well.

Problems with Windows 2000 Server Security

With all these great security features in Windows 2000, what could possibly go wrong? I can just start using Windows 2000, and all my problems will be gone, right? Well, no. There are still some things that you might want to look out for.

First of all, all this functionality does come with a price. Part of the price you will need to pay is in the form of hardware cost. Creating a secure domain requires machines that are dedicated to be domain controllers. In a large environment, this might mean several machines dedicated just to the process of providing authentication services. As your organization grows geographically, you may find it necessary to place domain controllers from other domains at remote locations to speed up the authentication process and provide

For Managers

Defining a Security Policy

Defining a security policy for your organization is a serious undertaking and should not be treated lightly. It does not matter whether your organization handles billions of dollars in transactions per day, or just handles manufacturing or other nonfinancial information; data is the lifeblood of your organization. In the wrong hands, the information stored on your IT systems could be damaging to the entire future of your enterprise.

Organizing an effort to understand the types of data you are storing, moving, using, and creating is the first step to a sound security policy. If you have not done so yet, consider looking at some of the excellent publications available in bookstores that deal with data security issues. If you can afford it, consider bringing in a security consultant to at least discuss some of the red-flag areas that you should be looking at. If nothing else, take the bull by the horns and organize a cross-functional effort yourself. As the manager responsible for your organization's data, you should lead the efforts to secure that data.

Start by understanding your organization's information sets. Can you place your organization's data into no more than five or six different security classifications? If not, you need to better understand what you are working with. Get together with other managers from the different areas that make up your customer base. Understand what they are dealing with. If nothing else, use this question: "If this information were compromised by loss, exposure, or unauthorized access, what would it cost?" You might then be able to see some patterns emerging. For some things, you might answer "Nothing! In fact, we want this information out in public to anyone who will read it!" Other types of information might fall into the "This would cost our R&D department three months of competitive advantage" category. As you see these patterns emerging, you have the foundation of your

Continued

security policies. You now have things you can call Company Confidential, For Internal Use Only, For Public Viewing, and so on. If you wish, you can use terms such as Top Secret, Secret, Unclassified, or even Red, Green, Blue. It really doesn't matter as long as everyone in the organization has an understanding of what the cost would be if the data in question were to escape or be otherwise compromised.

After these classifications are determined, apply the technology to create safe havens for each of the classifications you have defined. You could create a matrix such as the one illustrated in Table 10.2.

Table 10.2 A Simple Security Matrix

Data classification	Must reside on an encrypted file system	Must not reside on a networked computer	Must not leave the building	Must be clearly labeled when printed
Secret	Yes	Yes	Yes	Yes
Confidential	Yes	No	No	Yes
Distributable	No	No	No	Yes
Open	No	No	No	No

With a matrix such as this in hand, you can create the environment needed to satisfy these requirements. Remember, it should be the responsibility of the data owner/creator to determine the data classification, and the responsibility of the IT team to provide sufficient technology and processes to support them. Don't get stuck owning the security classification of each memo in the building; that is not your job.

Finally, perhaps most important is the social engineering aspect of the job. It is the responsibility of an IT manager to work with the management and executive staff to ensure that the security policy is understood by all members of the organization.

fault tolerance against network failures. Hardware is getting cheaper by the day, but still it is not free, and there is always a management cost associated with every box.

Of specific concern is the relative openness of the Microsoft computing platform. While it is not anywhere close to the mindset of the increasingly popular idea of the open source movement, Microsoft does make a huge portion of its operating system visible via the various Application Programming Interface sets, which encourage the development of software for use on the Windows 2000 environment. They are also published, and some are made freely available to anyone who wishes to create software. Many of the Internet's viruses do their work through calls to these API functions. An interesting cultural issue is involved here. By creating openness in the computing platform, we have the ability to use our tools for both good and evil. The wide publication of Microsoft standards allows only the development of software not only for constructive use, but for destructive use as well. There really is something to be said for attempting "security through obscurity."

The use of the standard Microsoft tools to secure your servers and network may make violation of your security policies difficult, but to get true best-of-breed security tools, you may be forced to go outside the Windows 2000 box and investigate other tools. This is not an affront to Microsoft's products; it is just that when a bank's finances are concerned, one might be better off with tools whose inner workings are not available at the local library or the latest "hack-and-crack" newsgroups. In a sense, Microsoft has fallen victim to its own success here.

Windows 2000 and Security Summary Points

Before we can discuss a product's ability or inability to deliver in the area of security, we must first have a common set of terms and a framework for understanding what security is and why it is needed.

Only then can a conversation be held to determine security policy for an organization. This policy discussion needs to be cross-functional, and it should involve as many stakeholders as possible. Once these questions are answered on an individual organization basis, the IT group can then begin the process of evaluating technological solutions and a process evangelism plan that will promote support of the security policies.

Windows 2000 security inherits the strengths of Windows NT security. These strengths include the usability and integration features that are common to most Windows platforms. The learning curve should be short and administration fairly straightforward. Some of the new features include a pervasive Kerberos authentication mechanism that will become the core of Windows 2000 security from this point forward. Kerberos is a well-documented, secure, and mature method of authentication that should serve the needs of the Windows network community quite well. The addition of PKI and the Encrypted File System to promote data integrity and privacy are welcome new features that make Windows 2000 a more plausible environment in which to store data that might be security-sensitive.

All these features are either transparent to administrators, or are made easily manageable through the usual administrator-friendly tools. After policies have been established and processes defined, administrators who do not need to be security experts themselves should easily accomplish managing the daily administration tasks. Distributed and partitionable management responsibilities via the MMC and Active Directory also go a long way to promote simple manageability.

On the downside, there exists the possibility of compromise due to the simple fact that Microsoft operating systems are so extensively used and documented. While there is really no way to determine the extent of the compromise that will be seen, it is a fairly good bet that several thousand self-proclaimed hackers will be actively pursuing ways to attack Windows 2000 security features. This is an unfortunate side effect of being one of the largest computer software manufacturers in the world. You can be assured that the Internet news groups, chat boards, and such will be full of ways to get around Windows 2000 security features within minutes of its release. All the Black Hats in the world will want to claim ownership of one or more ways to compromise Windows 2000.

FAQs

Q: What is this Kerberos stuff, and where does it come from?

A: Kerberos is an open specification for authentication. In the strictest sense, it is an algorithm. It originated at MIT and has been widely used in large information systems. It is well tested, mature, and regarded as being very secure. In its complete implementation, it is also fairly complicated. The full specification can be found at http://nii-server.isi.edu/info/kerberos.

Q: Can I let different administrators administer different security aspects of my environment?

A: Yes! By using the MMC and creating custom MMC consoles for each administrator or administrative role, you can allow different administrators to manage various aspects of your network and its security policy.

Q: We don't have a security plan. How can I get or make one?

A: You might consider starting with the suggestions presented in this chapter, and seeing where that takes you. There are more books on the subject of computer and information system security now than have been available before, and your local bookstore is a great place to start. If you have the budget, you might consider retaining a security consultant, even if just to look at your organization and make suggestions. Full-service consulting organizations are a good place to go for this type of assistance, even if you are just looking for advice. If you find later that you are in over your head, you can always go back to the consulting firm as your needs arise. You might also want to take a look at the many newsgroups that discuss security issues in general, and Windows security specifically.

Q: How secure is IPSec, and can I trust my network if I use it?

A: IPSec is a framework for implementing security components at several stages of the data transmission process. If they are used diligently, IPSec-specified techniques are not only a good idea, but an absolute must if you plan to conduct business across the Internet. It might be a good idea to consider some of the ways IPSec architecture and techniques might be used inside your organization, behind your firewall as well. You need to understand what it is you are protecting, from whom, and why, before any security architecture will be of any benefit.

Q: What is PKI?

A: Public Key Infrastructure is a framework for providing a public/private encryption scheme. Implemented in many forms, the basic idea is that you have a public key that is widely circulated (wide being relative to your organization or sphere of public exposure) and a private key to which only you have access. If you send something to me, you can encrypt it first by using your private key. Then, when I receive the information, I can attempt to decrypt it with your public key. If I am successful, then the assumption is that the data must have been encrypted with your private key. The conclusion is that the data is authentic or has a degree of integrity based on this assumption. Many companies have emerged lately in the business of being a certificate authority, or CA. They create public and private keys for individuals, industry, and government.

Q: Where can I go to learn more about Windows 2000 security and be kept abreast of any holes that come up as they are found?

A: Keep an eye on the newsgroups that address Windows Security. Make sure you subscribe to the various BackOffice newsletters that Microsoft publishes for free. The most authoritative source of security notifications is probably CERN, which maintains a notification distribution list that you can subscribe to at no charge. Their Web site is at http://consult.cern.ch/cnls/.

Several other Windows operating system security mailing lists may be viewed or subscribed to at http://xforce.iss.net/.

A good source for learning about IT Security in general is the Planet IT security Web page at http://www.planetit.com/techcenters/security.

If you have access to an NNTP news server, you might consider browsing or subscribing to one of the following:

- comp.os.ms-windows.nt.admin.security
- microsoft.public.access.security
- microsoft.public.win2000.beta.security
- comp.security.announce (general info, but some Windows stuff here too)

Index

B

M

P

Managing Software by Using Group Policy

Solutions in this chapter:

- **Deploying Software**

- **Creating Software Packages**

- **Maintaining Software**

- **Removing Software**

Introduction

This chapter focuses on one of the new features of software installation and Group Policy with Windows 2000. Group Policy, much like the Windows NT 4.0 System Policy Editor, is a way to define configurations for users and computers in your Windows 2000 domain. Group Policies enable you to restrict access, manage computer configurations, and control users' desktops and their environment. Group Policy is also used to determine which groups of users or computers receive software packages. One of the most exciting features of Windows 2000 is the ability to deploy, manage, upgrade, and remove software packages with the Software Installation snap-in for the Microsoft Management Console (MMC). You can create software packages, or you can use packages that are designed for the Windows 2000 Installer. You have full control over deploying these packages in an easy-to-use interface that is built right into Windows 2000, without the need to purchase and integrate expensive third-party software installation and management utilities.

Introduction to Managing Software Deployment

As computers continue to become dominant in large organizations with one (or more) computer on each desktop, they are increasingly difficult to manage. More technicians are required in order to install, maintain, and troubleshoot these computers, which comes at a high cost for companies and organizations. The Total Cost of Ownership (TCO) is far greater than the price of the actual computer. Companies need to factor in the cost for software, upgrades, maintenance, and technical support.

In order to lower TCO, many companies are looking into software programs from Microsoft and third-party vendors to allow remote software deployment. This can dramatically decrease the cost and the number of hours a technician would normally be required to visit the workstation.

With these programs, you can choose the software you would like to install, choose the computers that will receive the software, update the software, and even remove the software. All of these options can be scheduled to run during nonbusiness hours. All it takes is a skilled software deployment technician and the right software; in this case, Microsoft's Group Policy.

Deploying Software

The first step of software installation on remote computers using Microsoft's Group Policy is deploying the software. You need to determine whether the software will be assigned or published.

- Published software is optional, and users can browse the available software and determine if they need the application.

- Assigned software is software that a user is required to have on his or her computer, such as a service pack or operating system upgrade. If the application is assigned, it will be installed automatically.

When you publish software, it will be listed in the Add/Remove Programs applet in the Control Panel. With published software, unlike assigned software, the user will not be forced to install the software. The software will not automatically be installed unless a user clicks on a file that is associated with the software. In this case, you are telling the computer you would like to have this application installed to view the file that is associated with the software. For example, if you do not have Microsoft Word installed, but you click on a Word document (.doc) that a coworker sent you, Windows 2000 will then install Microsoft Word (if it is in the list of published applications) so you can view this document. The user can also remove the published software at any time. If the published application is removed, the user can install it at anytime in the future using the Add/Remove Programs applet, provided the software is still being published.

When you assign software to a *user*, in contrast to a *computer*, it will be available for the user as a Start menu shortcut, Desktop shortcut, or from the Add/Remove Programs applet in the Control Panel. After the Administrator assigns the software, it will be available for the user to install at the next logon. If a user does not install the software, but clicks on a file that is associated with the software, the software will automatically be installed. The user can remove the assigned software, but it will reappear from the install point where it was originally offered at the next logon.

When you assign software to a *computer*, in contrast to a *user*, it will be installed the next time the computer reboots. This means the user will not have to install the software, and it will not be offered as a Start menu shortcut, Desktop shortcut, or from the Add/Remove Programs applet in the Control Panel. However, it will create a shortcut to the application like every program does. This is not to be confused with the shortcut to install the program. The user cannot remove the software; only an Administrator can.

Before you begin installing and maintaining your software, you should have your Group Policy in order. Group Policy is used to define user and computer configurations to restrict access to resources, enforce desktop settings, and control the users' work environment. These policy settings are stored in Group Policy Objects (GPOs). These GPOs are created using the Group Policy snap-in for the MMC, and can be used as a stand-alone tool or as an extension to the Active Directory snap-ins.

Group Policy uses Administrative Templates in the form of .adm files that determine the Registry settings that can be modified. In Windows 2000, these Administrative Templates can be modified in the Group Policy snap-in user interface. The .adm files are text files that contain the Registry information to modify the computer's Registry, which includes restrictions or default values.

Just like Windows NT 4.0 system policies, you have separate settings for users and computers. The computer configuration consists of settings such as operating system behavior, the desktop, Startup and Shutdown scripts, security settings, and application settings. These settings will affect every user who logs on to this computer.

They are stored in the HKEY_LOCAL_MACHINE (HKLM) portion of the Registry. User configuration consists of user-related policies such as logon and logoff scripts, assigned and published applications, and folder redirection options. They are stored in the HKEY_CURRENT_USER (HKCU) portion of the Registry. With your Group Policy in order, it is time to begin deploying software. We will continue with the creation of software packages.

Creating Software Packages

Software installation and maintenance is made easier with the new Windows Installer, which standardizes the way applications are installed on multiple computers. Using the Windows Installer will allow you to take advantage of new program installation features, such as the ability to roll back an unsuccessful install. Using programs that are compliant with the new Windows Installer makes them easier to package. You can also be more comfortable that the program will install correctly. Using applications that are compliant with Windows 2000 offers a much greater benefit than noncompliant applications. Microsoft lists the following regulations for compliance:

- Application-specific .dll files are placed in the Application folder.
- Applications do not overwrite system .dll files.
- Applications only write to their own areas of the Registry, and will not modify existing keys of the Registry.
- System .dll files can only be updated by installing a service pack.
- Users do not need permission from the local Administrator to install applications.

This addresses several issues that plagued network Administrators in the past with .dll problems, such as a .dll being overwritten by an older application. Using the Windows Installer ensures that applications will adhere to the *Windows Installer format,* which means Windows 2000 will install the application on the application's behalf, therefore creating a uniform installation routine. A Windows Installer package will have the extension .MSI, and will be located in the root of the source, whether that source is the uncompressed files, or files compressed in a cabinet (.cab) format.

Windows Installer can install applications in one of four states:

- Installed on the local hard drive, which installs the files needed on the local computer.
- Installed to run from a server, either on the server hard disk or shared CD-ROM.
- Advertised, which means they exist on the source but can be installed on the local hard drive at any time.
- Not installed, which means no files will be copied.

Another feature of Windows Installer is the ability to add components of a program later that were not selected in the first run of setup. This is possible with non-Windows Installer applications, but you have to rerun the setup program; with Windows Installer, you do not. This means all features of the product are available, even if they are not installed. This is referred to as *feature-level* advertisement.

Windows Installer can also perform checks of the program installation and make repairs if needed. When an application calls the Windows Installer service, the service will automatically check for components that have been installed on the machine. Next, the Windows Installer service will check that all components are correctly installed. If the component is corrupt, a repair will be performed.

If during an application install using Windows Installer, the application is not correctly installed, you can return to a working state before the application was installed. This is very important because many times application installs that don't finish correctly can often leave the computer in an unstable state. Another reason this is important is because a user may be installing the application, encounter problems, and can then return to a working state without any technical intervention by support personnel. This will eliminate downtime if the user rolls back the installation until a later time when technical support can be present. However, the installation cannot be rolled back once it has successfully completed; it must be uninstalled.

Another feature of the Windows Installer is the ability to "patch" applications, and to keep this patch cached on the computer that received the patch. Before this, you would have to apply the patch each time you installed a component that required the original source files. Whenever the Windows Installer service needs to be invoked, it will verify that the application's core files are not corrupt or missing. If these files are missing or corrupt, the Windows Installer service will apply the patch that has been cached on the computer.

The "Designed for Microsoft Windows" logo will ensure that applications use the standards for Windows Installer in order to be compliant.

Creating a Non-Windows Installer Package File

If you are not using programs that are Windows Installer compatible, they can still be packaged. Before this program can be used for installation and maintenance, it will have to be packaged into a .zap file. These are text files that are similar to .INI files that describe how to install the program, and the properties of the program. The finished .zap file is stored in the same directory as the program that contains the setup file for that program.

The following is an example of a .zap file provided by Microsoft. Notice the underscore (_) symbol, which indicates the line should be continued, but has been wrapped to the next line.

```
; ZAP file for Microsoft Excel 97

[Application]
; Only FriendlyName and SetupCommand are required,
; everything else is optional
```

```
; FriendlyName is the name of the application that
; will appear in the software installation snapin
; and the add/remove programs control panel.
; REQUIRED
FriendlyName = "Microsoft Excel 97"

; SetupCommand is the command line that we use to
; Run the applications setup. if it is a relative
; path, it is assumed to be relative to the
; location of the ZAP file.
; Long file name paths need to be quoted. For example:
; SetupCommand = "long folder\setup.exe" /unattend
; or
; SetupCommand = "\\server\share\long _
; folder\setup.exe" /unattend
; REQUIRED
SetupCommand = setup.exe

; Version of the application that will appear
; in the software installation snapin and the
; add/remove programs control panel.
; OPTIONAL
DisplayVersion = 8.0

; Version of the application that will appear
; in the software installation snapin and the
; add/remove programs control panel.
; OPTIONAL
Publisher = Microsoft

; URL for application information that will appear
; in the software installation snapin and the
; add/remove programs control panel.;
; OPTIONAL
URL = http://www.microsoft.com/office

; Language for the app, in this case US English.
; OPTIONAL
LCID = 1033
```

```
; Architecture, in this case, intel.
; OPTIONAL
Architecture = intel

; the [ext] [CLSIDs] and [progIDs] sections are
; all optional

[ext]
; File extensions that this application will
; "auto-install" for. They are not required if you
; do not want the application. This entire section
; is OPTIONAL.

; note you can put a dot in front or not, as you like
; text after the first = is optional and ignored
; but the first = is required (or the whole line
; will be ignored)
XLS=
XLA=
XLB=
XLC=
XLM=
XLV=
XLW=

[CLSIDs]
; CLSIDs that this application will "auto-install"
; for. This entire section is OPTIONAL.

; Format is CLSID with LocalServer32,
; InprocServer32, and/or InprocHandler32 (in a
; comma separated list) after the =.

{00024500-0000-0000-C000-000000000046}=LocalServer32
{00020821-0000-0000-C000-000000000046}=LocalServer32
{00020811-0000-0000-C000-000000000046}=LocalServer32
{00020810-0000-0000-C000-000000000046}=LocalServer32
{00020820-0000-0000-C000-000000000046}=LocalServer32
```

```
[progIDs]
; progIDs that this application will "auto-install"
; for. This entire section is OPTIONAL.

; format is a CLSID, with the corresponding progid
; listed after the = sign
{00024500-0000-0000-C000- _
000000000046}=Excel.Application
{00024500-0000-0000-C000- _
000000000046}=Excel.Application.8
{00020821-0000-0000-C000-000000000046}=Excel.Chart
{00020811-0000-0000-C000-000000000046}=Excel.Chart.5
{00020821-0000-0000-C000-000000000046}=Excel.Chart.8
{00020810-0000-0000-C000-000000000046}=Excel.Sheet.5
{00020820-0000-0000-C000-000000000046}=Excel.Sheet.8
{00020820-0000-0000-C000-000000000046}=Excel.Sheet
{00020820-0000-0000-C000-000000000046}=Excel.Template
{00020820-0000-0000-C000-000000000046}=Excel.Workspace
```

With all of the software packages you have created, you will need to specify a distribution point on the network. This will include Windows Installer packages, ZAP files, and the files needed for the program to install.

You will need to create this software distribution point by creating the network share, the appropriate folders, copying the packages and executables to the folder, and then setting the permissions on the folder. Users should have the Read permission, and Administrators should have the Full Control permission.

We will be using this newly created Excel 97 ZAP file in a future exercise. It is helpful if you place this ZAP file in a network share with the permissions we described in the previous section. We will be using a network share called "Distribution" that will contain this ZAP file and the source files necessary to install Microsoft Excel 97.

The Global Knowledge Advantage

Global Knowledge has a global delivery system for its products and services. The company has 28 subsidiaries, and offers its programs through a total of 60+ locations. No other vendor can provide consistent services across a geographic area this large. Global Knowledge is the largest independent information technology education provider, offering programs on a variety of platforms. This enables our multi-platform and multi-national customers to obtain all of their programs from a single vendor. The company has developed the unique CompetusTM Framework software tool and methodology which can quickly reconfigure courseware to the proficiency level of a student on an interactive basis. Combined with self-paced and on-line programs, this technology can reduce the time required for training by prescribing content in only the deficient skills areas. The company has fully automated every aspect of the education process, from registration and follow-up, to "just-in-time" production of courseware. Global Knowledge through its Enterprise Services Consultancy, can customize programs and products to suit the needs of an individual customer.

Global Knowledge Classroom Education Programs

The backbone of our delivery options is classroom-based education. Our modern, well-equipped facilities staffed with the finest instructors offer programs in a wide variety of information technology topics, many of which lead to professional certifications.

Custom Learning Solutions

This delivery option has been created for companies and governments that value customized learning solutions. For them, our consultancy-based approach of developing targeted education solutions is most effective at helping them meet specific objectives.

Self-Paced and Multimedia Products

This delivery option offers self-paced program titles in interactive CD-ROM, videotape and audio tape programs. In addition, we offer custom development of interactive multimedia courseware to customers and partners. Call us at 1-888-427-4228.

Electronic Delivery of Training

Our network-based training service delivers efficient competency-based, interactive training via the World Wide Web and organizational intranets. This leading-edge delivery option provides a custom learning path and "just-in-time" training for maximum convenience to students.

Global Knowledge Courses Available

Microsoft
- Windows 2000 Deployment Strategies
- Introduction to Directory Services
- Windows 2000 Client Administration
- Windows 2000 Server
- Windows 2000 Update
- MCSE Bootcamp
- Microsoft Networking Essentials
- Windows NT 4.0 Workstation
- Windows NT 4.0 Server
- Windows NT Troubleshooting
- Windows NT 4.0 Security
- Windows 2000 Security
- Introduction to Microsoft Web Tools

Management Skills
- Project Management for IT Professionals
- Microsoft Project Workshop
- Management Skills for IT Professionals

Network Fundamentals
- Understanding Computer Networks
- Telecommunications Fundamentals I
- Telecommunications Fundamentals II
- Understanding Networking Fundamentals
- Upgrading and Repairing PCs
- DOS/Windows A+ Preparation
- Network Cabling Systems

WAN Networking and Telephony
- Building Broadband Networks
- Frame Relay Internetworking
- Converging Voice and Data Networks
- Introduction to Voice Over IP
- Understanding Digital Subscriber Line (xDSL)

Internetworking
- ATM Essentials
- ATM Internetworking
- ATM Troubleshooting
- Understanding Networking Protocols
- Internetworking Routers and Switches
- Network Troubleshooting
- Internetworking with TCP/IP
- Troubleshooting TCP/IP Networks
- Network Management
- Network Security Administration
- Virtual Private Networks
- Storage Area Networks
- Cisco OSPF Design and Configuration
- Cisco Border Gateway Protocol (BGP) Configuration

Web Site Management and Development
- Advanced Web Site Design
- Introduction to XML
- Building a Web Site
- Introduction to JavaScript
- Web Development Fundamentals
- Introduction to Web Databases

PERL, UNIX, and Linux
- PERL Scripting
- PERL with CGI for the Web
- UNIX Level I
- UNIX Level II
- Introduction to Linux for New Users
- Linux Installation, Configuration, and Maintenance

Authorized Vendor Training
Red Hat
- Introduction to Red Hat Linux
- Red Hat Linux Systems Administration
- Red Hat Linux Network and Security Administration
- RHCE Rapid Track Certification

Cisco Systems
- Interconnecting Cisco Network Devices
- Advanced Cisco Router Configuration
- Installation and Maintenance of Cisco Routers
- Cisco Internetwork Troubleshooting
- Designing Cisco Networks
- Cisco Internetwork Design
- Configuring Cisco Catalyst Switches
- Cisco Campus ATM Solutions
- Cisco Voice Over Frame Relay, ATM, and IP
- Configuring for Selsius IP Phones
- Building Cisco Remote Access Networks
- Managing Cisco Network Security
- Cisco Enterprise Management Solutions

Nortel Networks
- Nortel Networks Accelerated Router Configuration
- Nortel Networks Advanced IP Routing
- Nortel Networks WAN Protocols
- Nortel Networks Frame Switching
- Nortel Networks Accelar 1000
- Comprehensive Configuration
- Nortel Networks Centillion Switching
- Network Management with Optivity for Windows

Oracle Training
- Introduction to Oracle8 and PL/SQL
- Oracle8 Database Administration

Custom Corporate Network Training

Train on Cutting Edge Technology

We can bring the best in skill-based training to your facility to create a real-world hands-on training experience. Global Knowledge has invested millions of dollars in network hardware and software to train our students on the same equipment they will work with on the job. Our relationships with vendors allow us to incorporate the latest equipment and platforms into your on-site labs.

Maximize Your Training Budget

Global Knowledge provides experienced instructors, comprehensive course materials, and all the networking equipment needed to deliver high quality training. You provide the students; we provide the knowledge.

Avoid Travel Expenses

On-site courses allow you to schedule technical training at your convenience, saving time, expense, and the opportunity cost of travel away from the workplace.

Discuss Confidential Topics

Private on-site training permits the open discussion of sensitive issues such as security, access, and network design. We can work with your existing network's proprietary files while demonstrating the latest technologies.

Customize Course Content

Global Knowledge can tailor your courses to include the technologies and the topics which have the greatest impact on your business. We can complement your internal training efforts or provide a total solution to your training needs.

Corporate Pass

The Corporate Pass Discount Program rewards our best network training customers with preferred pricing on public courses, discounts on multimedia training packages, and an array of career planning services.

Global Knowledge Training Lifecycle

Supporting the Dynamic and Specialized Training Requirements of Information Technology Professionals

- Define Profile
- Assess Skills
- Design Training
- Deliver Training
- Test Knowledge
- Update Profile
- Use New Skills

Global Knowledge

Global Knowledge programs are developed and presented by industry profession-als with "real-world" experience. Designed to help professionals meet today's inter-connectivity and interoperability challenges, most of our programs feature hands-on labs that incorporate state-of-the-art communication components and equipment.

ON-SITE TEAM TRAINING

Bring Global Knowledge's powerful training programs to your company. At Global Knowledge, we will custom design courses to meet your specific network require-ments. Call (919)-461-8686 for more information.

YOUR GUARANTEE

Global Knowledge believes its courses offer the best possible training in this field. If during the first day you are not satisfied and wish to withdraw from the course, simply notify the instructor, return all course materials and receive a 100% refund.

REGISTRATION INFORMATION

In the US:
call: (888) 762–4442
fax: (919) 469–7070
visit our website:
www.globalknowledge.com